International union
for the scientific study
of population

The International Union for the Scientific Study of Population Problems
was set up in 1928, with Dr Raymond Pearl as President. At that time the
Union's main purpose was to promote international scientific co-operation
to study the various aspects of population problems, through national
committees and through its members themselves. In 1947 the International
Union for the Scientific Study of Population (IUSSP) was reconstituted into
its present form. It expanded its activities to:
- stimulate research on population
- develop interest in demographic matters among governments, national
  and international organizations, scientific bodies, and the general
  public
- foster relations between people involved in population studies
- disseminate scientific knowledge on population.

The principal ways through which the IUSSP currently achieves its aims are:
- organization of worldwide or regional conferences
- operations of Scientific Committees under the auspices of the Council
- organization of training courses
- publication of conference proceedings and committee reports.

Demography can be defined by its field of study and its analytical methods.
Accordingly, it can be regarded as the scientific study of human populations
primarily with respect to their size, their structure, and their development.
For reasons which are related to the history of the discipline, the demographic method is essentially inductive: progress in the knowledge results
from the improvement of observation, the sophistication of measurement
methods, the search for regularities and stable factors leading to the formulation of explanatory models. In conclusion, the three objectives of demographic analysis are to describe, measure, and analyse.

International Studies in Demography is the outcome of an agreement con-
cluded by the IUSSP and the Oxford University Press. The joint series is
expected to reflect the broad range of the Union's activities and, in the first
instance, will be based on the seminars organized by the Union. The
Editorial Board of the series is comprised of:

Differential Mortality

Methodological Issues and
Biosocial Factors

edited by
LADO RUZICKA
GUILLAUME WUNSCH
PENNY KANE

CLARENDON PRESS · OXFORD

Oxford University Press, Walton Street, Oxford OX2 6DP

Oxford New York

Athens Auckland Bangkok Bombay
Calcutta Cape Town Dar es Salaam Delhi
Florence Hong Kong Istanbul Karachi
Kuala Lumpur Madras Madrid Melbourne
Mexico City Nairobi Paris Singapore
Taipei Tokyo Toronto

and associated companies in
Berlin Ibadan

Oxford is a trade mark of Oxford University Press

Published in the United States
by Oxford University Press Inc., New York

First published in hardback 1989
First issued in paperback 1995
Hardback edition reprinted 1995

British Library Cataloguing in Publication Data

Differential mortality: methodological issues and biosocial factors.—(International
studies in demography)
1. Developing countries. Man. Mortality rate
I. Ruzicka, Lado. II. Wunsch, Guillaume III. Kane, Penny, 1945–
IV. Series 304.6'4'091724

ISBN 0–19–828651–1

Library of Congress Cataloging in Publication Data

Differential mortality: methodological issues and biosocial factors /
edited by Lado Ruzicka, Guillaume Wunsch, Penny Kane.
p. cm.—(International studies in demography)
Papers from the IUSSP-NIRA Joint Seminar on Biological and Social Correlates of
Mortality Nov. 24–27, 1984.
Bibliography: p. Includes index.
1. Mortality—Congresses. 2. Vital statistics—Congresses.
I. Ruzicka, Lado (Lado Theodor), 1920–. II. Wunch, Guillaume. III. Kane,
Penny. IV. IUSSP-NIRA Joint Seminar on Biological and Social Correlates of Mortality
(1984: Tokyo, Japan) V. International Union for the Scientific Study of
Population. VI. Sōgō Kenkyū Kauhatsu Kikō (Japan) VII. Series
HB1321.D54 1989 304.6'4—dc19 88-31297 CIP

ISBN 0–19–828651–1
ISBN 0–19–828882–4 (Pbk)

3 5 7 9 10 8 6 4 2

Printed and bound in Great Britain by
Biddles Ltd., Guildford and King's Lynn

Foreword

The Scientific Committee on Biological and Social Correlates of Mortality, established by the International Union for the Scientific Study of Population (IUSSP) decided at its meetings in December 1982 and March 1983 to focus its activities on issues related primarily to mortality transition in the less developed countries, and on the investigation of biological and socio-economic factors affecting infant and child survival. Attention was to be given to socio-economic differences in mortality in general, and in infant and child mortality in particular, both within and among countries; to the inter-country variations in the transition from high to low mortality and their determinants; and to social and cultural systems and institutions that facilitate or obstruct, as the case may be, such transition.

The committee approached the National Institute for Research Advancement (NIRA) in Tokyo and reached an agreement on a programme for a joint seminar that would satisfy the IUSSP committee's objectives and meet NIRA's own research interests. NIRA undertook the sponsorship of the seminar and the funding of most of the participants as well as providing the conference facilities and services.

The seminar, entitled the IUSSP–NIRA Joint Seminar on Biological and Social Correlates of Mortality, was held from 24 to 27 November 1984, and attended by 34 participants from 15 countries. It was organized in six formal sessions, which were held at the National Women's Education Centre (Nihon Daigaku Kaikan). The closing, seventh, session was held at the Nihon University in Tokyo, and to this a wider audience of Japanese scholars and officials of the Government was invited by NIRA.

There were 20 invited papers presented and discussed in the formal sessions; an additional set of four papers was tabled for the participants' information.

The seminar was formally opened and the participants were welcomed by N. Kurakake, executive vice-president of NIRA and chairman of the local organizing committee, on behalf of NIRA, and L. T. Ruzicka, chairman of the IUSSP Scientific Committee, on behalf of the IUSSP. The president of IUSSP, M. Concepcion, attended the seminar, and she and the executive vice-president of NIRA were the principal speakers at the closing session.

The primary concern of the seminar was the socio-biological conditions which lead to, or sustain, high levels of mortality in the less developed countries. To keep this objective in focus, for this book a selection of papers which primarily address these issues was made.

The committee's collaboration with NIRA benefited from the negotiation and liaison undertaken by S. Kono, who had much to do with its success. In the preparation of this volume the editors were assisted by members of the committee: L. Adeokun, J. Chackiel, S. D'Souza, and H. W. Mosley. They are also grateful for the support of the IUSSP Secretariat, in particular M. Lebrun. Last but not least, the two annonymous reviewers of an earlier draft of the volume, by their critical comments, greatly assisted the editors, and their contribution is acknowledged.

Contents

Contributors

Eduardo E. Arriaga	US Bureau of the Census
Andre Bouckaert	Catholic University of Louvain, Belgium
Stan D'Souza	UNDP, Cotonou, RP Benin
Josianne Duchêne	University of Louvain, Belgium
Nusret H. Fisek	Hacettepe University, Ankara, Turkey
Ronald H. Gray	Johns Hopkins University, Baltimore
José Miguel Guzman	CELADE, Santiago, Chile
Shiro Horiuchi	United Nations
Meiwita Budiharsana Iskandar	University of Indonesia, Jakarta, Indonesia
Penny Kane	University College, Cardiff, Wales
George C. Myers	Duke University, Durham, North Carolina
Alberto Palloni	University of Wisconsin, Madison, Wisconsin
Lado Ruzicka	Australian National University, Canberra, Australia
Budi Utomo	University of Indonesia, Jakarta, Indonesia
Guillaume Wunsch	University of Louvain, Belgium

Part I

Introduction

Problems and Issues in the Study of Mortality Differentials

LADO RUZICKA

Demography Department, Australian National University, Canberra, Australia

Demographers and epidemiologists have long been aware that chances of a child surviving through infancy and early childhood are primarily determined by the resources available in the child's family. These resources are not only economical, such as family income, quality of housing, and, associated with these, the physical environment in which the family lives and social amenities to which it can gain access. Equally important are the social resources: characteristics of the parents, such as education, beliefs, social norms, and traditions they hold. These affect the family life-style and behaviour in many respects which are directly or indirectly related to the active promotion and protection of health, and intervention in the case of ill health. The economic resources are usually measured by a range of indicators, such as income (of individual members or of the family as a whole), possession of household chattels, occupation of household head, type of house in which the family lives (construction material, number of rooms and the density of their occupation), and so on. Among the social resources the indicators most often encountered are the educational level of the parents, family type and size, religion (or some measure of religiosity), and caste (or other indicator of social status).

The direct association between child survival—usually measured in terms of infant or early childhood mortality or both—and a range of indices of economic and social resources available to the family has been demonstrated in studies covering a wide range of societies. The relationship holds true irrespective of the overall level of mortality in the national population, and exists in its geographic subdivisions, including urban–rural subdivisions. It has been shown that over time, despite any general decline of mortality, the differences in the chances of child survival among various socio-economic subgroups of the national population persist; whether they become narrower or wider does not appear, on currently available evidence, to be quite so clear.

Investigations of the differences in child survival by socio-economic characteristics of the families in which they live have been undertaken with at least two objectives in mind. The first is to attempt an assessment of the degree to which national development policies and strategies can be specifically related to the trends in child survival. Not dissociated with this aim is the other objective, namely the attempt to identify the most vulnerable groups of the population, which appear to have been left behind, or are lagging in participation, in the benefits accruing from social and economic development. In the more narrow sense of health protection, remedial actions are expected to be directed towards these groups in the design of policies and assignment of priorities. Both research goals have, apart from their intrinsic value in shedding some light on the determinants of mortality transition, important implications for health policy orientation. As Mosley (1985*a*) succinctly points out: 'if it is not feasible to explain any of the past mortality trends and current differentials on the basis of past national development strategies and programs, then it would be quite hazardous to speculate what might be the mortality change in the future on the basis of a change in health strategy that would incorporate P[rimary] H[ealth] C[are] programs'.

One of the problems of analysis of empirical data in the studies of mortality differentials by social and economic strata of the population has been the fact that the indicators of such stratification are highly correlated with each other. For instance, a parent's occupation is closely related to his or her education; individual income is related to occupation; family income depends on the size of the family as well as on the stage of the family life cycle—how many children there are in the family, how many of them are dependants, and how many contribute to family income. Individual and family income determine, to some extent, the housing and living conditions and the family's wealth. Most demographic studies in the past which addressed the problem of differential child mortality used to consider each socio-economic variable in isolation or, at best, in a combination of two or three. Typically, this took a form of a cross-tabulation by rural–urban division, and by education (of mother, father, or both) and father's occupation (Mitra, 1979; D'Souza *et al.*, 1982). Such analyses could not provide an answer to what has been, explicitly or implicitly, the ultimate goal of the investigations of differential mortality: to identify from the complex web of social and economic factors those which could be isolated as the most important, and to map out the causal links between socio-economic conditions and survival chances. Admittedly, in the past only a very limited range of indices of social and economic indicators was available for such studies, and most of the indices depended on data on areal variations in mortality and corresponding areal variations in the distribution of the social and economic parameters. In addition, the choice of parameters was limited to what the secondary data sources—most often vital registration and census—provided.

Only comparatively recently, with the advent of major demographic

surveys (and, in particular, the World Fertility Survey) and access to individual records, has the scope for analysis widened. Various forms of multivariate analysis have been applied and, in some instances, conceptual
models developed to outline the assumed causal paths between mortality
differentials and social and economic environment. In addition to information on individual or family characteristics, data started to emerge on the
social and other amenities available to communities and to be incorporated
in the study design: in particular, data on access to health services, sources
of water for various purposes, the disposal of sewage, and so on.

Typically, the conceptual models developed by demographers place great
emphasis on demographic factors (age of the mother and her parity, for
instance) and on social and economic variables. In some instances, however,
the role of institutional developments is also recognized. An example of a
more complex model of this type is the conceptual framework developed by
I. D. Pool (1982) which he used in the analysis of non-Maori mortality
trends in New Zealand.

Pool discerned three types of variables which he assumed played a role in
mortality transition in that population:

Explanatory variables
(a) *At macro-level*:
— health care infrastructure and technology (hospitals, clinics, ambu-
  lance services; high-cost technology: X-rays, clinical and surgical
  equipment; low-cost technology: chemotherapeutics, vaccines,
  insecticides);
— health administration and health regulations (organization and delivery of health care, bureaucratic supporting structures; acts and regulations relating to sanitation);
— environment;
— socio-economic and socio-cultural organization and change ('socio-
  cultural' is, in Pool's study, primarily related to ethnicity, but could
  encompass religion and fertility behaviour; 'socio-economic' includes
  social organization and change, wealth, income, education, economic
  change loosely defined, the system of production and distribution of
  commodities, especially those which meet the 'basic needs, political
  change);
— sanitation (sewerage, water purification and distribution, and so on,
  and the construction and implementation of sanitation).
(b) *At micro-level*:
— medical practice;
— hygiene (personal; in the household; in the immediate environment);
— personal life-style; individual socio-economic status; socio-cultural
  and biosocial characteristics ('biosocial' being defined as age, gender,
  and parity); genetic factors.

Intermediate variables
— preventive medicine and health measures;
— curative medicine and health measures;
— disease mechanisms.

The system, however, appears to give little explicit role to biological factors: thus, for instance, nutritional status does not appear on the list of biosocial explanatory variables. Pool justified this omission specifically (p. 13):

good nutrition is important for the prevention of ill health, but its prime antecedents are socio-economic and socio-cultural organisation and change. Without adequate incomes, efficient agriculture, transport and communications, populations will not be able to generate and sustain continuously satisfactory levels of diet and nutrition. Thus, although diet and nutrition have medical implications, ultimately differentials [in mortality] are explained by differences in the status levels of individuals or differences in the socio-economic levels of societies. Similar remarks could be made about a range of other basic needs such as lifestyles, access to medical care and housing.

Pool's is only one of a range of conceptual frameworks used in mortality analysis. It was mentioned here because it is an example of the more complex ones. Of a different type, because they are underpinned by different theoretical concepts, are analytical frameworks used by economists (for instance Schultz, 1985). However, all of them appear to leave out the biological risks of morbidity and mortality, how these risks are influenced by various patterns of human behaviour, and the conditions under which various population groups live.

In most instances demographic research on infant and child mortality differentials has not been able to provide answers as to how particular attributes and characteristics of individuals, families, or communities operate on levels, changes, and patterns of mortality; their *modus operandi* is, at best, conjectural. For instance, the negative association between relatively close spacing of births and the chances of infant and child survival has been recognized for a long time and firmly established from analysis of empirical data (see, for instance, a review of such studies in Cleland and Sathar, 1983; Hobcraft *et al.*, 1983). Yet the causal mechanisms are not at all clearly established and are rarely discussed (Winikoff, 1983). Similarly, a plethora of studies has demonstrated the positive effect of parents' education (and, in some instances, that of the mother in particular) on children's survival. For a long time the educational level of parents—a variable about which it was easier to obtain information than, for instance, family income—was largely considered a proxy for socio-economic status of the family, and the association with mortality was interpreted accordingly. It was only a few years ago that Caldwell (1979; Caldwell and McDonald, 1981) suggested that maternal education is linked with reduced infant and child mortality through a range of such factors as a reduction in fatalism in the face of a child's illness; a change in the traditional balance of family relationships that gives the mother more influence in decisions concerning family issues and, in particular, child care and treatment in case of illness, food allocation to children and adults, and so on; and a greater capability in understanding the 'modern world', such as, for instance, knowing where health care facilities are available and how to avail herself of them. Ware (1984, 194–5) pointed out that it may sometimes be difficult to separate the effects of income and education in matters of child care. In the case of food allocation within the family, for instance, it may well be that where there is food enough to go around, the decisions, irrespective of mother's education, will be different from those in a situation where difficult choices have to be made about who will get how much from the very limited food available.

It is often surmised that education imparts knowledge of the association between hygiene, cleanliness, and health protection—the 'germ theory' of disease causation. However, at least one study, based in a rural area of Bangladesh (Lindenbaum, 1983), found that both illiterate women and the majority of those with some education (except for the few with more than primary education) tended to share traditional beliefs about the causation of illness; neither did they differ in attitudes toward the appropriateness of various types of intervention and treatment of sick children, though those with some education might turn to an allopathic physician sooner, particularly if a modern health centre was nearby. However, women's education fostered 'upward social mobility' behaviour and an identification with the 'modern world' and its values—a clean house, neatness, and better personal hygiene—which were also transmitted to the children. Such behavioural patterns not only serve to convey higher social status but also generate beneficial health-protecting effects, resulting in better nutrition and care and, if not in lower morbidity, at least in lower case-fatality.

The complex web of links between the environmental, economic, social, cultural, and behavioural factors leading, on the one hand, to protection and preservation of health and, on the other hand, to illness and, in extreme cases, to death, obviously requires that a full recognition is given to the fact that some basic biological mechanisms operate between the former set of factors and the risks of the latter outcomes. An explicit recognition of biological processes within the conceptual framework of mortality causation is to be found in recent attempts to establish a firmer basis for the study of mortality transition and explanation of differentials between as well as within societies. In one of such attempts, for instance, Mahadevan (1984) developed a list of 'life affecting variables', some of which, because of 'their greater and immediate influence on mortality', he assigned a special position in his framework, labelling them 'imminent variables'. His framework makes specific reference to selected biological factors, such as infections and the morbidity pattern, nutritional deficiency and physiological weakness, biogenetic factors and immunity levels, and injuries.

In a similar vein, Venkatacharya (1985) attempted to organize in a systematic fashion the factors which affect the 'life process from birth to death of an individual'. Focusing on survival of children from birth to age five, he identified in his model several transitions: from birth to a healthy state; from birth to a morbid state; from health to malnutrition; from health to exposure to infection; from exposure to disease and mal-nutrition to low resistance and to morbid state; and from morbid state or low resistance to recovery. Associated with each of these transitions are conditions which, according to their closer or more remote effect on the transition process, he stratified as more proximate, proximate, and less proximate. The *more proximate* factors are predominantly biological: birth-weight, sex, gestational age, genetic endowment, maternal health, birth practices and pregnancy spacing, weaning (also, cultural or traditional practices affecting sex differentials in the timing of weaning). The *proximate* variables are largely socio-economic attributes of the family and its members and living conditions. Examples are education of mother, stan-dards of living of the household, marital status of the mother, attitudes affecting child-rearing, level of fertility, housing quality and crowding. Finally, the *less proximate* or *remote* factors describe environmental condi-tions in which the families live. They include the national level of social and economic development and national income, geography and physical environment, climate, food production and distribution, level and distribu-tion of health services and their orientation (preventive or predominantly curative), family-planning services, degree of urbanization, and so on. He also examines, at least in principle, which statistical models would be suited for analysis of such a complex system and how the necessary data could be obtained.

The most comprehensive and systematic conceptual framework sug-gested so far has been developed by Mosley (1980, 1985*a*, 1985*b*) and further elaborated upon by Mosley and Chen (1984). It focuses specifically on infant and child survival, which is viewed as the consequence of a limited number of 'proximate determinants'—that is, behaviourally mediated biological mechanisms. The framework identifies 14 proximate deter-minants of infant and child mortality which are then grouped into five cat-egories related to: (1) maternal fertility; (2) environmental contamina-tion; (3) nutrient availability; (4) injuries; and (5) disease control.

The model is based on the following set of assumptions (Mosley and Chen, 1984, 27): that the reduction of the child's survival chances is due to the operation of social, economic, biological, and environmental forces; the socio-economic forces (independent variables) operate through more basic proximate determinants and these, in turn, influence the risk of disease and the outcome of the disease processes; the biological indicators of the opera-tions of these proximate determinants are specific diseases and nutrient defi-ciencies observed in the surviving population. The dependent vari-ables—growth-faltering and, ultimately, mortality in children—are the cumulative consequences of multiple disease processes: a child only infrequently dies from a single isolated disease episode. In this model, 'a specific disease state in an individual [is] an indicator of the operation of the proximate determinants rather than . . . a "cause" of illness and death' (ibid., 28).

This framework is probably the most pronounced novelty in the approach to the study of differentials in child survival. Earlier, epidemiological studies attempted to identify all known causes of disease and death in individuals of a population, and then made inferences about the social and economic factors contributing to morbidity and mortality in order to develop rational control measures. Mosley and Chen approach the problem from a different angle: they search for and identify basic mechanisms, proximate determinants, common to all or most diseases. Through these mechanisms all socio-economic determinants must operate.

There is a strong interaction among the proximate determinants: the adverse effects generated by the contamination of the environment may be aggravated by the child's reduced ability to resist infection. Injury, low birth-weight, or immaturity at birth make the child more vulnerable; in contrast, adequate nutrition or vaccination may increase the child's capacity to resist infection. The interactions—labelled *biological synergy*—have been described by Chen (1981) in the case of diarrhoea and infections. Martorell and Ho (1984) cite examples of high incidence of complications with, and high fatality of, measles in malnourished children. Malnutrition reduces the host's resistance and increases the risk of infection and of a more severe disease outcome. Infections reduce appetite and cause unnecessary metabolic wastage of nutrients; as a result, they precipitate or aggravate malnutrition.

Mosley introduced in his earlier work (1985a) the concept of *social synergy* in risk factors. This is based on the observation that 'the same social determinant, e.g. poverty, can operate independently on more than one intermediate variable [proximate determinant in the model described here] to influence the risk of infant mortality, resulting in a combined risk that is more than would be expected by the simple sum of the operation of each intermediate variable'. The evidence of the impact of such a social synergy has been, in particular, strongly pronounced in the demographic studies which examined the effect of maternal education on child survival. A mother's education can affect the early child survival through differential pre-natal care, safe delivery, and her own nutritional status; her educational level gives her skills and expands the choices which she may make in practising health care, nutrition, hygiene, preventive care, and disease treatment (Caldwell, 1979). Such a social synergy may be the explanation of the sometimes-observed limited effect of direct medical interventions, and of the often striking impact on child survival of social changes (such as in women's education and role in the society) in the absence of major economic progress.

A conceptual framework organizes in a systematic fashion the various mechanisms and processes which produce the outcome under observation: in this case, growth-faltering and death of children. To be able to assist analysis of empirical data, the concepts have to be translated into measurable indicators (for more on this see Duchêne and Wunsch, in this volume). Mosley and Chen (op. cit.: 32–40) give examples of direct and indirect measures of the proximate and socio-economic determinants which they used in the model described above. However, it is very likely that investigation of some and perhaps even most of the concepts outlined in the framework may not be possible in the same field survey. A different method of investigation may be necessary to establish, for instance, differentials in levels and patterns of morbidity and mortality to the method which would investigate the mechanisms through which mother's education affects the chances of her children's survival. It is also likely that some of these mechanisms operate differently in different societies, or change over time (among different generations) in the same society. In investigations of the mechanisms through which a social synergism operates it may be that research approaches and methodology developed in social anthropology will yield significant returns, as the work of Caldwell and associates has shown (Caldwell *et al.*, 1982; Caldwell, 1985).

The conceptual framework suggested by Mosley and Chen (1984) is useful not only for the design of new surveys but also for drawing together findings from existing studies, or designing additional studies to fill in the gaps in knowledge on operation of biological and social synergisms. Its value has been demonstrated, for instance, in a study of squatter settlements in Jordan (Tekçe and Shorter, 1984), not only for its intrinsic advantage in facilitating specifications of the different orders of causality (and possible interactions) among the socio-economic and biological factors, but also for its potential for giving policy-makers insights into health-related development strategies.

Scientific research is based upon viable theories, suitable methods of analysis, and reliable data. Demography has often been criticized as lacking general theory. Many of its methods are adopted from statistics. In most instances it has to deal with data of poor quality. Yet, despite such drawbacks, significant advances have been made in the knowledge and understanding of the processes which affect the growth and structure of human populations. The development of conceptual frameworks for analysis of mortality and for the investigation of mortality determinants is an important step towards advancement of knowledge in this special area. Moreover, the results also bear a promise of practical importance for formulation of intervention policies on a wider scale than merely narrowly defined health intervention actions.

————

The chapters in this book are grouped into three sections. The first deals with methodological and conceptual problems in the study of differential mortality; in the second section, regional and country studies of mortality differentials, or specific aspects of such differentials—such as spacing of births, and health dynamics in old age—are presented. The third section is devoted to the impact upon health and mortality of crisis situations.

The path from concéptual framework or explanatory theory to its empirical testing is explored by J. Duchêne and G. Wunsch. Concepts and relations specified in a verbal framework have to be translated into operational definitions or indicators. These indicators and postulated relationships form an auxiliary theory which can then be submitted to empirical tests in the form of a statistical model. As the authors stress, the choice of a statistical model depends on the type of problem, that is, on the characteristics of the auxiliary theory, not vice versa as is unfortunately quite often the practice.

New, promising concepts, in particular those developed by W. H. Mosley alone or with L. C. Chen, are taken up in the subsequent chapter by R. Gray. He reviews approaches to field studies of health in developing countries and suggests some practical modifications by means of which demographic studies could provide more information on health. His critical appraisal of various algorithms for the identification of diseases or disease processes which may provide useful indicators for the proximate determinants of mortality (using Mosley's terminology) is followed by consideration of risk factors which influence the probability of disease, the severity of illness, and the effects of medical care. Finally, the chapter addresses epidemiological approaches to the study of risk factors which could be integrated with demographic studies.

Demographic analysis of time trends and differentials in mortality is always complicated by the concurrent structural changes in the population. Some of them may be a result of demographic processes, others the result of social and economic forces, or a combination of both. Neglect of such possibilities may lead to erroneous and misleading conclusions with potential adverse implications for decisions on population policy and strategies. S. Horiuchi addresses such problems as they are encountered specifically in analysis of mortality trends. He identifies six factors that may potentially lead to erroneous appraisal of mortality change: (1) differential declines in fertility and in population growth as they affect inter-country comparisons and regional estimates of mortality levels; (2) heterogeneity of populations with respect to susceptibility of subgroups to mortality; (3) differentials in the age structure of subsections of the national population and the changes in such age patterns; (4) improved completeness of data—not only of birth and death registration but also of retrospective reporting of births and deaths in a series of surveys; (5) improved accuracy of age reporting in censuses and surveys; (6) alternative measures of mortality, which may yield inconsistent results. He suggests that the apparent slowing down of mortality decline, where detected, should be carefully examined for those potential sources of bias, and points out ways to circumvent some of the problems. In many instances, however, detailed data needed for such analysis may not be readily available in less developed countries.

The transition of mortality from high to moderate and low levels is a result of the changing structure of causes of death. By how much a current level of mortality in a country or in a particular population subgroup might be reduced depends largely on the prevailing causes of death and on the assessment of the extent to which individual diseases may be controlled: either by the deployment of suitable medical technologies; or by improving standards of living, nutrition, sanitation, and so on; or by a suitable combination of a range of such measures. To measure the potential of mortality reduction, attempts have been made to develop an index of 'preventable deaths'. S. D'Souza discusses methodological issues involved in the process of the development of such an index and presents the results of his own attempt to derive an index of preventable infant mortality. Examples of the application of his methodology are shown in his chapter for a wide range of situations from countries with high to low mortality levels.

The transition from high through moderate to low levels of mortality has not been a smooth and continuous process in many developing countries. It has often been interrupted by temporary setbacks due to political unrest and disruption, and temporary food shortages, or even famines, usually following crop failures occasioned by droughts or floods or major political and economic crises. In the 1970s there were disconcerting signs in some countries of a slowing down of mortality decline, at levels still too high not to be amenable to further reduction given the existing medical technologies. Furthermore, certain population subgroups appeared to have been disadvantaged in the process of transition: for instance, young children, pregnant women and mothers, socially and economically deprived groups, and country-dwellers have benefited least from whatever progress has been made in disease control and the improvement of health conditions. According to E. Arriaga, mortality trends in the 1960s presented fewer similarities among the eleven developing countries he studied (seven in Latin America and four in South and East Asia) than was the case in the 1950s: in some of them the rapid fall of mortality continued, in others signs of stagnation set in. Infant and child mortality appear to have fallen faster than adult mortality. Also, in the 1960s, mortality reduction appears to have been more dependent on social and economic conditions in each individual country than it did in the previous decade. The diversity continued, and became even more pronounced, in the 1970s. It is unfortunate that reasonably dependable statistics are available only for the countries which, by then, had achieved comparatively low or at least moderate levels of mortality and, hence, may not be typical of the less developed countries as a group. This constrains our ability to generalize about the conditions of mortality decline and of its stagnation. Arriaga uses new methodology, for the estimation of the contribution to life expectation at birth of mortality change by age and causes of death, which deserves wider application.

J. Guzman, comparing the trends in infant mortality among social and economic subgroups of the populations in five Latin American countries, concludes that decline was a rather general phenomenon, in particular in the 1970s. Infants born to rural families and to less-educated parents, to agricultural labourers and farmers, benefited in the process, except in Peru, where progress was comparatively slower than in the other four countries. In middle-class families (that is, in the generally better-educated groups) additional declines in infant mortality were slower and, in some instances, the rates showed a tendency to stagnate at levels of around 40 deaths per thousand live births. By and large, the tendency has been towards a reduction of the differentials in infant mortality among various social and economic groups and between geographical areas; despite that, however, significant variations still persist. Guzman suggests that further reduction of the differentials and their eventual disappearance may depend less on a more general access to medical care and services than on a more equitable distribution of 'social surplus'.

In Indonesia, wide differentials in infant and child mortality have been documented in a number of studies reviewed by B. Utomo and M. B. Iskandar. It appears that the quite impressive overall decline of infant mortality (from 135 to 98 between 1971 and 1980) did not significantly reduce many of the existing disparities in the country. Infant mortality is still three times higher in Nusa Tenggara province than in Yogyakarta province in central Java. The range of infant mortality variation among urban areas (from 50 to 142) is relatively similar to that among the rural areas (from 66 to 194). In a few provinces the urban-rural gap is now, admittedly, negligible (of the order of 2 to 7 deaths per thousand births) but in others it is still high, at 50 to 70. In conclusion the authors suggest a range of developmental and health measures that need to be undertaken if a reduction of infant and child mortality is to be achieved overall, and if existing inequalities among population subgroups and regions are to be eliminated or, at least, markedly reduced.

Underutilization of existing health services in the rural areas of Turkey is emphasized by N. Fisek as an explanation of persistently high infant and child mortality in those areas. Although infant and child mortality in the country as a whole has been reduced over approximately the last twenty years, it is still quite high in the rural areas. One of the reasons, in the author's opinion, is the failure of the parents to seek medical help in time and to follow the advice of the health personnel. Despite the fact that health services are within comparatively easy reach, only about two-thirds of deceased children were seen by a physician during their terminal illness even in the more developed rural areas; this proportion was no more than about one-third in the least-developed areas. Fisek reports in detail the results of a survey conducted in a district adequately covered with curative and preventive services. The findings suggest that more than half of the children who died during the period of the study could have been effectively treated with the available facilities. The constraint on parents' utilization of these facilities was neither cost nor distance from such facilities but, rather, ignorance and general neglect of child care, possibly associated with fear of modern medical techniques. Even when parents were advised by the visiting nurse-midwife about proper child care, or the need for the child to be taken to a physician or a hospital, 44, 91, and 66 per cent of parents, respectively, did not follow the advice. Needless to say, child mortality was significantly higher in the families where the parents did not comply with the advice given to them.

The deleterious effects on maternal health, and chances of child survival, of the narrow spacing of pregnancies and birth were first documented about sixty years ago (see Gray, 1981; Winikoff, 1983). Since then, and in particular during the last decade or so, strong evidence has been presented about the extent of the excess risk to child survival due to short inter-birth intervals surrounding the child at risk (index child). Many of the studies, however, have contributed surprisingly little to clarifying the complexity of causal links between pregnancy spacing and the health of the mother and her children. The major drawback has been the diversity of approaches found in these studies and the lack of comparability of their findings—both, partly at least, resulting from the use of data which were originally collected for other purposes. Another comparatively little-explored area of mortality research has been the high risk to infants and young children in the families which had previously experienced child loss. The 'familial' level of infant and child mortality and its causes are still inadequately explained.

A. Palloni studies the impact of narrow child spacing in twelve Latin American countries, using as control variables birth order and mother's age at birth of the index child, her education, place of residence (whether urban or rural area), length of the preceding interval, survival status of the preceding sibling, and length of the subsequent birth interval. The findings confirm, once again, the increased risk of death to children born within comparatively short intervals, whether preceding or subsequent, as well as the effect of familial levels of mortality. In the countries studied, the hypothetical reduction of mortality between birth and age five which would result from a change in the pattern of child-bearing that eliminated disadvantaged spacing categories would be, on average, at least 12 and possibly as much as 20 per cent. One of the hypotheses about mechanisms through which the negative effects of short birth intervals operate has been the potential undermining of the older sibling's chances of survival due to early weaning—itself a result of the new pregnancy. This is a rather difficult point to prove but Palloni makes an attempt, using data on breast-feeding collected in the World Fertility Survey interviews (breast-feeding information was collected only for the last and next-to-last birth). The results, presented for Peru in the chapter, lead to a qualified conclusion that breast-feeding is probably not the main mechanism through which the birth interval effect operates.

Although the primary concern of the seminar was the conditions which sustain high levels of mortality in the less developed countries, it is realized that, with the gradual decline of mortality, new health problems emerge with social, economic, demographic, and policy implications.

G. Myers reviews the current state of research into the consequences of the reductions in mortality and increases in survival—even at advanced ages—for the future: are further reductions of mortality likely in the face of apparent biological restraints on lifespan? What diseases have been responsible for past declines of mortality and are they likely to be involved in future trends? Has the increase in survival been accompanied by a disproportionate increase in handicap and disablement? What are the societal and individual implications of these trends—for instance for health planning, population growth, and alternative population structures? A number of conceptual, methodological, and data problems have emerged which will need the collaboration of demographers, epidemiologists, health statisticians, and health planners if our present knowledge in this comparatively little-developed area of mortality research is to be advanced.

Famines and epidemics have been, in the past, the main cause of wide fluctuations of mortality, often ravaging the population over a comparatively short period of time and raising mortality levels many times above the long-term average. Although major epidemics appear now to be history, famines still represent a major danger to many societies and population groups living at the margin of subsistence level. In many parts of the developing world, it has been suggested that such marginal groups are increasing, not merely in numbers, but proportionately.

A. Bouckaert sets out, in a systematic way, concepts and a theoretical framework for the study of disasters in human populations. He defines what constitute the characteristics of catastrophic (in contrast to fluctuating) mortality; draws a distinction between man-made and natural disasters; and elaborates upon the importance of the pattern of human settlements, and the organization of society, for the severity of the sequelae of disasters.

The Chinese famine of 1959–61, its causes and implications, demographic, social, economic, and political, are discussed in P. Kane's chapter, which is a preliminary report on a major study now in progress. Certain features of the Chinese demographic and social responses to famine are similar to those identified in the studies of famine in other societies. However, there are important differences, some of which are undoubtedly due to the fact that China's is a centrally controlled economy. Both types of findings may help to further our understanding of how people respond to this particular type of disaster within the constraints of social, economic, and political structures and institutions.

The selection of discussions presented in this book is an attempt to promote further investigations of determinants of mortality differentials and to invite discussion about more effective ways of doing so. Modern health systems interact—at the community and family level—with traditional social systems, and often with strongly held cultural values. This interaction has to be explored jointly by biomedical and social scientists: demographers, sociologists, social anthropologists, epidemiologists, and health system analysts. The task is a complex one, and it would be rather naïve to expect that all the problems involved could be resolved in the course of one short meeting and in a score of papers.

Nevertheless, it is hoped that this volume will stimulate further study of differential mortality in a range of environmental and social settings, and that the methodological and conceptual approaches discussed here will contribute to such further explorations.

References

Caldwell, J. C. (1979), 'Education as a Factor in Mortality Decline: An Examination of Nigerian Data', *Population Studies* 33(3), 395–414.

—— (1985), 'Strengths and Limitations of the Survey Approach for Measuring and Understanding Fertility Change: Alternative Possibilities' in J. Cleland and J. Hobcraft (eds.), *Reproductive Change in Developing Countries: Insights from the World Fertility Survey*, Oxford University Press, Oxford, 45–63.

—— and P. F. McDonald (1981), 'Influence of Maternal Education on Infant and Child Mortality: Levels and Causes', *IUSSP International Population Conference, Manila 1981*, vol. 2. International Union for the Scientific Study of Population, Liège, 79–96.

—— P. H. Reddy, and P. Caldwell (1982), 'The Causes of Demographic Change in Rural South India: A Micro Approach', *Population and Development Review* 8(4), 689–727.

Chen, L. C. (1981), 'Diarrhea and Malnutrition: Interactions, Mechanisms, and Interventions', workshop on Interactions of Diarrhea and Malnutrition, Bellagio, Italy, 11–15 May 1981.

Cleland, J., and Z. Sathar (1983), 'The Effect of Birth Spacing on Childhood Mortality in Pakistan', World Fertility Survey, WFS/TECH 2163, London.

D'Souza, S., A. Bhuiya, and M. Rahman (1982), 'Socioeconomic Differentials in Mortality in a Rural Area of Bangladesh' in *World Health Organization, Mortality in South and East Asia: A Review of Changing Trends and Patterns, 1950–1975*, World Health Organization, Manila, 195–214.

Gray, R. H. (1981), 'Birth Intervals, Postpartum Sexual Abstinence and Child Health' in H. J. Page and R. Lesthaeghe (eds.), *Child Spacing in Tropical Africa: Traditions and Change*, Academic Press, London, 93–110.

Hobcraft, J., J. McDonald, and S. Rutstein (1983), 'Child-spacing Effects on Infant and Early Childhood Mortality', paper presented at the annual meeting of the Population Association of America, Pittsburgh, 14–16 April 1983.

Lindenbaum, S. (1983), 'The Influence of Maternal Education on Infant and Child Mortality in Bangladesh', International Centre for Diarrhoeal Disease Research, Dhaka, Bangladesh, August 1983 (mimeographed).

Mahadevan, K. (1984), 'Mortality, Biology and Society: Analytical Framework and Conceptual Model', paper presented at a seminar on Society and Population Dynamics, held at the SV University, Tirupati, India, 4–9 January 1984.

Martorell, R., and T. J. Ho (1984), 'Malnutrition, Morbidity and Mortality' in W. H. Mosley and L. C. Chen (eds.), *Child Survival: Strategies for Research*, Population and Development Review, supplement to vol. 10, 49–68.

Mitra, S. N. (1979), 'Infant and Child Mortality in Bangladesh: Levels and Differentials', MA thesis, Development Studies Centre, Australian National University, Canberra.

Mosley, W. H. (1980), 'Social Determinants of Infant and Child Mortality: Some Considerations for an Analytical Framework', discussion paper presented at a conference on Health and Mortality in Infancy and Early Childhood, held in Cairo, 18–20 May 1980.

—— (1985*a*), 'Will Primary Health Care Reduce Infant and Child Mortality? A critique of some Current Strategies, with Special Reference to Africa and Asia' In J. Vallin and A. Lopez (eds.), *Health Policy, Social Policy, and Mortality Prospects*, Ordina Editions, Liège, 103–138.

—— (1985*b*), 'Biological and Socioeconomic Determinants of Child Survival: A Proximate Determinants Framework Integrating Fertility and Mortality Variables', *IUSSP International Population Conference, Florence 1985*, International Union for the Scientific Study of Population, Liège, 189–208.

—— and L. C. Chen (1984), 'An Analytical Framework for the Study of Child Survival in Developing Countries' in W. H. Mosley and L. C. Chen (eds.), *Child Survival: Strategies for Research*, Population and Development Review, supplement to vol. 10, 25–45.

Palloni, A. (1985), 'Health Conditions in Latin America and Policies for Mortality Change' In J. Vallin and A. Lopez (eds.), *Health Policy, Social Policy and Mortality Prospects*, Ordina Editions, Liège, 465–92.

Pool, I. D. (1982), 'Is New Zealand a Healthy Country?', *New Zealand Population Review* 8 (2), 2–27.

Schultz, T. P. (1985), 'Household Economics and Community Variables as Determinants of Mortality', *IUSSP International Population Conference, Florence 1985*, vol. 2, International Union for the Scientific Study of Population, Liège, 225–36.

Tekçe, B., and F. C. Shorter (1984), 'Determinants of Child Mortality: A Study of Squatter Settlements in Jordan' in W. H. Mosley and L. C. Chen (eds.), *Child Survival: Strategies for Research*, Population and Development Review, supplement to vol. 10, 257–80.

Venkatacharya, K. (1985), 'An Approach to the Study of Socio-biological Determinants of Infant and Child Morbidity and Mortality', *IUSSP International Population Conference, Florence 1985*, vol. 2, International Union for the Scientific Study of Population, Liège, 237–53.

Ware, H. (1984), 'Effects of Maternal Education, Women's Roles and Child Care on Child Mortality' In W. H. Mosley and L. C. Chen (eds.), *Child Survival: Strategies for Research*, Population and Development Review, supplement to vol. 10, 191–214.

Winikoff, B. (1983), 'The Effects of Birth Spacing on Child and Maternal Health', *Studies in Family Planning* 14 (10), 231–45.

Part II

Methodological Issues

1 Conceptual Frameworks and Causal Modelling

JOSIANNE DUCHÊNE and GUILLAUME WUNSCH

Department of Demography, University of Louvain, Belgium

Proof/n. Evidence having a shade more of plausibility than that of unlikelihood. The testimony of two credible witnesses as opposed to that of only one.

Ambrose Bierce: *The Devil's Dictionary*

Theory purports to explain a set of facts. Without theory facts are not interpretable. As Pierre Duhem has written, interpretation substitutes for the concrete given, gathered by observation, abstract and symbolic representations which correspond to the given by virtue of the theories admitted by the observer. (See R. Ariew (1984) for a major review of Duhem's views on scientific theories, presently known as the Duhem–Quine theses.) The elaboration of a theory is composed of various stages. Using Blalock's (1968) terminology, one distinguishes firstly a *general theory* made up of abstract concepts and relations. As concepts are not observable, they have to be translated into measurable indicators; these indicators, and their interrelations, compose the *auxiliary theory*. Finally, as one of the present authors has argued (Wunsch, 1984), a third stage in theory-building should be added to Blalock's two-level approach, namely the *statistical model* which links, through various assumptions, the auxiliary theory to the 'concrete given', to go back to Duhem's terminology.

The purpose of this chapter is to discuss some aspects of this three-level model of theory-building. In the first section, we will define the various relationships which can link concepts together, in a general theory. The second section will discuss the passage from concept to indicator, in a conceptual framework approach. The third section considers a causal model specifically designed to take into account both concepts and indicators, that is, covariance structure analysis. We will use throughout Caldwell's theory (1979) on the role of education as a factor in mortality decline as an example. This theory is well defined and parsimonious; it has been tested by Caldwell himself, in the above-mentioned article, and by Martin *et al*. (1983).

Concepts, Relations, and Causal Graphs

General theories are usually expressed in a verbal form. For example, following Caldwell, the impact of education on child mortality can work through three channels: educated mothers become less 'fatalistic' about illness; an educated mother is more capable of drawing advantages from the modern world; and education of women changes the balance of familial relationships. Caldwell is especially concerned with the last channel: education influences family decision-making; changes in the latter will eventually reverse the direction of net intergenerational wealth flows, increase child-centredness, and improve the situation of children. Let e represent education of mother, f family decisions, g intergenerational wealth flows, and i illness. Caldwell's statement can be transformed into $e(R)f(R)g(R)i$, where the Rs stand for relationships to be defined. The main purpose of a general theory is to define the concepts used (e, f, g, and i in the present example) and to specify the various relations (R) between the concepts. Some assumptions have also to be made about the concepts not included in the system, such as the supposition that they have a random effect on the concepts included. (This assumption is sometimes called the 'weak closure' of the system.) In the present example, if we want to avoid spurious results we should also integrate as controls in the framework the other channels through which education can influence illness, *per se* or as a proxy for socio-economic status.

Before defining the various relationships that can be postulated between concepts, something should be said about the concepts themselves. Concepts reflect ideas and can therefore be understood differently from person to person. If the theory is to be comprehended by others, concepts need to be defined in a more or less precise way. At the very least, their scope should be delineated. This obvious recommendation is, in fact, rarely followed in the demographic literature; most theories are therefore probably understood correctly (if at all) by their authors alone! A second reason for giving the content of a concept is that it facilitates the choice of indicators. Furthermore, if a concept is understood differently between various investigators, it is probable that the operational definitions of this concept will also differ from person to person. Bohrnstedt (1970) has therefore suggested that the domain covered by each concept be stratified into its various meanings, each stratum being further subdivided if necessary in order to reach a *single dimension*. The content of the original concept is thus decomposed into its various dimensions. The search for unidimensionality is justified in order to avoid the same concept having different independent meanings. A set of indicators of a concept should all measure just one latent trait; this is impossible to achieve from the start if the concept is itself multidimensional. Unidimensionality of constructs can therefore be considered as a prerequisite to causal modelling (see Anderson and Gerbing, 1982).

Consider now the various relationships which can be postulated between concepts in the conceptual framework. Following Suppes (1975), one can define the event $B_{t'}$ as a prima-facie (positive) *cause* of the event A_t if and only if

$$t' < t, \tag{1}$$
$$P(B_{t'}) > 0, \tag{2}$$
$$P(A_t/B_{t'}) > P(A_t). \tag{3}$$

A prima-facie (positive) cause increases the probability of occurrence of the event A_t. Conversely, $B_{t'}$ is a prima-facie (negative) cause of A_t if the non-occurrence of $B_{t'}$ (i.e. $\bar{B}_{t'}$) is a prima-facie (positive) cause of A_t. In the social sciences, one often considers relations between non-dichotomous variables. Following Suppes once again, we may write that 'The property $y_{t'}$ is *a* (weak) *prima-facie* (positive) *quadrant cause* of the property X_t if and only if

$$t' < t, \tag{4}$$
For all x and y if $P\,(y_{t'} \geqslant y) > 0$ then $P(X_t \geqslant x/Y_{t'} \geqslant y) \geqslant P\,(X_t \geqslant x)$.
$$\tag{5}$$

The term quadrant is used because (5) may be rewritten as

$$P(X_t \geqslant x, Y_{t'} \geqslant y) \geqslant P\,(X_t \geqslant x)\,P(Y_{t'} \geqslant y). \tag{6}$$

If a property $Y_{t'}$ is a (weak) prima-facie negative quadrant cause of property X_t, then its opposite, $-Y_{t'}$, is a (weak) prima-facie (positive) quadrant cause of X_t. A causal relationship between two variables $Y_{t'}$ and X_t supposes that one can order, either temporally or logically, the occurrence of both events or the change of states in both variables. A causal relation will be represented by the arrow $Y \rightarrow X$. If no temporal or logical order can be assumed a priori, the possible relation will be called an *association* and will be represented by the link $Y \leftarrow X$.

A typology of causal relations has been given by Nowak (1975), considering an independent X variable, a confounding variable T, and a dependent variable Y.

First Case

When X and T are statistically independent, the order of X and T is irrelevant. T and X may either belong to the same sufficient condition for Y (if the partial relationship between X and Y increases for T and disappears for $\bar{T}$) or to different alternative causes of Y (if the partial relationship between X and Y is positive and approximately equal both for T and $\bar{T}$).

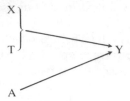

Figure 1.1

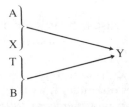

Figure 1.2

Second Case

When X and T are positively associated and T preceeds X, T may be either a part of two sufficient conditions for X and Y (in this case, the relationship between X and Y is spurious and disappears both for T and T̄) or T produces

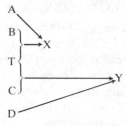

Figure 1.3

Y both directly and indirectly by producing X. In this case, X and T either belong to the same sufficient condition of Y or belong to different alternative causes of Y.

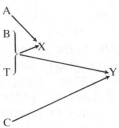

Figure 1.4

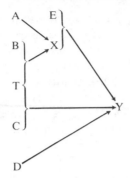

Figure 1.5

Third Case

When X and T are positively associated and X precedes T, X may be either an indirect cause of Y if the relationship between X and Y disappears both for T and T̄ or X produces Y both directly and indirectly by producing T. In this latter case X and T arc cither supplementary causes for Y or belong to alternative causes of Y. Causal graphs are similar to the two last figures of the second case, with X taking the place of T and vice versa.

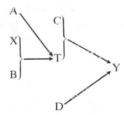

Figure 1.6

A *feedback* relationship is a particular form of a causal chain. It can be represented by Figure 1.7. X is a component of a sufficient cause of Y which is itself a component of a sufficient cause of X . . .

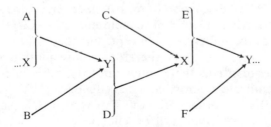

Figure 1.7

Variables X and Y are part of an interdependent system in permanent change, never reaching equilibrium: a change of X at t'' increases the probability of a change of Y at t', and therefore of the probability of a change in X at t.

The last relationship to be taken into account is the *interaction* effect. Following Boudon (1970), interaction exists between k variables when the impact of each of these k variables on a dependent variable is influenced by one or more of the remaining $(k - 1)$ variables. Interaction exists between all interdependent causes of Y: in other words, interaction cannot exist between the independent causes of Y.

The general theory is now complete: unidimensional concepts have been defined, their hierarchy has been postulated, and their interrelations have been predicted. A causal diagram has been drawn to represent the theory. Though no test of the theory has yet been made, this exercise is by itself already very fruitful: the investigator has been forced to clarify his/her concepts, and to assemble them in a causal order, distinguishing between explanatory and intermediate variables, and between direct and indirect effects on the endogenous variables in the system. Possible contradictions in the theory will have appeared. Relevant concepts have been retained, and the others discarded. Amid the concepts which have been kept, some have possibly been chosen as predictors and others as controls. Finally, assumptions have been made concerning the closure of the system. One can now proceed to the choice of indicators for the concepts, and to establishing the auxiliary theory.

Valid and Reliable Indicators: A Conceptual Framework Approach

Indicators have to be both reliable and valid. Reliable indicators have small random measurement error:[1] they are precise, though not necessarily valid. Validity, on the other hand, is the property of an indicator to be a true image of the underlying concept. Good indicators should be both reliable and valid, that is, precise and exact.

Translating concepts into indicators is a crucial step in the measurement model. If operational definitions are inadequate, the auxiliary theory will be a biased image of the general theory, and the results may be meaningless (for a recent non-technical discussion of measurement error, see Blalock, 1984). Few rules exist for the derivation of reliable and valid indicators. Hopefully, indicators reflect the underlying concept, but they may be tapping other traits too. If possible, one should therefore choose multiple indicators for a concept, in order to attenuate the impact of these other factors. Some indicators may be equivalent across contexts (Blalock (1982) calls these 'reference indicators') while others are not. This is a further reason to opt for multiple indicators, as some can be chosen as reference indicators and others as specific to the setting. Another distinction has been made recently

---

[1] Not to be confused with sampling error. A reliable instrument should yield the same measure on repeated trials on the same individuals.

by Bollen (1984) between 'cause' and 'effect' indicators. In the first case, a change in the indicator causes a change in the latent variable; in the second case, indicators are determined by the underlying concept.

A brief overview of reliability and validity estimation can be found in Wunsch and Duchêne (1985); the subject is covered more extensively in, for example, Carmines and Zeller (1979 and 1980). In this section, we will consider mostly interval-level indicators and assume that the latter are linearly related to their latent traits. Linear measurement models and especially factor-analytic techniques can then be used under these assumptions, though it should be stressed that if these conditions are not met the use of factor analysis can bring about misleading results (see, for example, Hattie, 1984).

In addition to these assumptions, the two following axioms will be postulated:

Axiom 1: If a set of indicators of an underlying concept comprises two (or more) independent factors, then the underlying trait is multidimensional, as a concept may not cover different independent meanings.

Axiom 2: Indicators and concepts are temporally simultaneous.

We now define 'cause' and 'effect' indicators as follows: an indicator is a 'cause' of a concept if a change of state of an indicator logically (as indicators and concepts are simultaneous—axiom 2) entails a change of state of the concept; or, vice versa, a change of state in the concept logically leads to a change of state in an 'effect' indicator. For example, income change may bring about a change in socio-economic status (SES): income level will therefore be a 'cause' indicator of SES. On the other hand, changes in SES may lead to changes in residence; residence is therefore an 'effect' indicator of SES. If all indicators in a set of multiple indicators are 'effect' indicators, then all these indicators will be highly correlated if they are valid indicators of an underlying dimension (Bollen, 1984). They should therefore all load heavily (positively or negatively) on a sole common factor. (It is important to keep in mind that correlated variables are not necessarily redundant and substitutable; see Guttman, 1977.) If all (or some) indicators in the set are 'cause' indicators, they need not be intercorrelated (Bollen, 1984), and therefore they may load on different independent factors. In this case, according to axiom 1, they will represent different concepts. We should therefore be wary when we mix together cause and effect indicators in a set of multiple indicators.

If we accept the assumptions of a factor-analytic measurement model,[2] the validity of a set of multiple indicators can be tested using confirmatory factor analysis (CFA). Consider, for example, Caldwell's theory as tested

---

[2] In various situations, we may consider these assumptions to be too strong to be acceptable; one should avoid, in these cases, structuring the problem according to the structure of the method (see Ratcliffe, 1983).

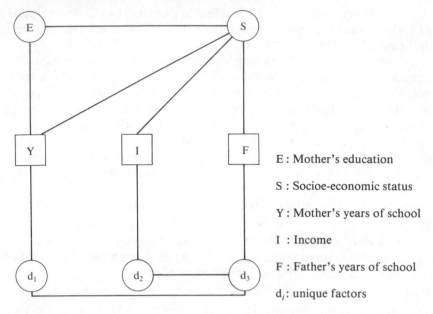

E : Mother's education

S : Socioe-economic status

Y : Mother's years of school

I : Income

F : Father's years of school

d_i: unique factors

Figure 1.8. Concepts and indicators for Caldwell's independent variables
Source: Martin *et al.*, 1983.

by Martin *et al.* One can schematically represent the 'independent' variables
in the theory by the diagram in Figure 1.8. We have restricted the model to
the predictor 'mother's education' (E) and to the control 'socio-economic
status' (S). These concepts (circles) are represented by the indicators (rec-
tangles) 'mother's years of school' (Y), 'income of father' (I), 'father's
years of school' (F). One postulates that E is linked to Y but not to I and F; S
is considered to be represented by all three indicators. In an exploratory
factor-analytic model, links would also be assumed between E, I, and F.
The confirmatory model assumes these links are nil. Variables d_i represent
the 'unique' factors, that is, errors in variables (common and unique factors
are assumed to be uncorrelated). Correlations have been assumed to exist
between Y and F, as well as between I and F. On the other hand, the correlation between Y and I has been constrained to zero. We may therefore write
the following equations, assuming a linear factor model and standardized
variables:

$$Y = l_{YE}F + l_{YS}S + d_1$$
$$I = 0E + l_{IS}S + d_2$$
$$F = 0E + l_{FS}S + d_3$$

where l_{ij} stands for loadings between indicator i and concept j.
   In matrix notation, one has:

$$\begin{bmatrix} Y \\ I \\ F \end{bmatrix} = \begin{bmatrix} l_{YE} & l_{YS} \\ 0 & l_{IS} \\ 0 & l_{FS} \end{bmatrix} \begin{bmatrix} E \\ S \end{bmatrix} + \begin{bmatrix} d_1 \\ d_2 \\ d_3 \end{bmatrix}$$

or, in general form:

$$x = D c + d$$

where x, c, and d respectively stand for vectors of observed indicators, concepts (common factors), and errors in variables (unique factors), and D is the matrix of factor loadings.

Furthermore, one considers the variance–covariance matrix among common factors

$$P = \begin{bmatrix} p_{EE} & p_{ES} \\ p_{SE} & p_{SS} \end{bmatrix}$$

where p_{kk} represents the variance of factor k and p_{kr} the covariance between factor k and factor r. In the confirmatory model, one assumes that $p_{kr} = p_{rk}$.

One also has a variance–covariance matrix covering the unique factors; in the present example, one may write:

$$T = \begin{bmatrix} t_{11} & 0 & t_{13} \\ 0 & t_{22} & t_{23} \\ t_{31} & t_{32} & t_{33} \end{bmatrix}$$

The diagonal elements correspond to the variances of the unique factors, and the off-diagonals to their covariances. In this example, $t_{12} = t_{21}$ has been constrained to zero.

If Z represents the variance–covariance matrix between the indicators, it can be shown (see, for example, Long, 1983) that the following covariance matrix equation holds:

$$Z = DPD' + T, \text{ where } D' \text{ is } D \text{ transposed.}$$

If the model is *identified*, the covariance equation can be solved for the parameters in the matrices, D, P, and T, using a fitting function.

As one sees, CFA differs from factor-analysing each set of multiple indicators separately, in that it simultaneously takes into account all of the observed variables and latent factors in the conceptual framework. CFA is also different from the more usual form of (exploratory) factor analysis, as noted previously, because it places constraints on some of the relationships on the basis of the conceptual framework.

If one accepts the assumptions of the factor-analytic approach, CFA is therefore a particularly suitable measurement model when a conceptual framework has been developed. The loadings matrix D indicates the degree of linkage between abstract concepts and their operational definitions as postulated by the conceptual framework. If some of the loadings are low, this indicates that some of the assumed relationships between concepts and indicators are not valid. The squared correlation between an indicator and its underlying concept measures the proportion of valid variance. Low loadings (or correlations) therefore indicate that the measure is either not valid or unreliable.[3] An excellent example of the application of CFA to measurement of data quality in surveys, on the basis of a conceptual framework, can be found in Andrews (1984); for a longitudinal design, see, for instance, Hanna (1984).

Structural Relations and Measurement Models

When all the variables in the framework are observed, causal modelling is well covered by classical econometric techniques (see, for instance, Duncan, 1975). Direct and indirect effects can be examined through the use of path analysis, both for continuous data (see Asher, 1976; Kendall and O'Muircheartaigh, 1977) and for discrete data (Winship and Mare, 1983). Relationships between sets of independent and dependent variables can be treated by the canonical correlation approach, or by the more recently developed set correlation method (Cohen, 1982). When the structural relationships have been developed between concepts (unobserved variables), as in the case of the 'general theory' component of a conceptual framework, standard multivariate techniques are, however, not applicable. Such is the case, for example, of Caldwell's theory of mortality decline: the causal model is elaborated in terms of unobserved concepts, but it can obviously be tested only on the basis of the operational definitions of these concepts.

Structural modelling in terms of unobserved concepts measured by empirical indicators can be undertaken by having recourse to covariance structure analysis (CSA). In the field of demography, this approach has been used, among others, by E. Thomson (1983) in her analysis of individual or couple utility of another child. This approach is largely the result of Jöreskog's work on structural equation modelling. Much of the literature on CSA is highly technical, but readable accounts can be found among others in Jöreskog and Sörbom (1982) and Long (1981 and 1983). Jöreskog and Sörbom have also developed a computer program, known as LISREL (distributed by Scientific Software, Inc.), which performs the analysis of covariance structures, as well as confirmatory factor analysis. LISREL is particularly suited to testing conceptual frameworks on the basis of operational definitions, data being given on continuous or order scales. Latent variable structural equation modelling with categorical data is not currently handled by LISREL; it can, however, be performed using recent developments presented by Muthén (1983 and 1984). The measurement model of

---

[3] When variables are standardized, loadings are equivalent to correlations between concepts and indicators in the case of orthogonal common factors (see, e.g., Kim and Mueller, 1978). As noted previously, reliability could be tested (at least in principle) by repeated measurement on the same individuals.

CSA relies on linear factor analysis; eventual extensions could possibly cover polynomial factors and interaction terms between factors, as developed by Etezadi-Amoli and McDonald (1983). Further assumptions relate to the linear simultaneous equation model used to estimate relationships between concepts, as pointed out below.

As CSA considers the relations between 'independent' (exogenous) and 'dependent' (endogenous) concepts, one has this time two measurement models of the CFA-type, linking indicators to their respective concepts. The X-indicators are related to their concepts by the matrix equation $x = D_x c_x + d_x$, the Y-indicators are represented by a similar equation $y = D_y c_y + d_y$ where D_i ($i = x$ or y) represents the matrix of factor loadings, c_i are vectors of concepts (latent factors), and d_i are vectors of unique factors, that is, errors of measurement in variables.

To these two CFA-type measurement models is now added a set of structural equations linking dependent and independent concepts. In matrix notation, one may write: $c_y = B c_y + G c_x + e$. The vector e stands for errors in equations, and the B and G matrices comprise the structural coefficients relating the endogenous concepts to one another (B matrix) and the exogenous concepts to the endogenous concepts (G matrix).

Furthermore, seven variance–covariance matrices are distinguished. Four matrices relate to the measurement models and express the associations between the observed independent and dependent indicators, and between their respective errors in variables. Let us call them Z_x, Z_y, T_x, and T_y, as in the CFA model. Finally, three variance–covariance matrices correspond to the structural latent concepts: the first (K) corresponds to the associations between the endogenous concepts, the second (N) to the exogenous concepts, and the third (M) to the errors in equations. A complicated equation (see, for example, Long, 1983, 58–9) relates the variances and covariances between the indicators (Z) to the parameters of the model contained in the eight matrices D_x, D_y, B, G, N, M, T_x, and T_y (K does not appear as such in the *reduced form* of the structural equations).

The main assumptions of CSA are the following. First, both structural equations and factor equations are linear. Second, concepts and measurement errors are uncorrelated. Third, measurement errors and errors in equations are uncorrelated across equations. Fourth, exogenous variables are not correlated with errors in equations. All variables are, furthermore, measured from their means. The first condition is required for all linear models. The second condition is necessary for the measurement models, while the fourth is assumed for the structural equation model. The third assumption is needed for pooling together the measurement and structural models. Finally, it is assumed, as usual in structural equations, that the matrix I–B is non-singular,[4] where I is the identity matrix.

---

[4] This implies no redundancy in the reduced-form equations.

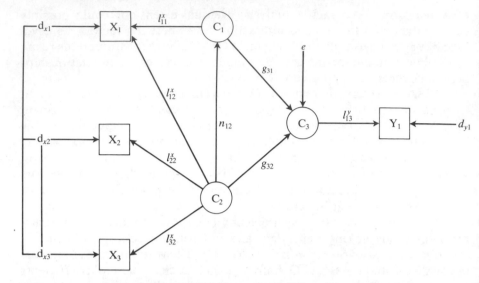

Figure 1.9.   Structural relations and measurement models for Caldwell's thesis

As in CFA, parameters can be constrained in the two measurement models. Furthermore, parameters can be restricted to zero in the B and G structural matrices, implying the absence of causal relationships between specific variables. This corresponds to dropping arrows in the causal diagram representing the conceptual framework. For example, Figure 1.9 presents the causal diagram related to a simplified version of the Caldwell thesis. C_3 is child mortality represented by age of child at death (y_1). C_1 and C_2 stand respectively for mother's education and for socio-economic status. C_1 is represented by years of school of mother (x_1), while socio-economic status is operationally defined by x_1 as well as by income (x_2) and years of school of father (x_3). In this example, one has assumed that all indicators are 'effect' indicators. Parameters g_{31} and g_{32} are structural coefficients representing the impact of the exogenous concepts C_1 and C_2 on the endogenous concept C_3. The ds are errors in variables for the x and y indicators, while the ls are the corresponding factor loadings. The covariance between the two exogenous concepts is n_{12}. The error in equation, representing the fact that C_1 and C_2 do not perfectly 'explain' C_3, is noted by the variable e.

The major problem in CSA is identification. The model *must* be identified, or else parameter estimation is meaningless. No easy method exists to test the identification of the covariance structure model. The problem is especially important in non-recursive models, models including simultaneous causality represented by double-way arrows in the causal diagram.[5] If

---

[5] We have argued previously that, at least in principle, double-way arrows should not exist, for if C_1 causes C_2, C_2 may not be simultaneously a cause of C_1.

identification has been proven by showing that the variances and covariances of factors can be solved in terms of the variances and covariances of indicators, a tedious but necessary procedure, estimation may proceed on the basis of a suitable fitting function. LISREL VI presently estimates the parameters, at the user's option, by the method of instrumental variables, by unweighted, two-stage, or generalized least squares, or by maximum likelihood. Standard errors of the parameter estimates may be calculated, under assumptions of normality.

One sees that CSA combines a psychometric approach to measurement error (confirmatory factor analysis) with the econometric techniques of causal modelling. CSA is therefore, at present, the most powerful statistical technique dealing with conceptual frameworks translated into suitable auxiliary theories through the use of operational definitions. On the other hand, CSA requires that a number of assumptions be met; these assumptions, added to those already contained in the auxiliary theory, may not be to everyone's taste. In that case, more modest techniques may be preferred: in the case of ill-structured problems, approaches other than well-structured quantitative techniques may even be more suitable, as Ratcliffe (1983) has argued. It should also be stressed that the auxiliary theory may lead to an unidentified model, or to one which poorly fits the data. When these situations arise, the conceptual framework has to be changed accordingly, on the basis of theory, on the one hand, and of the structure which, it is hoped, is contained in the data, on the other.

Conclusion

A conceptual framework is a way of structuring reality according to one's assumptions; as such, it does not constitute reality itself. Though theories are not the *laws of nature*, and reality cannot be considered *per se* independently from theory and measurement, there should at least be some congruence between one's theoretical propositions and the 'concrete given'. The purpose of this chapter has been to cover various phases in the passage from theory to data, stressing mainly the importance of defining unidimensional concepts and adequate relationships between concepts, as well as the need to test the reliability and validity of the concepts' operational definitions.

Confirmatory factor analysis and covariance structure analysis are powerful tools to use in measurement and causal models. It must be remembered, however, that these methods rely on a series of rather strong assumptions. As the general theory itself is already but one's view of reality, and as a set of conditions must also be satisfied if indicators are to correspond to concepts, the whole process of scientific discovery seems to be based on somewhat fragile grounds! No wonder, then, that widely divergent theories may sometimes fit the data more or less equivalently. Though the arbitrary nature of Science cannot be avoided (after all, the rules of Science are man-made), we can at least try to play the game correctly. If we do, we may hopefully end up one day like Lewis Carroll's mad gardener:

> He thought he saw a Garden-Door
> That opened with a key:
> He looked again, and found it was
> A Double Rule of three:
> 'And all its mystery, he said,
> Is clear as day to me!'

References

Anderson, J. C., and D. W. Gerbing (1982), 'Some Methods for Respecifying Measurement Models to Obtain Unidimensional Construct Measurement', *Journal of Marketing Research* 19, 453–60.

Andrews, F. M. (1984), 'Construct Validity and Error Components of Survey Measures: A Structural Modeling Approach', *Public Opinion Quarterly* 48, 409–42.

Ariew, R. (1984), 'The Duhem Thesis', *British Journal Philosophy and Science* 35, 313–25.

Asher, H. B. (1976), *Causal Modeling*, Sage Publications, Beverly Hills.

Blalock, H. M. (1968), The Measurement Problem: A Gap between the Languages of Theory and Research' in H. M. Blalock and A. B. Blalock (eds.), *Methodology in Social Research*, McGraw Hill, New York, 5–27.

—— (1982), *Conceptualization and Measurement in the Social Sciences*, Sage Publications, Beverly Hills.

—— (1984), *Basic Dilemmas in the Social Sciences*, Sage Publications, Beverly Hills.

Bohrnstedt, G. W. (1970), 'Reliability and Validity Assessment in Attitude Measurement' in G. F. Summers (ed.), *Attitude Measurement*, Rand MacNally & Co., Chicago.

Bollen, K. A. (1984), 'Multiple Indicators: Internal Consistency or no Necessary Relationship?', *Quality and Quantity* 18, 377–85.

Boudon, R. (1970), *L'Analyse mathématique des faits sociaux*, Plon, Paris.

Caldwell, J. C. (1979), Education as a Factor in Mortality Decline: An Examination of Nigerian Data, *Population Studies* 33(3), 395–414.

Carmines, E. G., and R. A. Zeller (1979), *Reliability and Validity Assessment*, Sage Publications, Beverly Hills.

Cohen, J. (1982), 'Set Correlation as a General Multivariate Data-Analytic Method', *Multivariate Behavioral Research* 17, 301–41.

Duncan, O. D. (1975), *Introduction to Structural Equation Models*, Academic Press, New York.

Etezadi-Amoli, J., and R. McDonald (1983), 'A Second Generation Nonlinear Factor Analysis', *Psychometrika* 48(3), 315–42.

Guttman, L. (1977), 'What is Not What in Statistics', *The Statistician* 26(2), 81–107.

Hanna, G. (1984), 'The Use of a Factor-analytic Model for Assessing the Validity of Group Comparisons', *Journal of Educational Measurement* 21(2), 191–9.

Hattie, J. (1984), 'An Empirical Study of Various Indices for Determining Unidimensionality', *Multivariate Behavioral Research* 19, 49–78.

Jöreskog, K. G., and D. Sörbom (1982), 'Recent Developments in Structural Equation Modeling', *Journal of Marketing Research* 19, 404–16.

Kendall, M. G., and C. A. O'Muircheartaigh (1977), 'Path Analysis and Model Building', *Technical Bulletins* (WFS) 2, 1–27.

Kim, J. O., and C. W. Mueller (1978), *Introduction to Factor Analysis*, Sage Publications, Beverly Hills.

Long, J. S. (1981), 'Estimation and Hypothesis Testing in Linear Models containing Measurement Error: A Review of Joreskog's Model for the Analysis of Covariance Structures' in P. V. Marsden (ed.), *Linear Models in Social Research*, Sage Publications, Beverly Hills.

—— (1983*a*), *Confirmatory Factor Analysis*, Sage Publications, Beverly Hills.

—— (1983*b*), *Covariance Structure Models*, Sage Publications, Beverly Hills.

Martin, L. G. *et al.* (1983), 'Covariates of Child Mortality in the Philippines, Indonesia and Pakistan: An Analysis Based on Hazard Models', *Population Studies* 37(3), 417–32.

Muthén, B. (1983), 'Latent Variable Structural Equation Modeling with Categorical Data', *Journal of Econometrics* 22, 43–65.

—— (1984), 'A General Structural Equation Model with Dichotomous, Ordered Categorical, and Continuous Latent Variable Indicators', *Psychometrika* 49(1), 115–32.

Nowak, S. (1975), 'Causal Interpretations of Statistical Relationships in Social Research' in H. M. Blalock *et al.* (eds.), *Quantitative Sociology: International Perspectives on Mathematical and Statistical Modeling*, Academic Press, New York, 79–132.

Ratcliffe, J. W. (1983), 'Notions of Validity in Qualitative Research Methodology', *Knowledge: Creation, Diffusion, Utilization* 5(2), 147–67.

Suppes, P. (1975), 'A Probabilistic Analysis of Causality' in H. M. Blalock *et al.* (eds.), *Quantitative Sociology: International Perspectives on Mathematical and Statistical Modeling*, Academic Press, New York, 49–77.

Thomson, E. (1983), 'Individual and Couple Utility of Children', *Demography* 20(4), 507–18.

Winship, C., and R. D. Mare (1983), 'Structural Equations and Path Analysis for Discrete Data', *American Journal of Sociology* 88, 54–110.

Wunsch, G. (1984), 'Theories, Models, and Knowledge: The Logic of Demographic Discovery', *Genus* 40(1–2), 1–17.

—— and J. Duchêne (1985), 'From Theory to Statistical Model', paper delivered at IUSSP General Conference, Florence.

Zeller, R. A., and E. G. Carmines (1980), *Measurement in the Social Sciences*, Cambridge University Press, Cambridge.

2 The Integration of Demographic and Epidemiologic Approaches to Studies of Health in Developing Countries

RONALD H. GRAY

School of Hygiene and Public Health, The Johns Hopkins University, Baltimore, United States

Demographers and biomedical scientists, particularly epidemiologists, have long had common interests in population-based studies of health problems in developing countries. Demographers have traditionally been concerned, among other issues, with measuring levels of mortality, and differentials in mortality associated with socio-economic characteristics such as education and income. However, demographic inquiries seldom address problems of the disease processes leading to death. Epidemiologic studies, on the other hand, have tended to focus on specific diseases or constellations of diseases, and their modes of transmission, prevention, or treatment.

These differences in disciplinary focus are reflected in basic study methodology, in explanations of mortality levels, trends, and differentials, and in policy prescriptions for future mortality reduction. However, there is a growing consensus on the need for disciplinary integration at both a descriptive and explanatory level. Mosley and Chen (1984) have provided a major step toward disciplinary convergence by the recent development of a framework for analysis of child survival which incorporates both the underlying socio-economic determinants of mortality commonly addressed by demographers, and the proximate determinants of mortality (risk factors, disease processes, prevention, and treatment) commonly addressed by epidemiologists.

There is, however, a recognized need to operationalize this conceptual framework by the integration of epidemiologic and demographic methodologies. The rationale for operationalizing this framework is the need for improved health information in developing countries:

(a) To provide descriptive data measuring the relative magnitude of different health problems so as to establish health priorities;

(b) To identify differentials which might define risk factors or subgroups at highest risk, so as to identify causal relationships and devise interventive strategies; and (*c*) To provide baseline and post-intervention data needed for the evaluation of health interventions or related activities.

The object of the present chapter is to review approaches to field studies of health in developing countries, and to suggest some practical modifications. The basic question is: how can integration of demographic and epidemiologic studies provide better information on the proximate and underlying determinants of morbidity and mortality. Much can be learned from available experience, and the intention is to suggest a synthesis rather than to develop totally new methodologies.

The following review will consider issues of mortality and morbidity within the Mosley–Chen (1984) framework, and suggest alternative study strategies. The initial discussion will focus on the use of algorithms for the identification of diseases or disease processes which may be used as indicators or markers for the proximate determinants of mortality, and on how such information can be obtained from surveys of morbidity or mortality. Then consideration will be given to the risk factors for disease, which implies measurement of the underlying determinants and factors such as maternal characteristics, environmental conditions, diet, and so on, which influence the probability of disease, the severity of illness, and the effects of medical care. I will then address epidemiologic approaches to the study of risk factors which could be integrated with demographic studies.

Studies of Mortality

Demographic studies generally employ estimates of vital rates derived from registration data, or retrospective information on mortality obtained by interview in censuses or sample surveys and from multi-round surveys. Because deaths are relatively rare events, there is a need to study large populations, and the logistics often require relatively brief death registration forms or interview schedules which limit the amount and quality of information on mortality determinants. The primary emphasis has been on the complete recording of events and basic information on the characteristics of the deceased, or in the case of child mortality on the characteristics of the parents, rather than the underlying diseases leading to or associated with death. In many countries demographic estimation is based on robust indirect techniques using retrospective data, particularly maternity histories or, more recently, information on the outcome of last pregnancy (United Nations, 1983; MacRae, 1979). Epidemiologic studies of mortality in developing countries have been mainly prospective cohort-type investigations which estimate mortality rates among individuals with and without certain predisposing conditions (for example, malnutrition), or trials of preventive and therapeutic measures with specific disease endpoints (such as vaccination or oral rehydration).

Registration or surveillance systems generally record 'cause of death', but these data are frequently defective, since the symptoms or mode of death are reported rather than the underlying disease or condition leading to death. Thus, a high proportion of deaths are attributed to ill-defined symptoms such as senility, fever, and so on (World Health Organization, 1980). In many situations registration is performed by lay workers, and WHO has attempted to systematize the lay classification of causes of disease and death (World Health Organization, 1978). However, the personnel responsible for registration are often insufficiently trained, supervised, and motivated to permit adequate reporting using the WHO system. Also, the WHO lay reporting system covers a large number of conditions, many of which are difficult to diagnose in the absence of clinical data. The average lay reporter or registrar would find it hard, if not impossible, to learn and use the twenty groups of morbid conditions listed, and to code them appropriately. Even in the Matlab demographic surveillance area, lay diagnosis based on local terminology of illness provided suboptimal cause-specific mortality data (Chen *et al.*, 1980*a*; Islam *et al.*, 1982).

Very few demographic surveys have attempted to obtain data on 'cause of death', in part because of the difficulties with retrospective lay diagnosis, and in part because of the limitations on interview time and questionnaire complexity. However, recent developments in infectious disease epidemiology and experience with specialized mortality studies may provide methodology to obtain more data on 'cause of death' in demographic inquiries. Essentially, the diagnosis of a given disease is based on a series of questions, addressed to surviving relatives, regarding symptoms and signs which are reasonably specific to the condition, and which have been directly or indirectly validated by independent means. Clearly, not all diseases can be diagnosed in this manner, but many of the major disorders leading to infant or child death can potentially be identified by diagnostic algorithms, and can serve as marker diseases for the proximate determinants suggested by Mosley and Chen (1984).

As a preamble to the discussion of diagnostic algorithms and their application to demographic surveys, it is first necessary to consider the concept of 'cause of death'. Traditionally, classification of the cause of death has been based on the assumption that there is an underlying disease which, through a sequence of morbid conditions, leads to death (World Health Organization, 1980). The WHO International Classification of Diseases (ICD) provides complex coding systems to establish sequences and to decide on the 'underlying' cause. Allowance is made for coding parallel disease processes contributing to death but which are not a part of the underlying disease sequence. The system is complex, and, even with physician diagnoses in industrialized countries, it has been shown that cause-of-death data are frequently inaccurate due to misdiagnosis, misclassification, coding errors, and 'diagnostic habit': that is, physician's preference for certain diagnoses (World Health Organization, 1980). Moreover, analysis of data using multiple causes of death has shown that the concept of an 'underlying cause' is untenable in many situations, especially at the extremes of age, where in many cases death is due to multiple causes (World Health Organization, 1980; Goodman *et al.*, 1982).

In developing countries the majority of deaths in childhood cannot be attributed to a single disease or 'cause'. Death often results from the cumulative effects of multiple recurrent illness in combination with impaired nutrition (Chen *et al.*, 1980*b*; Heywood, 1982, Mata, 1978; Martorell and Ho, 1984; Mosley and Chen, 1984; Puffer and Serrano, 1973). We therefore have to consider the constellation of diseases associated with death rather than single conditions. However, even this concept may have limited value, since, with some notable exceptions such as neo-natal tetanus or other neo-natal conditions, the sequence leading to death is often the lifetime burden of morbidity, whereas information collected during a terminal illness or after death may relate only to those conditions present shortly before demise. For example, in a recent Gambian study children with measles had persistently higher mortality than children without measles for nine months after the acute illness (Hull *et al.*, 1983). Nevertheless, the diseases occurring shortly before death can provide important information of relevance to public health priorities.

In summary, it is proposed that retrospective information on a limited number of diseases associated with death be obtained from relatives of deceased persons interviewed in demographic surveys, and that these conditions can be considered as markers for the proximate determinants of mortality.

Diagnostic Algorithms

Over the past two decades, numerous biomedical studies of specific diseases have provided diagnostic questions (algorithms) that can be used by lay workers in the field to obtain retrospective information from relatives regarding the illnesses preceding death. In particular, maternal interview data have been used to diagnose illness in dead and living children.

Potential diagnostic algorithms and their validation and limitations are described for neo-natal deaths, post-neonatal or childhood deaths, and certain adult conditions. The sensitivity and specificity of these algorithms (that is, the ability to detect true cases and non-cases of disease) and predictive value cannot be precisely quantified. Moreover, the predictive value would vary with prevalence of the disease, and all three measures might vary with the time period between death and interview, and cultural or educational factors affecting respondent recall (Barker and Rose, 1979). The principles of validation are illustrated in Figure 2.1.

True diagnosis

		Positive	Negative
Algorithm Diagnosis	Positive	a	b
	Negative	c	d

Sensitivity $= a/(a+c) =$ (True positives detected)
Specificity $= d/(b+d) =$ (True negatives detected)
Predictive Value $= a/(a+b)$

Figure 2.1.   Principles of validation
Source: Barker and Rose, 1979.

Many algorithms appear sufficiently pathognomonic to estimate the frequency of certain illnesses in field studies, and where diseases are recognized by the population, local terminology could be used to supplement these algorithms. The following section gives examples of algorithms, and although they are not exhaustive, the illustrations encompass most childhood diseases of major importance in developing countries.

Neo-natal Deaths

Neo-natal Tetanus

Neo-natal tetanus was once noted for its 'peculiar quietness', and although recognized in many cultures, was frequently underdiagnosed and under-reported by health authorities. The disease is caused by contamination of the umbilical cord stump with spores of *Clostridium tetani* due to unhygienic methods for the ligation and dressing of the severed cord. The organism grows in the necrotic tissue and releases a toxin which results in muscle spasm, and protection can be provided by vaccination of the mother. Thus, neo-natal tetanus reflects obstetrical care (vaccination), delivery practices, and environmental contamination as sources of tetanus spores (Foster, 1984; Stanfield and Galazka, 1984).

The WHO Expanded Program of Immunization (EPI) has conducted numerous surveys and hospital-based studies, and has devised an algorithm which appears relatively specific for neo-natal tetanus (Stanfield and Galazka, 1984; World Health Organization EPI, 1983). This is shown here.

1. Babies born alive who die between the third and thirtieth day of life.
2. History of normal suckling and crying at birth and for at least two days after birth.
3. Onset of illness between three and 28 days of age.

4. History of an inability to suckle followed by stiffness and/or unremitting muscle spasm ('convulsions').

Source: World Health Organization EPI, 1983.

This lay diagnosis has been validated by the following criteria:

(*a*) The age distribution of putative tetanus deaths conforms to the expected distribution based on physician diagnosis (mean age of death between 7 and 10 days), and differs from the age distribution of other neo-natal conditions which occur predominantly within two days of birth (Figure 2.2).

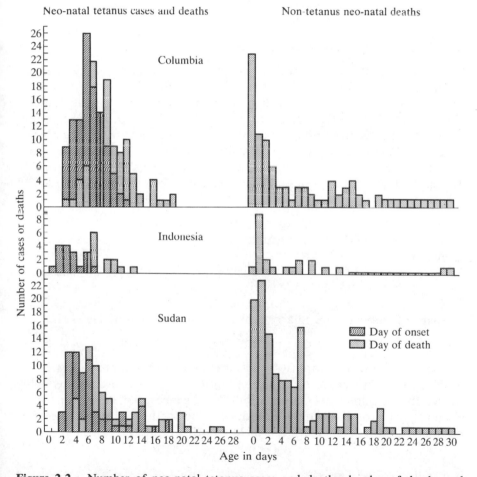

Figure 2.2. Number of neo-natal tetanus cases and deaths, by day of death, and number of non-tetanus neo-natal deaths, by day of death, in Colombia (1961–6), Indonesia (Jakarta, 1981–2), and Sudan (1981)
Source: Stanfield and Galazka, 1984.

(*b*) Putative tetanus cause-specific mortality is negligible if mothers received two or more tetanus toxoid vaccinations during pregnancy, or if traditional birth attendants (TBAs) are trained in proper aseptic care of the umbilical cord stump.

(*c*) Total neo-natal mortality is reduced if mothers in populations with prior evidence of a high incidence of neo-natal tetanus have received tetanus toxoid vaccination.

(*d*) Putative neo-natal tetanus deaths are more frequent in rural areas where contamination of the cord stump with animal excreta containing tetanus spores is more frequent. The disease is also more common in societies which use animal excreta to dress the cord stump or as material for housing construction.

Low Birth-weight, Birth Trauma, and Asphyxia

Low birth-weight due to intra-uterine growth retardation is prevalent in many developing countries as a result of poor maternal nutrition, short birth spacing, or infections during pregnancy, particularly with malaria (Villar and Belizan, 1982; McGregor *et al.*, 1983). Birth trauma and asphyxia are usually due to complications of delivery associated with poor obstetric care. These three conditions generally lead to death during the early perinatal period. Although diagnostic algorithms have not been carefully devised and tested, the potential for these conditions can be diagnosed by this algorithm.

1. Stillborn infant or infant dying within the first week of life.
2. Failure to suckle or cry normally after birth and at any time prior to death.
3. Very small infant (suggestive of low birth-weight due to intrauterine growth retardation or prematurity).
4. History of prolonged or complicated labour.
5. Signs of trauma, particularly bruising or indentation of the skull.

Source: Adapted from World Health Organization, 1978.

There is a need for simplified measures to identify infants of low birth-weight, since most births occur in the home where scales are not available for weight measurement. One possibility is the measurement of upper arm circumference, and research should be done to determine whether this permits the correct identification of low birth-weight.

Congenital Abnormalities

Even in industrialized countries congenital abnormalities are frequently underdiagnosed at birth (Christianson *et al.*, 1981). However, major external deformities such as anencephaly, spina bifida, or limb reduction defects are easily recognized by the mother, and death frequently occurs in the early neo-natal period.

In summary, if a death is reported during the first month of life it should be possible to discriminate between neo-natal tetanus, birth trauma/asphyxia and low birth-weight, or external congenital abnormalities.

Post-neonatal and Childhood Deaths

Diarrhoea/Dysentery

Numerous studies have shown that diarrhoea is associated with infant and child deaths, particularly among infants not breast-fed or during supplementation and weaning. The age-specific incidence of diarrhoea or diarrhoeal deaths varies with feeding practices in different societies, and the rates show marked seasonal variation. Investigation of the bacterial, viral, or parasitic aetiology shows a common transmission mechanism of faecal contamination of food or water through poor personal hygiene, inadequate sanitation and water supplies, and unhygienic food preparation or storage. Also, poor nutrition is associated with a longer duration of diarrhoea, and conversely diarrhoea may impair nutrition, both during the acute phase of the illness and cumulatively over the longer term. Rehydration using oral rehydration therapy can markedly reduce the case fatality from diarrhoea (Black *et al.*, 1982, 1983; Mata, 1983). Thus diarrhoea mortality reflects environmental conditions, nutritional status, and medical care.

In most studies an episode of diarrhoea can be defined as a history of three or four or more liquid stools per day, and an episode of dysentery as the passage of frequent liquid stools containing blood and mucus. In addition, acute diarrhoeal deaths are generally associated with dehydration, which can be identified by maternal interview. The suggested algorithm is given here.

1. History of three, four, or more liquid stools per day (diarrhoea).
2. Passage of blood and mucus (dysentery).
3. Dry mouth, dry wrinkled skin, sunken eyes, lack of urine, and in young infants depressed fontanelle (dehydration).
4. The above conditions should have occurred immediately before the time of death.

Source: Adapted from Black *et al.*, 1982.

In a Bangladesh study, this definition was validated by obtaining a history from the mother and examining a single stool specimen. Agreement was obtained in 80 per cent of cases. Also, the mothers' subjective reports of diarrhoea were compared with reports based on the above definition, and agreement was obtained in 97 per cent of cases (Black *et al.*, 1982). However, a less stringent definition of diarrhoea used in the Machakos project led to an overestimation of diarrhoeal incidence based on maternal recall (Leeuwenburg *et al.*, 1984*b*). Validation has also been derived from studies of prevention or treatment.

Measles

Measles is a significant cause of infant and child mortality in developing countries. Case fatality is higher in younger children, children with severly impaired nutrition, and in incidents of more severe illness with associated complications such as diarrhoea or pneumonia (Foster, 1984; Hull *et al.*, 1983; Koster *et al.*, 1981; Morley *et al.*, 1963). Medical care can reduce mortality by the treatment of complications (Jacob *et al.*, 1980). Recent studies have also shown higher measles mortality to be associated with over-crowding (Loening and Coovadia, 1983) or with the occurrence of several cases within a single family (Aaby *et al.*, 1981), suggesting that severity of infection may be related to the infective dose. Vaccination can reduce short-term mortality (Hull *et al.*, 1983), although longer-term survival may not be improved due to the competing risk of other diseases (Kasongo Project Team, 1981). Thus, measles mortality is reflective of the epidemiology of the disease (epidemics and age of infection), preventive and curative measures, nutritional status, and environmental/socio-economic conditions (for instance, crowding).

The WHO EPI (1983) algorithm for the diagnosis of measles is given here. Lay diagnoses have been used successfully in numerous field studies of vaccine efficacy (Aaby *et al.*, 1981; Hull *et al.*, 1983; Leeuwenburg *et al.*, 1984*a*; Kasongo Project Team, 1981). In addition, the disease is commonly recognized by the community.

1. History of a blotchy rash lasting three or more days, followed by peeling of the skin.
2. History of fever.
3. History of cough, runny nose, and red eyes.
4. The above conditions should have occurred within three months of death.

Source: World Health Organization E P I, 1983; Leeuwenburg *et al.*, 1984*a*.

The Machakos project in Kenya examined the discriminating value of different signs of measles. It was shown that the rash and subsequent peeling skin (desquamation), cough, and conjunctival inflammation provided maximum discrimination between cases with confirmed measles and control children with other illnesses (Leeuwenburg *et al.*, 1984*a*). Figure 2.3 shows the sensitivity, specificity, and predictive value of measles diagnosis based on an algorithm of clinical signs, compared to laboratory diagnoses based on virus isolation or antibody titres. The sensitivity and predictive value of the algorithm exceed 90 per cent.

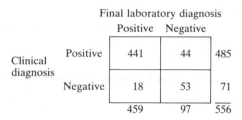

Sensitivity = 441/459 = 96 per cent
Specificity = 53/97 = 54 per cent
Predictive Value = 441/485 = 91 per cent
(See Figure 2.1 for explanation).

Figure 2.3. Validation of measles diagnosis
Source: Leeuwenburg *et al.*, 1984*a*.

Whooping Cough

Studies suggest that whooping cough (pertussis) is a significant cause of death in Africa (Morley *et al.*, 1966; Voorhoeve *et al.*, 1978; Muller *et al.*, 1984), and, as in the case of measles, mortality is higher in younger children and in cases with associated complications. Whooping cough adversely affects child nutrition and can lead to persistent respiratory symptoms (Morley *et al.*, 1966; Mata, 1978). The disease can be prevented by vaccination (Voorhoeve *et al.*, 1978; Muller *et al.*, 1984). Thus, whooping cough mortality reflects the disease epidemiology and preventive or curative care. The WHO EPI algorithm is given here.

1. History of severe cough persisting for two or more weeks.
2. Recurrent bouts of coughing with characteristic whoop.
3. Cough followed by vomiting.

Source: Adapted from World Health Organization EPI, 1983; Voorhoeve *et al.*, 1978.

In a Kenyan study using similar diagnostic criteria based on lay interviews, the diagnosis of whooping cough could be confirmed by more objective clinical investigations in 40 per cent of cases. In addition, when mothers of children with confirmed whooping cough were reinterviewed after an interval of 6–12 months, 96 per cent gave a concordant or affirmative history of previous whooping cough, suggesting reliability of recall for positive cases in which a clinical diagnosis had been made (Voorhoeve *et al.*, 1978). A number of vaccine trials have shown declines in whooping cough cases diagnosed by similar algorithms (Cook, 1978; Muller *et al.*, 1984).

Acute Lower Respiratory Tract Infections

Acute lower respiratory tract infections (ALRTI) such as pneumonia and bronchiolitis of bacterial and viral origin have been identified as major causes of child mortality, particularly in highland populations of Papua New Guinea (Riley *et al.*, 1981*a*), but they may also be important in the Indian subcontinent (Bulla and Hitze, 1978; Chen *et al.*, 1980*a*). The case fatality rate is higher among infants, undernourished children, and in over-crowded conditions, and antibiotic treatment can reduce mortality sub-stantially (Foster, 1984; McCord and Kielmann, 1978; Riley *et al.*, 1981*b*). Thus, like measles and pertussis, ALRTI reflect disease epidemiology (geographic area, age, season), nutrition, living conditions, and medical care.

An algorithm for ALRTI is given in here. Although not adequately valid-ated, vaccine trial data suggest these disorders can be diagnosed by history (Riley *et al.*, 1981*a*).

1. Cough and fever.
2. Difficulty in breathing or rapid respiration due to shortness of breath or chest pain.
3. Duration less than two weeks.

Source: Riley *et al.*, 1981*a*; Essex, 1978.

Tuberculosis

Tuberculosis in childhood is difficult to recognize due to its numerous mani-festations and chronic symptomatology. Shown here is a possible algorithm based on WHO suggestions which have not been evaluated (World Health Organization, 1978; World Health Organization EPI, 1983).

1. Chronic cough for three months or more (unresponsive to antibiotic treatment).
2. Weight loss.
3. Slight fever.
4. Blood in the sputum.
5. Abdominal swelling.
6. Painless swellings (lymph nodes) in neck, under the arms, or in the groin.
7. Swelling of the joints of slow onset.

Source: Adapted from World Health Organization, 1978; World Health Organization EPI, 1983.

Malnutrition

Protein–calorie malnutrition is well recognized as a serious health problem. Undernourished children have a higher probability of death, and of more severe or protracted illness from diseases such as diarrhoea, ALRTI, measles, and whooping cough, due to impaired immune response or impairment of other body defences (such as integrity of the mucus membrane of the gut or respiratory tract) (Black *et al.*, 1983; Mata, 1983; Martorell and Ho, 1984). Diagnosis of malnutrition or undernutrition is usually based on clinical signs or anthropometric measures and may be difficult to effect from history alone. Puffer and Serano (1973) conducted a Latin American study of childhood mortality in which a series of questions were asked about the previous nutritional status of dead children. They found that they could identify clinical malnutrition from retrospective data even though the death certificates often specified other underlying causes. The algorithm is given here.

1. History of weight loss (moderate or severe).
2. Did the child's arms, legs, body, or face become thinner?
3. Did the child's legs, body, or face become swollen (oedema)?
4. Could the ribs be seen more prominently through the skin?
5. Did the child's hair fall out, pull out easily, or change colour?
6. Does the child have difficulty moving around the house or in locating food or toys after dark, compared to other children of the same age? (vitamin A).

Source: Puffer and Serrano, 1973, Sommer *et al.*, 1980

Recent studies in Indonesia suggest that vitamin A deficiency, which is a known cause of blindness, may also be associated with increased risk of child mortality and a higher incidence of morbidity from diarrhoeal or respiratory disease (Sommer *et al.*, 1983 and 1984). Night blindness (known by mothers in Indonesia as *buta ayam*, 'chicken blindness') is a defect characteristic of vitamin A deficiency, and may provide a simple field test for this condition. Studies by Sommer *et al.* (1980) show that 97 per cent of children with night blindness have objective evidence of impaired vision on ophthalmic examination, and mean serum levels of vitamin A in children with night blindness (13.4 μg/dl $\pm$ SE 0.35) were significantly lower than for normal children (18.3 μg/dl $\pm$ SE 1.00). Moreover, a history of night blindness correctly identified 84 per cent of children with clinical evidence of vitamin A deficiency (xerophthalmia). Thus, night blindness appears to be a useful marker for vitamin A deficiency, which in turn is related to nutritional practices and to risks of morbidity and mortality.

Malaria

Although recognized as a serious cause of morbidity and mortality, and of low birth-weight, malaria is difficult to diagnose without laboratory investigations to demonstrate parasites in a peripheral blood smear (Bradley and Keymer, 1984; McGregor *et al.*, 1983).

WHO (1978) has suggested that intermittent high fever with chills and prostration can be used as a crude diagnostic algorithm, but this possibility has not been evaluated, and hospital studies of clinical diagnosis correlated with blood smears show considerable error (Essex, 1978). However, in areas where malaria is endemic the severe form of the disease (largely due to *P. falciparum*) is often a recognized entity, and has a local name which could help identification. Further studies are needed to establish whether diagnosis based on history is feasible.

Trauma

Deaths from trauma are not infrequent among both children and adults. Usually such deaths are easily identified (Chen *et al.*, 1980*a*; Fortney *et al.*, 1983), although recall may be affected by legal or cultural factors which make respondents reticent about admitting to injuries due to suicide or homicide. The WHO (1978) classification of causes of injury is given here.

1. Bites or stings of venomous animals.
2. Accidental burns.
3. Accidental drowning.
4. Accidental poisoning (other than food poisoning).
5. Transport (traffic) accidents (involving railway, boats, aircraft, motor vehicles, other vehicles, animals being ridden or drawing vehicle).
6. Other accidents.
7. Suicide, self-inflicted injury.
8. Homicide, assault.
9. Violence, unknown whether accident, self-inflicted, or assault.

Source: World Health Organization, 1978.

Maternal Mortality

Maternal mortality during pregnancy, labour, and the puerperium is poorly reported even in industrialized countries (Smith *et al.*, 1984). Limited studies in developing countries have shown extremely high levels of maternal mortality, particularly among very young or older mothers and primiparous and high-parity women, and maternal deaths may contribute substantially to total adult female mortality (Chen *et al.*, 1974; Rhinehart *et al.*, 1984).

Demographic surveys often obtain estimates of adult mortality from information on orphanhood or widowhood (United Nations, 1983). If a female death was identified it would be possible to inquire whether death occurred during pregnancy, labour, or the puerperium, and to identify certain conditions associated with death (such as abortion, convulsions, prolonged labour, haemorrhage, and sepsis).

Several investigations used routine registration, hospital-based data, health-care provider interviews and physician inquiries into maternal deaths, or linkage of birth and death records to estimate maternal mortality in developing countries. However, only two studies, in Egypt and Indonesia, have utilized lay workers to interview the relatives of deceased women of reproductive age (Fortney *et al.*, 1983). In Egypt, 1,135 deaths in women of reproductive age were identified from registration data, and relatives were interviewed within two months of death. The interview questionnaires were reviewed by a medical panel to reach a final diagnosis. When a 10 per cent sample of interviews was resubmitted to the panel, there was a high degree of consistency in allocating the death to maternal causes (Fortney *et al.*, 1983).

A possible algorithm to identify maternal mortality for use in surveys of adult mortality is given here.

1. Was the woman pregnant when she died, and if so, how many months had she been pregnant? (In some cultures it might be better to ask whether the woman was menstruating regularly in the month before death.)
2. When did death occur in relation to delivery (for example, before, during, or immediately after)?
3. Did the woman have a pregnancy which terminated within two months prior to death?
4. Was death associated with vaginal haemorrhage, prolonged labour (more than two days), high fever and shock (sepsis), convulsions (eclampsia)?
5. What was the outcome of the pregnancy (live birth, still birth, neo-natal death)?
6. What medical or traditional health care did the woman receive?
7. History of induced abortion.

Source: World Health Organization, 1978, Fortney *et al.*, 1983.

Problems and Limitations of Diagnostic Algorithms

Experience has shown that retrospective demographic inquiries encounter problems of omission of events, errors in the timing of events, misstatement of age, and so on. It is to be expected that these problems of recall and misstatement will be greater if retrospective techniques are used to obtain information on diseases preceding death. However, experience with specific diseases such as neo-natal tetanus is reassuring in this regard, and at least suggests the feasibility of studying certain conditions. There is need for further empirical research to determine which questions or groups of questions have most predictive value, and in some cases scoring systems may be required, to give greater weight to questions which have greatest predictive value.

Two further issues that need to be addressed are the duration of the interval between death and interview, and the interval between onset of disease and death. It is to be expected that omissions or recall errors will be greater with longer intervals prior to interview. For example, studies of neo-natal mortality and neo-natal tetanus in the Ivory Coast suggest that omissions are minimal for interviews conducted 1–7 months after birth, and that there is more marked underestimation for intervals longer than one year (Stanfield and Galazka, 1984). Although ascertainment and precision of diagnosis may be increased if only recent events are studied, larger sample sizes will be necessary to ensure sufficient numbers of events.

The interval between disease onset and death is more problematic. Chronic conditions of long duration which persist up to death do not present major difficulties. However, in the case of acute conditions such as measles, although the disease is of short duration, the subsequent debility due to the acute illness can increase the risk of death for a considerable period of time following the initial episode (Hull *et al.*, 1983). Clearly, the reference period may vary from one disease to another and there is a need to use multiple time intervals.

There is no simple solution to the question of appropriate reference periods, but it probably would be best to restrict inquiries to deaths within the past two to five years of interview, and to illnesses occurring within a three-month period preceding death. The latter time period could be subdivided into shorter intervals (for instance, at time of death, up to one week, up to one month, and so on).

Another question is how to identify the appropriate respondent and the unit of observation to be used. Information on infant or child deaths is usually obtained from the mother, but this practice excludes women who have died, and children of dead mothers may have a very different mortality risk to children whose mothers survive. Also, if women are the sole respondents it would not be possible to estimate female adult or maternal mortality from orphanhood or widowhood data.

Another issue is the importance of studying health problems in the family. There is much evidence to suggest that some women are prone to repeated child loss and that this may relate to family factors. Also, overcrowding is an important factor in infectious disease risk; disease transmission frequently occurs within families; and disease severity may be related to illness clustering within households. These and other considerations would suggest that the unit of observation should be the household or family, as in the Malaysian Family Life Survey, rather than an individual woman, as in the WFS surveys (Davanzo, 1984; World Fertility Survey, 1983).

Numerator data on the distribution of diseases associated with death could be used to establish public health priorities. Additionally, such numerator data can be related to population exposure data (for example, socio-economic characteristics) to estimate rates or proportions of outcomes for different exposure groups. However, this only partly addresses the issues raised in the Mosley–Chen (1984) framework, in that underlying socio-economic determinants are linked to markers of proximate determinants (in this case terminal illness), but there is limited information on the operation of the proximate determinants *per se*. To complete the schema, information is required on morbidity among survivors, and on the factors associated with disease risk or utilization of medical care, which influence both morbidity and case-fatality. These issues are considered in subsequent sections.

Studies of Morbidity

Demographic studies seldom measure morbidity, and this leaves a gap in the information on the causal chain linking underlying socio-economic characteristics with mortality. For example, in the association between maternal education and child survival, it is important to know whether children of poorly educated mothers have higher mortality because they suffer more frequent, or multiple, illness as a consequence of exposure or lack of preventive care, because these illnesses are more severe, perhaps as a consequence of undernutrition; or because they have less access to therapeutic care. This information is needed both to understand how education affects health and to devise appropriate interventions.

To provide these missing links, it is necessary to undertake morbidity surveys in conjunction with mortality surveys; since morbidity is a more frequent event than mortality, smaller study samples are required. Ideally, morbidity surveys could be conducted on random subsamples of populations surveyed for mortality, although if specific subgroups are of interest, purposeful selection could be made (for instance, for more educated women in populations with a low prevalance of higher education). Also, cluster sampling may provide a cost-effective approach in certain situations (Henderson and Sundaresan, 1983).

The methodology for morbidity measurement is well established in the epidemiologic literature and could be incorporated into demographic surveys. The disease algorithms previously described can easily be used for this purpose and questions can be asked about current status as well as illness over variable periods preceding interview.

In addition to a history of illness, it is possible to examine subjects for current illnesses, especially nasopharyngeal and skin infections, and to take anthropometric measurements for evaluation of nutritional status (Martorell and Ho, 1984). Simple observation can also detect disabilities such as blindness or paralysis, and an algorithm for polio is given as an example here. In an Indonesian study of 50 clinically confirmed cases of polio, 84 per cent were diagnosed by the lay interviewers using a similar algorithm (Ulfah *et al.*, 1981).

1. Flaccid paralysis of the leg(s), arm(s), and/or trunk with wasting of the affected muscles.
2. History of an acute illness with abrupt onset of paralysis developing fully within three days among children under six years.
3. History that paralysis was not present at birth or associated with serious injury and mental retardation.

Source: Adapted from World Health Organization, EPI, 1983; Ulfah *et al.*, 1981.

Finally, additional information can be obtained on other relevant factors such as sources of exposure, nutrition and breast-feeding, medical care-seeking behaviour, and preventive measures (vaccination, contraception, personal hygiene). These will be discussed further in the next section.

The appropriate recall reference period (for example, illness in the last three months, two weeks, or currently) would vary with the frequency of the disease and its duration. With acute illnesses of short duration, incidence measures (that is, new episodes in a given period) are of value, whereas for diseases of long duration, point prevalence measures (that is, current status) are more appropriate. However, for illnesses of short duration but high incidence, such as diarrhoea, prevalence measures are also useful (Black *et al.*, 1982; Black, 1984). The relationship between incidence and prevalence depends on the duration of illness; $P = I \times D$ (where P = prevalence, I = incidence, and D = duration).

The appropriate reference period will also depend on the recall ability of the respondent. With a disease such as measles which occurs only once in an individual's lifetime and has distinctive characteristics, longer recall periods can be used, whereas for common, recurrent, and less distinctive illnesses, such as diarrhoea, a shorter recall interval such as two weeks is more appropriate, to avoid either omission of episodes or the aggregation of repeated episodes.

Morbidity surveys can be applied to other demographic problems such as infertility. The proportions of women living in a marital situation who are childless at a given age (for instance, 35 or above) are a reasonable measure of the prevalence of primary infertility, and this information is routinely obtained from census or survey data. There is strong evidence to suggest that where primary infertility is a major problem (as where the proportions childless are over 10 per cent), the aetiology is likely to be sexually transmitted diseases (STDs), mainly due to gonorrhoea or chlamydia, and possibly postpartum or post-abortal infection. The common mechanism underlying infertility is pelvic inflammatory disease (PID) leading to obstruction or damage of the fallopian tubes (Muir and Belsey, 1980).

It is possible to obtain a history of PID in relation to prior STD or obstetric/abortion infection, so as better to assess the causes of infertility. A possible algorithm is given here.

1. History of lower abdominal pain and fever, with or without vaginal discharge (PID).
2. Timing of symptoms in relation to delivery or abortion or known episode of STD.
3. Urethral discharge in males (STD).

Source: World Health Organization, 1984; Arya *et al.*, 1980.

Information using comparable algorithms has been shown to be of predictive value. Arya *et al.* (1980) conducted aggregate-level studies in low- and high-fertility areas of Uganda, and found that a history of lower abdominal pain suggestive of PID, or a history of urethral discharge in males, was markedly more prevalent in the population which had a high proportion of primary infertility. In a WHO (1984) case–control study of acute PID in developing countries, a similar algorithm suggestive of prior infection was shown to be associated with an increased risk of a recurrent infection (the relative risks were 5.5 for one prior episode, 12 for two or three episodes, and 18 for four or more) (Gray, 1985). Other data show that repeated PID episodes increase the risk of infertility (Westrom, 1980). In a study of ectopic pregnancy, too, women who had a prior history of PID were found to have evidence of past infection at time of surgery in 69 per cent of cases (Gray and Campbell, 1985). This experience with aggregate- and individual-level data suggests that a putative diagnosis of PID or STD is associated with infertility, that a past history of PID is predictive of recurrent episodes and increases the risk of infertility, and that information obtained by interview can be validated by objective clinical evidence.

In summary, given that it is possible to identify diseases associated with morbidity as well as death, it is now necessary to turn to measurements of the risk factors affecting these markers of the proximate determinants.

Measurement of Risk Factors

A risk factor may be defined as an attribute or exposure that increases the probability of occurrence of disease or other outcome. Risk factors are measures of those antecedents of disease such as socio-economic status, environmental conditions, therapy, and so on, which influence the probability of illness, and the outcome in terms of mortality or growth faltering. The chain of events can be investigated in terms of morbidity and mortality, since both have shared antecedents.

The range of possible risk factors has been described elsewhere (Mosley and Chen, 1984; Ware, 1984), and need not be exhaustively covered in the present chapter. In brief, these factors comprise:

(a) Maternal risk factors such as age, parity, birth interval, and child care arrangements.

(b) Environmental risk factors or sources of exposure such as water supplies and sanitation; food preparation/storage, breast-feeding, supplementation, and weaning; housing conditions (including over-crowding and construction materials); personal hygiene (use of soap, and so on).

(c) Nutritional risk factors are food availability, types of foodstuffs, and their relative contributions to the diet; food distribution in the family with particular emphasis on inequalities by sex, age, or body size. This information is often difficult to obtain by interview because 24-hour dietary histories may be unreliable, especially for children (Brown, 1984). However, since detailed prospective studies are not usually feas-ible, dietary histories are of necessity the main source of data. Wherever possible, dietary history data should be validated on a subsample using more precise methods. In the Machakos study, semi-quantitative mater-nal recall data were compared with estimates of nutrient intake based on direct measurements of foods, and reasonable agreement was found for most dietary constituents (Kusin *et al.*, 1984). With infants and young children, breast-feeding, supplementation, and weaning are clearly important nutritional risk factors as well as measures of exposure, and in this regard the age of the child at supplementation or weaning is of critical importance (Jason *et al.*, 1984; Seward and Serdula, 1984).

(d) Risk factors for injury are patterns of maternal or surrogate child care, number of children under care, hazards such as cooking facilities (open fires) or unprotected water (for example, canals or tanks), motor vehicles, domestic and other animals.

(e) Risk factors measuring personal illness control are preventive measures such as vaccination, contraceptive use, antenatal care, or malaria prophylaxis. Curative measures such as cultural practices in response to illness (like traditional remedies or the withholding of food), self-medication using modern technologies (such as use of oral rehydration therapy, malaria therapy), and care-seeking behaviour (for instance, use of traditional practitioners or modern medical services). With regard to modern service utilization, it is necessary to consider acceptability and availability of services *per se* and accessibility in terms of distance or cost (Scrimshaw and Hurtado, 1984).

Finally, again drawing on the Mosley–Chen (1984) framework, underly-ing socio-economic determinants may be considered as indirect risk factors (operating through the above proximate risk factors) or as effect modifiers. These underlying determinants are individual-level variables such as par-ental education, occupation, tradition, attitudes, and normative beliefs and practices; household-level variables such as income or wealth; and community variables, like ecology, disease epidemiology, political economy, and health system. Some individual- or household-level variables can be easily quantified and are frequently measured (education, occupation, or income), others are more complex subjective states which are difficult to measure, and community-level variables present measurement problems beyond the scope of this chapter.

From the foregoing discussion, it is clear that the measurement of risk factors is lengthy, detailed, and difficult. The feasibility of obtaining reliable information varies from item to item, and sources of error or bias abound. Nevertheless, certain key variables have been measured in field settings.

For logistic reasons, information this detailed can only be obtained on limited numbers of subjects, and we next consider how such data may be collected so as to quantify the effects of risk factors on proximate disease indicators or mortality outcomes.

Application of Case–Control Methodology

Case–control studies are epidemiologic investigations in which cases are defined as individuals with a specified disease or outcome (such as growth faltering or death), and controls are defined as individuals free of the disease or outcome of interest. Controls should, however, be representative of the population from which cases are drawn. Comparisons are made between cases and controls with respect to risk factors, which may be individual characteristics, exposures, or behaviours. Case–control studies are retrospective in that information on antecedent risk factors is only obtained after the disease or outcome has occurred in case subjects, and, in a strict sense, such studies can only suggest, they cannot prove causality. The approach has been extensively applied to epidemiologic problems and there is a large literature on the design, conduct, analyses, and interpretation of case–control studies of acute or chronic disease, particularly in hospital settings (Schlesselman and Stolley, 1982). However, this study strategy has seldom been applied to problems of child survival in developing countries, due, in part, to the difficulty of identifying an unbiased sample of cases and controls. Recently, case–control methods have been applied to the study of risk factors for fatal and non-fatal outcomes of disease (Ryder *et al.*, 1985), and to the evaluation of vaccine efficacy (Ministry of Health, Honduras, 1985; Orenstein *et al.*, 1982).

The advantage of case–control studies is that information need be obtained only on limited numbers of cases or controls, rather than a whole survey sample or population, and simple procedures for estimating sample size are given in Schlesselman and Stolley (1982). This parsimony of sample size makes the collection of detailed information using lengthy interview and record forms more feasible in field settings. Case–control studies are particularly useful for the investigation of rare diseases or outcomes, but may be applied to more common conditions (Gray, 1984). It would, for example, be possible to define a case as a child death identified in the course of a demographic survey, and to define a control as a child which survived. Similarly, cases could be defined as children with growth faltering or with specified diseases identified in morbidity surveys, and controls would be children free of these conditions. In each example, data on risk factors could be obtained from interview with parents. Moreover, if the survey is a random sample of the population, then the cases and controls would constitute an unbiased sample.

The objective is to measure the frequency of occurrence of risk factors among cases and controls to assess the risk associated with a given factor. If exposure is greater in cases than controls it suggests an increased risk, and, conversely, if exposure is lower in cases than controls it suggests a reduced risk associated with the factor under study.

The basic tabulation of data is straightforward, as shown in Figure 2.4. The number of exposed and non-exposed cases is denoted by a and c, and the number of exposed and non-exposed controls as b and d, respectively. An odds ratio equal to 1 implies no association, OR >1 implies increased risk, and OR <1 implies a decreased risk or protective effect of the factor. A conventional Chi square test on one degree of freedom can be used as a test of statistical significance.

The odds of exposure among cases is a/c, and among controls b/d. The risk of disease or outcome in cases associated with exposure to the risk factor is measured by the odds ratio (OR):

$$OR = \frac{a/c}{b/d} = \frac{a \times d}{c \times b}$$

		Cases	Controls	
Exposure to risk factor	Yes	a	b	m_1
	No	c	d	m_2
		n_1	n_2	N

Figure 2.4.   Basic tabulation of data on frequency of occurrence of risk factors

Analysis is not restricted to binary variables, and continuous variables can be categorized to examine 'dose response relationships' or consistency of effect (for instance, maternal education can be divided into several sub-categories and the risk estimated relative to women in the highest education group). An example using household 'wealth' is given in Table 2.1.

The data may also be stratified or partitioned to examine associations in subgroups or between combinations of variables, and logistic regression

Table 2.1. Association between household wealth and child death

Household wealth class*	Deaths (cases)	Survivors (controls)	Odds ratios
1 (low)	114	167	2.4
2	70	136	1.8
3	74	161	1.6
4 (high)	44	155	1.0

* Household wealth based on a scoring system and divided into quantities.
Source: Gemert *et al.*, 1984.

procedures allow the estimation of odds ratios for multiple risk factors and the assessment of interaction between factors (Schlesselman and Stolley, 1982).

As with all non-experimental investigations, case–control studies are vulnerable to bias (Sacket, 1979). Selection bias may arise if cases or controls are unrepresentative of the true populations at riks: for example, if highly educated women utilize medical care facilities more than the poorly educated, then a hospital-based case–control study could be biased with respect to education, thus limiting the generalization of results. Also, selection bias may arise differentially between cases and controls if the latter are not identified from a comparable representative population (as when cases are identified in hospitals, and controls from non-hospitalized populations). Misclassification bias can occur if case diagnosis is incorrect (that is, true cases of disease are missed and classified as controls, or false cases of disease are incorrectly included). Such misclassification will dilute the true association between disease and risk factors.

Recall bias can occur if information obtained from case and control subjects differs systematically in completeness or accuracy. To avoid recall bias, it is necessary to use standardized questionnaires and interview procedures and, as far as possible, to keep the interviewers 'blind' with respect to the case or control status of the respondent. However, there are subjective factors which may influence recall: for example, the mother of a dead child may be motivated to provide more accurate data than the mother of a surviving child, or a highly educated mother may provide a better history than a poorly educated woman. To evaluate such recall bias one can compare case and control responses to variables suspected to be risk factors, which should be more frequent among cases, and neutral variables, which should be equally distributed between cases and controls.

Another major problem with observational studies is confounding, which implies that an apparent association between a risk factor and outcome is artifactual due to the operation of a third variable. For example, if younger women are more educated, and age is related to the risk of disease, then a spurious association may be observed between education and disease. Adjustment can control for confounding, for instance by examining the association between age and outcome after stratification on education.

Case–control designs have the advantage of parsimony if the outcome—such as death—is rare, but the approach is equally applicable to situations in which the risk factor of interest is rare. If tertiary education is infrequent in a population, it may not be possible to study the rates of disease or death among the highly educated because the numbers in this category are too few. However, one can do a case–control study in which individuals are selected by exposure and non-exposure to the risk factor rather than the outcome. In Figure 2.4 the odds of disease among the exposed is a/b and among the non-exposed c/d. Thus, the odds ratio of disease among the exposed versus non-exposed is $a/b \div c/d = (a \times d)/(b \times c)$. In other words, the odds of disease associated with a factor are the same as the odds of the factor associated with disease. This allows considerable flexibility of application to field studies.

Summary and Conclusions

Demographic and epidemiologic studies of child survival have in the past yielded important information on determinants of mortality. However, if we are to expand our understanding of health problems in developing countries it is necessary to integrate these two disciplinary approaches. This chapter has largely dwelt upon the application of epidemiologic methods to demographic surveys, but, equally, epidemiologists have much to learn from demographers. For example, cross-sectional and retrospective surveys could be used instead of logistically complex prospective surveillance studies of morbidity and mortality. This would result in great economies of cost and time, and in principle could yield similar information of relevance to health assessment.

In summary, it is proposed that both epidemiologic and demographic surveys be integrated to explore the use of algorithms for disease diagnosis based on retrospective interview data and direct current status observation; that surveys of mortality be accompanied by parallel surveys of morbidity in random subsamples; that interview information be obtained on risk factors; and that research designs such as case–control studies be more widely employed. Unless new and more cost-effective strategies are adopted, our knowledge of the determinants of mortality and our ability to evaluate the impact of health interventions will be constrained by incomplete information, surveillance of limited and possibly unrepresentative populations, and by the costs of field research. There is a need to develop further these interdisciplinary methodologies and to evaluate critically their feasibility in field settings.

References

Aaby, P., J. Bukh, I. M. Lisse, and A. J. Smits (1981), 'Measles Vaccination and Child Mortality', *Lancet* 2, 93.
—— —— —— —— (1984), 'Overcrowding and Intensive Exposure as Determinants of Measles Mortality', *American Journal of Epidemiology* 120, 49–63.
Arya, O. P., S. R. Taber, and H. Nsanze (1980), 'Gonorrhea and Female Infertility in Rural Uganda', *American Journal of Obstetrics and Gynecology* 138, 929–32.
Barker, D. J. P., and G. Rose (1979), *Epidemiology in Medical Practice*, 2nd ed. Churchill & Livingstone, New York, 116–24.
Black, R. E. (1984), 'Diarrheal Diseases and Child Morbidity and Mortality' in W. H. Mosley and L. C. Chen (eds.), *Child Survival: Strategies for Research*, Population and Development Review, supplement to vol. 10, 141–61.
—— , K. H. Brown, and S. Becker (1983), 'Influence of Acute Diarrhea on the Growth Parameters of Children' in J. A. Bellanti (ed.), *Acute Diarrhea: Its Nutritional Consequences in Children*, Nestle Vevey/Raven Press, New York, 75–83.
—— —— —— and M. Yunus (1982), 'Longitudinal Studies of Infectious Diseases and Physical Growth of Children in Rural Bangladesh: I. Patterns of Morbidity', *American Journal of Epidemiology* 115, 305–14.
Bradley, D. J., and A. Keymer (1984), 'Parasitic Diseases: Measurement and Impact' in W. H. Mosley and L. C. Chen (eds.), *Child Survival: Strategies for Research*, Population and Development Review, supplement to vol. 10, 163–81.
Brown, K. J. (1984), 'Measurement of Dietary Intake' in W. H. Mosley and L. C. Chen (eds.), *Child Survival: Strategies for Research*, Population and Development Review, supplement to vol. 10, 69–91.
Bulla, A., and D. Hitze (1978), 'Acute Respiratory Infection: A Review', *Bulletin of the World Health Organization* 56, 481–98.
Chen, L. C., M. C. Gesche, S. Ahmed, A. I. Chodhury, and W. H. Mosley (1974), 'Maternal Mortality in Rural Bangladesh', *Studies in Family Planning* 5(11), 334–41.
—— , M. Rahman, and A. M. Sarder (1980a), 'Epidemiology and Causes of Death among Children in a Rural Area of Bangladesh', *International Journal of Epidemiology* 9, 25–33.
—— , A. K. M. A. Chowdhury, and S. L. Huffman (1980b), 'Anthropometric Assessment of Energy–Protein Malnutrition and Subsequent Risk of Mortality among Preschool Aged Children', *American Journal of Clinical Nutrition* 33, 1836–45.
Christianson, R. E., B. T. Van den Berg, and F. W. Milkovich Land Oeschli (1981), Incidence of Congenital Anomalies among White and Black Live Births with Long-term Follow-up', *American Journal of Public Health* 71, 1333–41.
Cook, R. (1978), 'Pertussis in Developing Countries: Possibilities and Problems of Control through Immunization' in C. R. Manclark and J. C. Hill (eds.), *International Symposium on Pertussis*, DHEW publication with NIH 79-1830, Washington, DC, 283–6.

Davanzo, J. (1984), 'A Household Survey of Child Mortality Determinants in Malaysia' in W. H. Mosley and L. C. Chen (eds.), *Child Survival: Strategies for Research*, Population and Development Review, supplement to vol. 10, 307–22.

Essex, B. (1978), *Diagnostic Flow Charts*, A. R. Adams & Sons, Dover, England, 1–64.

Fortney, J. A., S. Saleh, S. Gadalla, and S. A. Rogers (1983), 'Causes of Death to Women of Reproductive Age in Egypt', paper presented at the 52nd annual meeting of the Population Association of America, Pittsburgh, 14–16 April 1983, 22.

Foster, S. O. (1984), 'Immunizable and Respiratory Diseases and Child Mortality' in W. H. Mosley and L. C. Chen (eds.), *Child Survival: Strategies for Research*, Population Development Review, supplement to vol. 10, 119–40.

Gemert, W., R. Slooff, J. K. Van Ginneken, and J. Leeuwenburg (1984), 'Household Status Differentials and Childhood Mortality' in J. K. Van Ginneken and A. S. Muller (eds.), *Maternal and Child Health in Rural Kenya: An Epidemiologocial Study*, Croom Helm, London, 271–80.

Goodman, R. A., K. G. Manton, T. F. Nolan, D. J. Bregman, and A. R. Hinman (1982), 'Mortality Data Analysis Using a Multiple Cause Approach', *JAMA* 247, 793–6.

Gray, R. H. (1984), 'Case Control Studies of High Risk Pregnancy: Work Book on Research on the Risk Approach in Maternal and Child Health Including Family Planning', Division of Family Health, WHO, Geneva.

—— and O. Campbell (1985), 'Epidemiologic Trends of PID in Contraceptive Use' in G. Zatuchni, A. Goldsmith, and J. J. Sciarra (eds.), *Intrauterine Contraception: Advances and Future Prospects*, Harper & Row, Philadelphia, 398–411.

Henderson, R. H., and T. Sundaresan (1983), 'Cluster Sampling to Assess Immunization Coverage: A Review of Experience with a Simplified Sampling Method', *Bulletin of the World Health Organization* 60, 253–60.

Heywood, P. (1982), 'The Functional Significance of Malnutrition: Growth and Prospective Risk of Death in the Highlands of Papua New Guinea', *Journal of Food and Nutrition* 39(1), 13–19.

Hull, H. F., J. W. Pap, and F. Oldfield (1983), 'Measles Mortality and Vaccine Efficacy in Rural West Africa', *Lancet* 1, 972–5.

Islam, M. S., M. M. Rahman, K. M. S. Aziz, M. Rahman, M. H. Munshi, and M. M. Patuari (1982), 'Infant Mortality in Rural Bangladesh: An Analysis of Causes during Neonatal and Postneonatal Periods' *Journal of Tropical Pediatrics* 28, 294–8.

Jacob, J. T., A. Joseph, T. I. George, J. Radhakrishnan, R. P. D. Singh, and K. George (1980), 'Epidemiology and Prevention of Measles in Rural South India', *Indian Journal of Medical Research* 72, 153–8.

Jason, J. M., P. Nieburg, and J. S. Marks (1984), 'Mortality and Infectious Disease Associated with Infant-feeding Practices in Developing Countries', *Pediatrics* supplement, Task Force on Infant-feeding Practices, 702–26.

Kasongo Project Team (1981), 'Influence of Measles Vaccination on Survival Pattern of 7–35 Month Old Children in Kasongo, Zaire', *Lancet* 1, 764–7.

Koster, F. T., G. C. Curlin, K. M. A. Aziz, and A. Haque (1981), 'Synergistic

Impact of Measles and Diarrhoea on Nutrition and Mortality in Bangladesh', *Bulletin of the World Health Organization* 59, 901–8.

Kusin, J. A., W. M. Van Steenbergen, S. A. Lakkani, A. A. J. Jansen, and U. Renquist (1984), 'Food Consumption in Pregnancy and Lactation' in *Maternal and Child Health in Rural Kenya: An Epidemiological Study*, Croom Helm, London, 127–42.

Leeuwenburg, J., W. Gemert, A. S. Muller, A. M. Voorhoeve, and P. W. Kok (1984*a*), 'The Epidemiology of Measles' in *Maternal and Child Health in Rural Kenya: An Epidemiological Study*, Croom Helm, London, 77–94.

—— —— —— and S. C. Patel (1984*b*), 'The Incidence of Diarrhoeal Disease' in *Maternal and Child Health in Rural Kenya: An Epidemiological Study*, Croom Helm, London, 109–18.

Loening, W. E. K., and H. M. Coovadia (1983), 'Age-specific Recurrence Rates of Measles in Urban, Periurban and Rural Environments: Implications for Vaccination', *Lancet* 2, 324–6.

MacRae, S. M. (1979), 'Birth Notification Data as a Source of Basic Demographic Measures, Illustrated by Specific Application to the Study of Childhood Mortality in the Solomon Islands', Ph.D. thesis, London Faculty of Medicine, London School of Hygiene and Tropical Medicine, University of London.

Martorell, R., and T. J. Ho (1984), 'Malnutrition, Morbidity, and Mortality' in W. H. Mosley and L. C. Chen (eds.), *Child Survival: Strategies for Research*, Population and Development Review, supplement to vol. 10, 49–68.

Mata, L. J. (1978), *The Children of Santa Maria Cauque: A Prospective Field Study of Health and Growth*, MIT Press, Cambridge, MA, 281–3.

—— (1983), 'Epidemiology of Acute Diarrhea in Childhood' in J. A. Bellanti (ed.) *Acute Diarrhea: Its Nutritional Consequences in Children*, Nestle Vevey/Raven Press, New York, 3–22.

McCord, C., and A. A. Kielmann (1978), 'A Successful Programme for Medical Auxiliaries Treating Childhood Diarrhoea and Pneumonia', *Tropical Doctor* 8, 220–5.

McGregor, I. A., M. E. Wilson, and W. Z. Billewicz (1983), 'Malaria Infection of the Placenta in The Gambia, West Africa, its Incidence and Relationship to Stillbirth, Birthweight and Placental Weight', *Transactions of the Royal Society of Tropical Medicine and Hygiene* 77, 232–44.

Ministry of Health, Honduras (1985), 'Clinical Efficacy of Trivalent Oral Polio Vaccine Tested', *EPI Newsletter* 7, 1–4.

Morley, D., L. Wood, M. Wood, and W. J. Martin (1963), 'Measles in Nigerian Children', *Journal of Hygiene* 61, 115–34.

—— —— —— —— (1966), 'Whooping Cough in Nigerian Children', *Tropical and Geographical Medicine* 18, 169–82.

Mosley, W. H., and L. Chen (1984), 'An Analytic Framework for the Study of Child Survival in Developing Countries' in W. H. Mosley, and L. C. Chen (eds.), *Child Survival: Strategies for Research*, Population and Development Review, supplement to vol. 10, 25–45.

Muir, D. G., and M. A. Belsey (1980), 'Pelvic Inflammatory Disease and its Consequences in the Developing World', *American Journal of Obstetrics and Gynecology* 138, 913–28.

Muller, A. S., J. Leeuwenburg, and A. M. Voorhoeve (1984), 'The Epidemiology of Pertussis and Results of a Vaccine Trial' in J. K. Van Ginneken and A. S. Muller (eds.), *Maternal and Child Health in Rural Kenya: An Epidemiological Study*, Croom Helm, London, 95–108.

Orenstein, W. A., J. S. Marks, and C. R. Hogue (1982), 'Vaccine Efficacy: A New Application of Case–Control and Case–Exposure Methodology', Society for Epidemiologic Research, Cincinnati, Ohio, 16–18 June 1982.

Puffer, R. R., and C. V. Serrano (1973), 'Patterns of Mortality in Childhood', Scientific Publications no. 262, Pan American Health Organization, Washington, DC.

Rhinehart, W., A. Kols, and S. H. Moore (1984), 'Healthier Mothers and Children through Family Planning', *Population Reports*, series J, 27, 659–96.

Riley, I. D., and R. M. Douglas (1981), 'An Epidemiologic Approach to Pneumococcal Disease', *Review of Infectious Diseases* 3, 233–45.

—— —— , F. A. Everingham, and D. E. Smith (1981), 'Immunization with a Polyvalent Pneumococcal Vaccine', *Archives of Diseases in Childhood* 56, 354–7.

Ryder, R. W., W. C. Reeves, and R. B. Sack (1985), 'Risk Factors for Fatal Childhood Diarrhea: A Case–Control Study from Two Remote Panamanian Islands', *American Journal of Epidemiology* 121, 605–10.

Sacket, D. L. (1979), 'Bias in Analytic Research', *Journal of Chronic Diseases* 32, 51–63.

Schlesselman, J. J., and P. D. Stolley (1982), 'Case–Control Studies, Design, Conduct and Analysis', Oxford University Press Monographs in Epidemiology and Biostatistics.

Scrimshaw, S. C. M., and E. Hurtado (1984), 'Field Guide for the Study of Health-seeking Behaviour at the Household Level', *Food and Nutrition Bulletin* 6, 27–45.

Seward, J., and M. K. Serdula (1984), 'Infant Feeding and Growth', *Pediatrics* supplement, Task Force on Infant-feeding Practices, 728–62.

Smith, J. C., J. M. Hughes, P. S. Pekow, and R. W. Rochat (1984), 'An Assessment of the Incidence of Maternal Mortality in the United States', *American Journal of Public Health* 74, 780–3.

Smucker, C. M., G. B. Simmon, S. Bernstein, and B. D. Misra (1980), 'Neonatal Mortality in South Asia: The Special Role of Tetanus', *Population Studies* 34, 321–35.

Sommer, A., I. Tarwotjo, and J. Katz (1984), 'Increased Risk of Respiratory Disease and Diarrhea in Children with Pre-existing Mild Vitamin A Deficiency, *American Journal of Clinical Nutrition* 40, 1090–5.

—— —— G. Husani, and D. Susanto (1983), 'Increased Mortality in Children with Mild Vitamin A Deficiency', *Lancet* 2, 585–8.

—— —— —— —— and S. Sarossa (1980), 'History of Night Blindness: A Simple Tool for Xerophthalmia Screening', *American Journal of Clinical Nutrition* 33, 887–91.

Stanfield, J. P., and A. Galazka (1984), 'Neonatal Tetanus in the World Today', *Bulletin of the World Health Organization* 62, 647–69.

Ulfah, N. M., S. Parastho, T. Sadjimin, and J. E. Rhode (1981), 'Polio and Lameness in Yogyakarta, Indonesia', *International Journal of Epidemiology* 10, 171–5.

United Nations, Department of Economic and Social Affairs (1983), 'Indirect Techniques for Demographic Estimation' in *Population Studies No. 81, Manual X*, United Nations, New York.

Villar, J., and J. M. Belizan (1982), 'The Relative Contribution of Prematurity and Fetal Growth Retardation to Low Birthweight in Developing Countries', *American Journal of Obstetrics and Gynecology* 143, 793–8.

Voorhoeve, A. M., A. S. Muller, T. W. J. Schulpen, W. T. Mamnetje, and M. Van Rens (1978), 'The Epidemiology of Pertussis', *Tropical and Geographical Medicine* 30, 121–4.

Ware, H. (1984), 'Maternal Variables and Child Mortality' in W. H. Mosley and L. C. Chen (eds.), *Child Survival: Strategies for Research*, Population Development Review, supplement to vol. 10, 191–214.

Westrom, L. (1980), 'Incidence, Prevalence and Trends of Acute Pelvic Inflammatory Disease and its Consequences in Industrialized Countries', *American Journal of Obstetrics and Gynecology* 138, 880–92.

World Fertility Survey (1983), 'Findings of the World Fertility Survey on Trends, Differentials and Determinants of Mortality in Developing Countries', meeting of an expert group on mortality and health policy, International Conference on Population 1984, UN Population Division, Rome, 30 May–3 June.

World Health Organization (1978), *Lay Reporting of Health Information*, WHO, Geneva.

—— Division of Health Statistics Dissemination of Statistical Information (1980), *Manual of Mortality Analysis*, WHO, Geneva.

—— Weekly Epidemiology Record (1981), *Magnitude of Tuberculosis Problems in the World*, WHO, Geneva.

—— EPI (1983), 'Provisional Guidelines for the Diagnosis and Classification of the EPI Target Diseases for Primary Health Care, Surveillance and Special Studies, Expanded Program of Immunization EPI/GEN/83/4, WHO, Geneva.

—— Task Force on Intrauterine Devices (1984), 'PID Associated with Fertility Regulating Agents', *Contraception* 30, 1–21.

3 Some Methodological Issues in the Assessment of the Deceleration of the Mortality Decline

SHIRO HORIUCHI

Population Division/IESA, United Nations

The rapid decline of mortality that triggered the post-war population explosion appears to have slowed down in a number of less developed countries. The Population Division of the United Nations recognized the problem in the late 1970s:

Estimates suggest, tentatively but plausibly, that many national mortality downtrends in the less developed areas were more rapid in the first half of the post-war era than they have been in the second half. This would be consistent with the expectation that the causes of death most yielding to disease-control programmes have become relatively less important, while more resistant diseases have become relatively more prominent. (United Nations, 1979a, 24.)

Gwatkin (1980) elaborated and strengthened the above-described hypothesis, examined a wide range of international data, and found a variety of empirical evidence supporting the hypothesis. Palloni (1981) focused on Latin American countries and showed that mortality in those countries was not declining as much as expected. The deceleration of the decline of mortality became the subject of a session at the IUSSP International Population Conference in Manila, where the relevant conditions in Africa, Latin America, and Asia were discussed by Azefor (1981), Arriaga (1981), and Sivamurthy (1981), respectively. Furthermore, an analysis of mortality trends in 24 less developed countries selected for their relatively high data quality revealed that the average annual rate of increase in life expectancy at birth from the 1960s to the 1970s was lower than that from the 1950s to 1960s (United Nations, 1982a, table I.1).

Although these studies are sufficiently convincing on the declining pace of mortality reduction in some countries, a question remains unanswered as

The author greatly acknowledges the helpful comments of Eduardo Arriaga, Shunichi Inoue, and Guillaume Wunsch on earlier versions of this chapter. The author has also benefited from discussions on this subject with participants in the seminar. The opinions expressed herein are those of the author and should not be construed as necessarily representing the opinions of the United Nations.

to whether the deceleration is a dominant mortality trend in less developed regions. A variety of mortality trends are observed in different countries. The successful continuation of mortality reduction in some countries such as Costa Rica and Cuba merits attention. The recent release of demographic data in China led to the recognition of very rapid mortality decline there since the early 1960s (Brass, 1984; Coale, 1984; Ling, 1981). In addition, a recent thorough study of population dynamics in India showed that mortality in India was decreasing more rapidly than previously estimated (Bhat, Preston, and Dyson, 1984).

The expectation of life at birth (e_0) and the infant mortality rate (the number of deaths before the first birthday per 1,000 live births) for major regions of the world from 1950 to 1980, estimated by the Population Division of the United Nations in its 1982 assessment, are shown in Tables 3.1 and 3.2. Although e_0 for all less developed regions combined increased from 40.7 in 1955–60 to 54.8 in 1975–80, the increment in e_0 between two successive quinquennial periods decreased from 4.9 between 1955–60 and 1960–5 to 2.1 between 1970–5 and 1975–80. This is consistent with the expectation of stagnated mortality reduction. However, the systematic

Table 3.1. Expectation of life at birth, for world and major regions, 1950–80 (increase from the preceding quinquennial period in parentheses)

Region	1950–5	1955–60	1960–5	1965–70	1970–5	1975 80
World	45.8	45.7	49.9	52.6	55.4	57.3
More developed regions	65.1	68.4	69.8	70.5	71.4	72.1
		(3.3)	(1.4)	(0.7)	(0.9)	(0.7)
Less developed regions	41.0	40.7	45.6	49.4	52.7	54.8
		(−0.3)	(4.9)	(3.8)	(3.3)	(2.1)
Africa	37.5	39.6	41.6	43.5	45.5	47.6
		(2.1)	(2.0)	(1.9)	(2.0)	(2.1)
Latin America	51.0	53.9	56.5	58.5	60.6	62.5
		(2.9)	(2.6)	(2.0)	(2.1)	(1.9)
Northern America	69.0	69.7	70.1	70.6	71.5	73.3
		(0.7)	(0.4)	(0.5)	(0.9)	(1.8)
East Asia	42.5	37.0	46.2	53.4	60.1	65.3
		(−5.5)	(9.2)	(7.2)	(6.7)	(5.2)
South Asia	40.1	42.3	45.1	47.4	49.4	51.7
		(2.2)	(2.8)	(2.3)	(2.0)	(2.3)
Europe	65.3	68.0	69.7	70.6	71.4	72.2
		(2.7)	(1.7)	(0.9)	(0.8)	(0.8)
Oceania	61.0	62.7	64.0	64.4	65.9	66.4
		(1.7)	(1.3)	(0.4)	(1.5)	(0.5)
USSR	61.7	68.4	70.0	70.0	70.4	69.6
		(6.7)	(1.6)	(0.0)	(0.4)	(−0.8)

Source: United Nations, 1985*a*.

Table 3.2.   Infant mortality rate, for world and major regions, 1950–80 (percentile decrease from the preceding quinquennial period in parentheses)

Region	1950–5	1955–60	1960–5	1965–70	1970–5	1975–80
World	139	137	117	106	94	89
		(1)	(15)	(9)	(11)	(5)
More developed regions	56	41	31	26	21	19
		(27)	(24)	(16)	(19)	(10)
Less developed regions	159	158	136	120	106	100
		(1)	(14)	(12)	(12)	(6)
Africa	185	172	160	149	138	127
		(7)	(7)	(7)	(7)	(8)
Latin America	126	112	100	90	80	70
		(11)	(11)	(10)	(11)	(13)
Northern America	29	27	25	22	18	14
		(7)	(7)	(12)	(18)	(22)
East Asia	124	150	107	86	62	45
		(−21)	(29)	(20)	(28)	(27)
South Asia	182	166	151	139	128	120
		(9)	(9)	(8)	(8)	(6)
Europe	62	48	37	30	24	19
		(23)	(23)	(19)	(20)	(21)
Oceania	68	62	55	51	43	43
		(9)	(11)	(7)	(16)	(0)
USSR	73	44	32	26	26	29
		(40)	(27)	(19)	(0)	(−12)

Source: See Table 3.1.

trend to diminishing increments is not found for Africa and South Asia. Although the increase in e_0 for Latin America from 1950–5 to 1960–5 exceeds that from 1960–5 to 1970–5, which agrees with the observations of Palloni (1981) and Arriaga (1981), the trend for Latin America does not appear parallel with that for all less developed regions combined. A substantial steady decrease in the increment of e_0 on the regional level is found only for East Asia. The declining increment in e_0 for less developed regions, therefore, seems simply to have echoed the steeper decrease in the gain of e_0 for China, which at present accounts for about 85 per cent of the population of East Asia.

It can be speculated, however, that the apparent decrease in the gain of e_0 for East Asia may be attributable to the characteristics of the measure e_0 rather than a slowing down in the improvement of socio-economic conditions and public health programmes that affect the mortality level of the population. A decelerated growth in e_0 might be seen if it was more difficult to achieve the same amount of gain in e_0 at lower levels of mortality. If this is true, the deceleration would be more apparent when e_0 is growing more rapidly. Given the fact that the mortality rate has been declining very steeply in East Asia, this speculation does not appear too implausible.

Table 3.2 reveals that the infant mortality rate for all less developed regions combined has also been declining. Estimates for the five quinquennial periods from 1955 to 1980 are 158, 136, 120, 106, and 100, respectively, so that the absolute decrements between the two successive five-year periods are 22, 16, 14, and 6, showing a relatively steady trend of reducing decrements. However, the trend may also be a statistical artefact, because the percentile decrements for the same periods are 14, 12, 12, and 6, exhibiting a less prominent trend. In addition, the proportional decrease for less developed regions from 1970–5 to 1975–80 is 6 per cent, which is lower than any of the proportional decrements for Africa, Latin America, East Asia, and South Asia. This puzzle gives rise to a suspicion that the small proportional decline in the infant mortality rate for less developed regions in the 1970s may be another statistical artefact.

The brief examination of mortality trends given above on the basis of the United Nations regional-level estimates suggests than an inappropriate selection of measures of mortality change and statistical mechanisms of aggregation might produce an apparent deceleration of mortality decline. It seems, therefore, quite important to recognize the methodological problems that could lead to an underestimation of mortality decline. The purpose of the present chapter is to identify and discuss those problems, which should lead to caution in studies of the deceleration of mortality decline.

Interrelationships among Fertility, Mortality, and Growth

It is known that high fertility tends to be associated with high mortality both on the international and intranational level, both in cross-section and time-series statistics. It is also held empirically that the population of countries, or groups within a country, of higher levels of fertility and mortality are likely to grow faster than those of lower levels of fertility and mortality, as far as population dynamics in the period after World War II are concerned. Their greater numbers of births imply that an increasingly greater weight is given to countries (or subnational groups) of relatively high mortality levels in aggregating the mortality measures of the countries (or subnational groups).

This leads to a slowing down of mortality reduction on the aggregated level. Bucht and Chamie (1982; also United Nations Secretariat, 1982) indicated that the reduced pace of the decline in the average infant mortality rate for the less developed regions is mainly attributable to a change in the regional contributions to the infant mortality rate. This can be shown using the latest United Nations estimates of infant mortality rates (United Nations, 1984). The average infant mortality rate for the less developed regions decreased from 159 in 1950–5 to 100 in 1975–80, as shown in Table

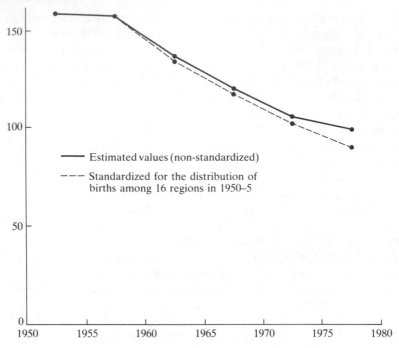

Figure 3.1.   Estimated infant mortality rate for less developed regions, 1950–60

3.2. However, if the distributions of births among the 16 less developed sub-regions had remained constant from 1950–5 to 1975–80, the average infant mortality rate for less developed regions would have been 91 in 1975–80 (see Figure 3.1). The increasing proportion of infants born in countries where there is a relatively high mortality level made the decline in the infant mortality rate, for the total of the less developed regions, smaller than those in many of the subregions. The same mechanism can be expected to operate at the national level as well, because the proportion of total births in those subnational populations which have high levels of fertility and mortality tends to increase.

This type of bias is not restricted to the infant mortality rate. Groups that grow faster than others increase their contributions to mortality measures such as crude death rates and life expectancy at birth (e_0) for the total population, and those groups tend to have relatively high mortality levels.

Heterogeneity

It can be reasonably assumed that human populations are heterogeneous in terms of frailty. Thus, there are individual differences in the susceptibility to mortality. Because weaker groups tend to die at younger ages and be reduced at a faster pace, the older population comprises a larger proportion of more healthy persons. As a result, the age trajectory of death rates for a population may be considerably different to the age pattern of mortality risk for individual members of the population (Vaupel, Manton, and Stallard, 1979).

For example, Horiuchi and Coale (1983) find that the rate of mortality change with age, defined as $d \log (m(x))/dx$, where $m(x)$ is the death rate at exact age x, follows a symmetrical bell-shaped pattern for middle-aged and old women in populations that have relatively accurate data. Among the widely known mathematical models of adult mortality, only the Perks logistic equation fits well the observed pattern of the rate of mortality change with age. The Perks model is derived from the assumption that the mortality risk of individuals follows the Makeham equation and that individual frailty is gamma-distributed. The results seem to suggest the significance of heterogeneity in mortality analysis and the usefulness of the gamma-distribution for approximating variation in individual frailty.

Although most studies of the effect of population heterogeneity on mortality have focused on age patterns of mortality, it could be expected that heterogeneity would have some impact on mortality trends. Improvements in the standard of living and advancement of medical technology enable relatively weak people who might otherwise die at younger ages to survive to old age. The population will thus include an increasing proportion of persons who are relatively susceptible to the risk of death, which makes the mortality decline in the population lower than that in a group of a given extent of frailty.

A few simple simulations have been conducted in order to assess the effect of heterogeneity, based on the heterogeneous population model proposed by Vaupel, Manton, and Stallard (1979). In the model, differential frailty within a population is expressed in terms of the proportionality of age-specific death rates. A person of frailty z follows the mortality schedule in which the risk of death at exact age a is expressed as $z.m_s(a)$, where $m_s(a)$ is the risk of death of age a for a person of average frailty and z is assumed to be gamma-distributed.

Two stationary populations have been generated. A person of average frailty in the first population follows the Coale–Demeny West model lifetable for females at level 13 ($e_0 = 50$). The risk of death at all ages for an average person in the second population is lower by 5 per cent than that for its counterpart in the first population. This implies that if groups of the same frailty level are compared, age-specific death rates for those in the second population are always lower by 5 per cent than those in the first population. The simulation shows, however, that the difference in the geometric means of age-specific death rates from age 0 to 80 between the two populations is only 4.5 per cent, because the second population includes a higher proportion of relatively frail persons.

The effect of population heterogeneity may operate even before birth. For instance, the advancement of obstetrics and perinatal medicine leads to a higher proportion of live births among high-risk foetuses that would otherwise be lost in miscarriages or still births. This may make the trend of declining infant mortality less apparent, because infant mortality among those high-risk births is likely to be higher than that of other births.

Finally, two cautionary remarks seem necessary. First, it should be noted that population heterogeneity may moderate mortality reduction at any state of its downwards trend and does not necessarily produce a deceleration of decline. It might be expected, however, that years of very steep fall in mortality are followed by a period in which the population includes a significantly higher proportion of frail persons than before.

Second, it should also be noted that the effect of heterogeneous frailty on mortality trends might be exaggerated in the illustration given here, because the simulation is based on assumptions that probably over-simplify reality. It was assumed that the probability of an individual's death at a certain age is determined by two factors: the level of environmental risk of death to which the person is exposed, and the susceptibility of the person to the risk. The latter is assumed to be a function of his/her frailty as determined at the time of birth, and his/her current age.

The former factor—the level of environmental risk of death—is considered to reflect the standard of living and the level of medical technology that is available. A higher standard of living generally reduces exposure to disease-causing agents and vectors, and also provides inhabitants with efficient protection from cold, heat, rain, wind, and so on. Advanced medical technology leads to better treatment of patients. Therefore, progress in both the standard of living and medical technology lowers the environmental risk of death to which individuals are exposed.

The very same determinants of mortality risk, however, also affect the susceptibility of individuals to that risk. Individuals are more likely to survive the same level of risk if they are better nourished, have healthier lifestyles, have been immunized against more diseases, and have never suffered from diseases that may leave long-lasting damage to health. It seems quite plausible that economic, social, and medical developments not only provide frail people with a comfortable environment in which they can easily survive but also help them to become healthier and stronger. Thus, the suppressing effect of population heterogeneity on mortality decline can be reduced to the extent that the susceptibility of individuals to environmental mortality risk is lowered by improvements in the standard of living and medical technology.

Differential Changes in the Age Structure of Subpopulations

As a mortality measure, one of the major advantages of the expectation of life at birth is that it is independent of the age structure of the population.

However, it is not widely known that the life expectancy is affected by differential changes in the age structure of subpopulations even when life tables of the subpopulations remain unchanged.

The impact of the age structure of a subpopulation on life expectation is clear when we consider a population in which there is cross-over mortality between subpopulations. Cross-over mortality, in this context, means that an excess mortality under a certain age of one group over another is reversed above that age. This has been observed for whites and non-whites in the United States (Nam *et al.*, 1978; Manton and Stallard, 1981). Suppose that a population is composed of two groups which have a cross-over mortality schedule, and that, for every age group, the higher mortality segment has greater weight. Such an age structure would lower the expectation of life at birth for the total population, and it could even be lower than that of any of those of its subpopulations. A similar mechanism, if operating in the opposite direction, could produce an e_0 for the total population which was higher than those of its subpopulations. In brief, the correlation between differences in age-specific death rates and those in age-group sizes among subpopulations affects e_0 of the total population.

Empirically, a positive correlation seems more plausible than a negative one, for the following reason. In general, populations with higher fertility and mortality levels tend to have younger age structures. It is also recognised that (proportional) differences in death rate are greater at younger ages between populations of different mortality levels. For example, in the United Nations 'general' pattern model life-tables for males, the ratio of age-specific death rate (*m*) in the life-table with $e_0 = 50$ years to that in the life-table with $e_0 = 70$ years keeps decreasing almost monotonically from 7.47 for ages 1–4 to 4.96 for ages 20–4, 3.69 for ages 40–4, 1.99 for ages 60–4, and further to 1.23 for ages 85 +, although it rises from 3.64 for age zero to 7.47 for ages 1–4 (United Nations, 1982b). Such a reduction of mortality ratio at older ages can be found in any model life-table systems that are widely used. It is therefore likely that the excess mortality of the younger subpopulation is greater at younger ages. Table 3.3 shows the ratio of the population of Malays to that of the Chinese by age, and the ratio of death rates of Malays to those of Chinese, in Peninsular Malaysia in 1981.

Table 3.3. The ratio of population of Malays to that of Chinese and the ratio of death rate of Malays to that of Chinese by age, Peninsular Malaysia, 1981

Age	Ratio of population	Ratio of death rate
0–4	2.08	1.96
5–14	1.72	1.70
15–39	1.60	1.10
40–64	1.57	1.28
65 +	0.99	1.04

Source: Malaysia, Department of Statistics, 1983.

Both of the ratios tend to decrease with age, although one anomaly can be observed.

It would thus be expected that the divergence (convergence) of age structures at the subnational level has a negative (positive) impact on the value of e_0 at the national level. Whether they are diverging or converging over time depends on the demographic and socio-economic conditions of the country. The index of dissimilarity in the age distribution between more developed and less developed regions increased from 0.134 in 1950 to 0.199 in 1980, according to the latest United Nations estimates (1984). Such a divergence of age structures contributes to an apparent reduction in the pace of mortality decline at the aggregated level.

Improved Completeness of Registration and Retrospective Reporting of Deaths

In a number of less developed countries, registration of deaths is substantially defective. This leads to an underestimation of mortality, unless the enumeration of persons is less complete than registration of deaths. An improvement in the vital registration system increases the completeness of death reporting. For example, it is estimated that the completeness of registration of deaths at age 5 and over in Sri Lanka improved from 87.6 per. cent in 1945–7 to 90.5 in 1952–4, 94.7 in 1962–4, and 98.0 in 1970–2 (United Nations, 1982, 338–9). Mortality decline in the period of improving registration will be underestimated, unless the number of registered deaths are corrected for under-registration. It is, therefore, very important to estimate the completeness of death registration in the past, as well as the current level of completeness. Because it is impossible to conduct a matching survey to check the coverage of death registration in the remote past, we need to estimate the completeness from consistencies between the age structure of persons, that of deaths, and that of growth. Various methods have been devised for this purpose (Bennett and Horiuchi, 1981; Brass, 1975; Palloni and Kominski, 1984; Preston *et al.*, 1980; Preston and Hill, 1980; United Nations, 1979*b*) and their comparative usefulness has been discussed (Preston, 1984).

The same problem arises when mortality data are collected in censuses and surveys. Typical data on mortality obtained at censuses and surveys include information on kin survivorship and deaths that occurred in the household during a certain period preceding the interview. Improved administration of data collection, and a rise in the educational level of inhabitants, lead to more complete reporting of deaths at more recent censuses and surveys, possibly resulting in an underestimation of mortality decline.

Improved Accuracy of Reported Ages

Reported ages, of enumerated persons and at deaths, are not sufficiently accurate in many developing countries (Ewbank, 1981). Although symptoms of both over- and understatement of ages are frequently observed, ages are more likely to be exaggerated than understated (see, for example, Gibril, 1975; Retherford and Mirza, 1982), particularly at old ages (Mazess, 1978; Medvedev, 1974). The age overstatement transfers some persons of relatively younger ages in which mortality is lower to older age groups with higher mortality. This, in general, leads to an underestimation of mortality rates at old ages and, in turn, an overestimation of the expectation of life. However, any rise in the educational level of the population and improvement of birth registration would reduce the upward bias in reported ages, thereby lowering the computed value of life expectancy, which possibly cancels part of the effect of actual mortality decline.

For example, an indication of old-age exaggeration may be found in the official life-table for Mexican females, 1970 (United Nations, 1974), when it is compared to the new United Nations model life-tables (United Nations, 1982b). Table 3.4 shows the expectation of life at different ages in the official life-table for Mexican females, together with the corresponding values of expectation of life at birth in the 'general' pattern of the new United Nations model life-tables. Although e_0 is 63.43, e_{65} and e_{75} are 15.22 and 9.87, which correspond respectively to 69.42 and 72.49 of e_0 in the United Nations 'general' pattern.

Table 3.4. Comparison of life expectancies for females in Mexico, 1970, and life expectancies in the United Nations general pattern model life-tables

Age x	e_x in the official life-table	e_0 in model life-tables that corresponds to e_x
0	63.43	63.43
10	60.78	64.61
20	51.45	64.69
30	42.58	65.05
40	34.09	65.89
50	25.93	66.94
60	18.47	68.29
65	15.22	69.42
70	12.34	70.78
75	9.87	72.49
80	7.82	75.19
85	5.96	76.79

Source: United Nations, 1975.

Horiuchi and Coale (1982) have developed a method for correcting life expectation for old-age exaggeration without using a model life-table. They have proposed an equation for estimating the expectation of life at an old age x (e_x) from the death rate and growth rate for the open interval $x +$. As long as the age transfer across the age x is not significantly large, the equation can be used to obtain an accurate estimate of e_x even when the age mis-reporting above x is considerable. The application of this method to Mexican data suggests that the age exaggeration is not considerable under age 65, and e_{65} of Mexican females in 1970 is 13.57 (Horiuchi and Coale, 1982, tables 3 and 4). This is lower by 1.65 years than the official figure, and corresponds to 62.38 of e_0 in the United Nations 'general' pattern. Correction of e_{65} from 15.22 to 13.57 results in a reduction of e_0 from 63.43 to 62.54. Although this is a result of demographic analysis, a similar reduction of e_0 could be produced if the quality of age data improved, and this might mask the actual increase in e_0 to some extent.

Another way to avoid the problem of age exaggeration among the old is to use temporary life expectations, as recommended by Arriaga (1981, 1984). The temporary life expectation from x to y is the average number of years that a group of persons alive at exact age x will live from age x to y years. Thus the measure is not affected by mortality data for age y and above.

Characteristics of Mortality Measures

The impression of a stagnation in mortality decline often arises from the basic characteristics of mortality measures themselves. The problem arises when the observed amount of absolute change in a mortality measure is examined for the analysis of mortality trends.

The expectation of life cannot keep increasing infinitely. It is expected that the increase in e_0 slows down when e_0 approaches the biological limit of human longevity. A given amount of increase in the expectation of life requires a greater rate of mortality decline in populations of lower mortality levels. This can be shown using model life-tables. For female life-tables following the United Nations 'general' pattern (United Nations, 1982b), for example, the increase in expectation of life at birth from 40 to 50, 50 to 60, and 60 to 70 years corresponds to reductions in the geometric mean of age-specific death rates by 31 per cent, 37 per cent, and 48 per cent, respectively. In other words, although a decline in mortality risk by about one-third increased life expectancy from 40 to 50 years, a reduction in mortality risk by about one-half is necessary in order to extend life expect-ancy from 60 to 70 years (United Nations, 1985b, chapter 3). The greater difficulty in increasing e_0 at the lower level of mortality can be shown using the quantity H, which has been developed by Keyfitz (1977, chapter 3) for measuring the proportionate increase in life expectancy corresponding to a small proportional decrease in the death rate of all ages. He showed that the value of H for United States female life-tables fell from 0.35 in 1919–21, when e_0 was 56.4 years, to 0.16 in 1959–61, when e_0 was 73.4.

One reason for the differential difficulty in increasing e_0 is the fact that changes in death rates at different ages make different contributions to e_0. In general, death rates at younger ages have greater impact on e_0. This property of e_0 seems to suggest the importance of decomposition of e_0 into contributions of improvement in age-specific death rates (Arriaga, 1984; Pollard, 1982; United Nations, 1982*a*, 11).

One way to circumvent this problem in comparing changes of e_0 in different periods is to set up a model schedule of mortality improvement to which observed changes in e_0 are compared. For example, Palloni (1981) fitted a logistic equation to the historical time-series of e_0 for England and Wales, France, and Sweden, in order to compute 'expected' gains of e_0 in Latin American countries, which were compared to observed gains there. Inoue and Yu (1979) found that the increase of e_0 was inversely related to the level of e_0 in more developed countries in 1950–75, and constructed a working model of mortality decline by averaging gains in e_0 for different levels of e_0 in those countries. Coale (1982, figure 5) showed the inverse relationship between e_0 and its gain for more developed countries from the 1930s to 1970s. The figure seems to imply that a simple linear equation fits the data quite well.

An alternative approach is to employ another measure of the overall mortality level in place of life expectation. For example, proportional change in the geometric mean of age-specific death rates was examined in an analysis of mortality trends in less developed countries (United Nations, 1982*c*, table 41). Since the lower bound (zero) of death rates makes it extremely difficult to achieve a substantial absolute amount of reduction of death rate at a low level of mortality, it seems more reasonable to infer mortality trends from proportional rather than absolute changes in death rates.

Another indicator of mortality change has been proposed by Arriaga (1981). The measure, which is described as the index of relative change in 'temporary life expectation', measures the gain in the number of years lived between two ages in relation to the maximum possible gain. The ingenuity of the idea seems to rest in the fact that it is considerably more reasonable to expect a nearly constant proportional decrease in the person-years lost than a nearly constant proportional increase in the person-years lived.

A third option is the annual rate of logistic growth of survival function,

$$(\text{logit } p(a,t_2) - \text{logit } p(a,t_1))/(t_2 - t_1)$$

where $p(a,t)$ is the life-table function at time t of probability to survive from birth to age a. The average of these rates over different ages may be meaningful when mortality changes over time are well approximated by Brass's single-parameter logit model. Such a pattern of mortality change has previously been hypothesized by Mitra (1983).

Most mortality measures other than the expectation of life are some types of mortality rates. Since mortality rates are non-negative, it is not valid to analyse mortality trends on the basis of absolute decrements of those rates. Simple procedures to circumvent this problem include
(1) computation of the proportional change in the mortality rates and
(2) comparison of observed changes with a logistic curve that is bounded to be non-negative.

Conclusion

Six factors that could lead to the underestimation of mortality decline have been discussed in this chapter. It should be noted that the purpose of the chapter is not to claim that the widely discussed issue of stagnation of mortality decline in less developed countries is only a statistical artefact, but to assert that any apparent slowing down of mortality decline in each country should be viewed with caution, in consideration of the above-mentioned sources of bias. The effects of those factors on observed mortality decline should be estimated if possible.

The problem in the use of absolute change in conventional mortality measures for assessing mortality trends can be avoided by selecting appropriate measures of mortality change and/or comparing observed changes with some 'standard' schedule of mortality decline. In many cases, the effects of changes in the completeness of death registration, and changes in age misreporting patterns, can, to some extent, be assessed by utilizing existing methods of demographic analysis. On the other hand, the adjustment of observed mortality decline for the other three factors (that is, the interrelationships of fertility, mortality and growth, heterogeneity and differential age structures) seem to require detailed mortality data on the subnational level and/or development of new methods and models.

References

Arriaga, E. E. (1981), 'The Deceleration of the Decline of Mortality in LDCs: The Case of Latin America' in *IUSSP International Population Conference, 1981*, vol. 2, International Union for the Scientific Study of Population, Liège, 143–64.

—— (1984), 'Measuring and Explaining the Change in Life Expectancies', *Demography* 21 (1), 83–96.

Azefor, M. N. A. (1981), 'Counteracting Forces in the Continued Decline of Mortality in Africa', in *IUSSP International Population Conference, 1981*, vol. 2, International Union for the Scientific Study of Population, Liège, 5–20.

Bennett, N. G., and S. Horiuchi (1981), 'Estimating the Completeness of Death Registration in a Close Population', *Population Index* 47 (2), 207–21.

Bhat, P. N. Mari, S. H. Preston, and T. Dyson (1984), *Vital Rates in India, 1961–1981*, National Academy Press, Washington, D C.

Brass, W. (1975), *Methods for Estimating Fertility and Mortality from Limited and Defective Data*, Laboratories for Population Statistics, University of North Carolina, Chapel Hill.

—— (1984), 'Mortality in China over the Past 50 Years', paper presented at the annual meeting of the Population Association of America, 28 April–1 May 1982, San Diego.

Bucht, B., and J. Chamie (1982), 'Estimates and Projections in Infant Mortality Rates', paper presented at the annual meeting of the Population Association of America, 29 April–1 May 1982, San Diego.

Coale, A. J. (1984), *Rapid Population Change in China, 1952–1982*, National Academy Press, Washington, D. C.

—— (1982), 'A Reassessment of World Population Trends', *Population Bulletin of the United Nations* 14, 1–16.

——, P. Demeny, and B. Vaughan (1983), *Regional Model Life Tables and Stable Populations*, 2nd ed., Academic Press, New York.

Ewbank, D. C. (1981), *Age Misreporting and Age-selective Underenumeration: Sources, Patterns and Consequences for Demographic Analysis*, National Academy Press, Washington, D C.

Gibril, M. A. (1975), 'Some Reporting Errors in the 1973 Gambian Census', M.Sc. thesis, University of London.

Gwatkin, D. R. (1980), 'Indications of Change in Developing Country Mortality Trends: The End of an Era?', *Population and Development Review* 33(3), 615–44.

Horiuchi, S., and A. J. Coale (1982), 'A Simple Equation for Estimating the Expectation of Life at Old Ages', *Population Studies* 36(2), 317–26.

—— —— (1983), 'Age Patterns of Mortality for Older Women', paper presented at the annual meeting of the Population Association of America, 14–16 April 1983, Pittsburg.

Inoue, S., and Y. C. Yu (1979), 'United Nations New Population Projections and Analysis of Ex Post Facto Errors', paper presented at the annual meeting of the Population Association of America, 25–8 April 1979, Philadelphia.

Keyfitz, N. (1977), *Applied Mathematical Demography*, John Wiley & Sons, New York.

Ling Rui-Zhu (1981), 'A Brief Account of 30 Years' Mortality of Chinese Population', *World Health Statistics Quarterly* 34(2), 127–34.

Lombardo, E. (1983), 'Estimation of Expectation of Life in the Case of Truncation of Survivorship Function at Old Ages: Some Considerations', *Genus* 39, 167–74.

Malaysia, Department of Statistics (1983), *Vital Statistics: Peninsular Malaysia, 1981*, Kuala Lumpur.

Manton, K. G., and E. Stallard (1981), 'Methods for Evaluating the Heterogeneity of Aging Process in Human Populations using Vital Statistical Data: Explaining the Black/White Mortality Crossover by a Model of Mortality Selection', *Human Biology* 53(1), 47–68.

Mazess, R. B. (1978), 'Health and Longevity in Vilcabamba, Ecuador', *Journal of the American Medical Association* 240.

Medvedev, Z. A. (1974), 'Caucasus and Altay Longevity: A Biological or Social Problem?', *Gerontologist* 14.

Mitra, S. (1983), 'A Simple Model for Linking Life Tables by Survival–Mortality Ratios', *Demography* 20(2), 227–34.

—— (1984), 'Estimating the Expectation of Life at Older Ages', *Population Studies* 38(2), 313–19.

Nam, C. B., N. L. Weatherby, and K. A. Ockay (1978), 'Causes of Deaths which Contribute to the Mortality Crossover Effect', *Social Biology* 25(4), 306–14.

Palloni, A. (1981), 'Mortality in Latin America: Emerging Patterns', *Population and Development Review* 7(4), 623–49.

—— and R. Kominski (1984), 'Estimation of Adult Mortality Using Forward and Backward Projection', *Population Studies* 38(3), 479–93.

Pollard, J. H. (1982), 'The Expectation of Life and its Relationship to Mortality', *Journal of the Institute of Actuaries* 109(2), 225–40.

Preston, S. H. (1984), 'Use of Direct and Indirect Techniques for Estimating the Completeness of Death Registration Systems' in *Data Bases for Mortality Measurement*, United Nations, New York.

—— and K. Hill (1980), 'Estimating the Completeness of Death Registration' *Population Studies* 34(2), 349–66.

—— A. J. Coale, J. Trussell, and M. Weinstein (1980), 'Estimating the Completeness of Reporting of Adult Deaths in Populations that are Approximately Stable', *Population Index* 46(2), 179–202.

Retherford, R. D., and G. M. Mirza (1982), 'Evidence of Age Exaggeration in Demographic Estimates for Pakistan', *Population Studies* 36(2), 257–70.

Sivamurthy, M. (1981), 'The Deceleration of Mortality Decline in Asian Countries', in IUSSP *International Population Conference, 1981*, vol. 2, International Union for the Scientific Study of Population, Liège, 51–76.

United Nations (1975), *Demographic Yearbook 1974,* New York.

—— (1979a), *Concise Report on the World Population Situation in 1977: New Beginnings and Uncertain Ends*, New York.

—— (1979b), 'Model Life Tables for Developing Countries: An Interim Report' (ESA/P.WP.63.), New York.

—— (1982a), *Levels and Trends of Mortality since 1950*, New York.

—— (1982b), *Model Life Tables for Developing Countries*, New York.

—— (1982c), *World Population Trends and Policies, 1981 Monitoring Report, Volume 1: Population Trends*, New York.

—— (1985a), *World Population Prospects: Estimates and Projections as Assessed in 1982*, New York.

—— (1985b), *World Population Trends and Policies, Population and Development Interrelations and Population Policies: 1983 Monitoring Report*, New York.

——, Secretariat (1982), 'Infant Mortality: World Estimates and Projections, 1950–2025', *Population Bulletin of the United Nations* 14, 31–53.

Vaupel, J. W., G. Manton, and E. Stallard (1979), 'The Impact of Heterogeneity in Individual Frailty on the Dynamics of Mortality', *Demography* 16(3), 439–54.

4 Measures of Preventable Deaths in Developing Countries: Some Methodological Issues and Approaches

STAN D'SOUZA

UNDP, Cotonou, RP Beniu

Worldwide interest in primary health care programmes and infant and child mortality control programmes has been aroused through the Alma Ata Conference (1978) and its declared goal of 'health for all by the year 2000'. Immunization, health education, and so on form an integral part of health strategies whose emphasis is on preventive rather than curative health care. Researchers are trying to develop mortality frameworks that are comprehensive enough to include both biological and social factors (Mosley, 1983), following a realization that improvements in health technology alone would not be sufficient to overcome the stagnation in mortality decline which has been noted recently (United Nations, 1980). It should be recognized, however, that public health workers have for several decades pointed out the need for social improvement in developing countries to ensure appropriate access to and use of available health technology (Gordon, 1956).

Against this background, policy-makers in developing countries have felt a growing need for indicators that can assess the level of 'preventable deaths' and provide simple measures of the efficacy of health programmes aimed at reducing such deaths, particularly since health resources are scarce and choices of health strategies are required (Evans *et al.*, 1981). In a report prepared for the World Health Organization, approaches to developing a Preventable Death Index (PDI), as well as background material regarding various measures used, have been described in detail (D'Souza, 1983). This chapter will briefly raise some methodological issues and problems related to the development of such measure. An application of the index to the situation in selected less developed countries will be made. The index will also be used to describe the epidemiological transition in China.

The opinions expressed herein are those of the author and should not be construed as necessarily representing the opinions of the United Nations.

Preventable Deaths

The concept of 'preventable deaths' should be clarified first. Deaths that may be considered 'preventable' in one country may not be so in another. Absolute criteria for determining preventable deaths do not exist and relative considerations have to be adopted. A norm or a standard has to be established. Considerations of cost and feasibility of preventing deaths from particular causes within realistic country settings are also important.

> Despite data limitations, it is clear that infectious and parasitic diseases—which have largely been eliminated in the more developed countries—still account for a very large proportion of all deaths in developing countries, especially among the very young. If to these deaths are added the deaths either caused by or associated with nutritional deficiencies, the proportion rises to a sizeable majority of all deaths. The number of deaths from the above causes can be reduced dramatically at relatively modest costs, and most of them must be characterised as preventable.
>
> (United Nations, 1980.)

The Expanded Program on Immunization (EPI) of the World Health Organization has focused on six vaccine-preventable diseases. Some estimates show that the elimination of neo-natal tetanus, pertussis, and measles through immunization would eliminate 3–4 million deaths annually (Foster, 1983). While vaccine-preventable diseases are a major contributing factor to high mortality rates, the long-term impact of such programmes on mortality levels may not be very great without improvements in the social and health environment and the reduction of malnutrition and diseases such as malaria (Foege, 1983).

The historical experience of developed countries is of great value in the understanding of mortality declines and control, but the changed health-technology situation in recent decades and the complex social and cultural settings of low-income countries impose caution in the use of such experience. The mortality declines registered in developing countries such as Sri Lanka, Cuba, and China provide important material for the selection of such standards. Mortality differentials within countries, whether based on socio-economic, ethnic, or sex differences, can also serve as relative frameworks to determine preventable deaths. Further, the experience of 'small area' controlled experiments, in which specific health or other inputs have been made, can also furnish criteria for determining which deaths are preventable within particular countries (D'Souza, 1984). The Khanna study in India (Wyon and Gordon, 1971) suggested broad categories of deaths that could be considered preventable within the Indian setting and with existing technological inputs. High death rates among the young from infection and malnutrition are considered preventable, whereas other causes of death are deemed less amenable to preventive measures. A more recent study in Chile also provides broad categories of theoretically preventable deaths (Castillo *et al.*, 1983).

Indicators and Standards

Indicators used to estimate preventable deaths are of various types. At one end there are quantitative estimates, such as counts of 'deaths averted'. The inclusion of cost estimates allowing for cost–benefit analyses would facilitate the choice of criteria for determining 'preventable deaths'. At the other extreme, one can utilize indicators implying various levels of preventable deaths on a qualitative scale. Estimates of mortality rates can be used to obtain global quantitative estimates of the number of preventable deaths, once the *standard* rates have been chosen on the basis of appropriate assumptions. Where estimates of mortality rates are available only through small area studies, indicators of preventable deaths are subject to similar limitations. The term 'index' in this chapter will be restricted to indicators that have been set on a quantitative scale graduated in a regular manner between a 'low' and 'high' level.

Walsh and Warren (1979) provided criteria for assessing which causes of death may be considered preventable in terms of setting priorities for mortality reduction in a given country. They include the following factors:

1. Prevalence/incidence of the disease.
2. Morbidity or severity of disability caused by the disease.
3. Risk of mortality.
4. Feasibility of control (including relative efficacy and cost of intervention).

Clearly, there are few developing countries where data on all these criteria are available. However, qualitative approaches are possible using as a standard the cause-of-death structure prevailing in countries where such data do exist. Historical data sets can also offer a standard. In Table 4.1, the major infectious diseases endemic in the developing world have been classified into three groups of priorities for disease control based on prevalence of the disease, mortality, morbidity, and feasibility of control (Walsh and Warren, 1979).

An illustration of the use of the mortality rates of a developed country to assess the number of preventable deaths in a developing country is found in a study by Taucher (1981) on Chile. The use of a standard from developed countries raises, however, conceptual problems. Some of the diseases encountered in developing countries were not of major importance for the developed countries. Data from developing countries at earlier stages of their development are largely from Latin America and thus may be insufficiently similar to the existing situations of developing countries of Asia and Africa.

The assessment of the number of preventable deaths through health programmes can be made by 'small area' controlled studies. Estimates of the deaths averted can be obtained by comparing results against a 'baseline' that includes both 'treatment' and 'control' areas, although the use of

Table 4.1. Priorities for disease control in the developing world based on prevalence, morbidity, mortality, and feasibility of control

Disease and priority for control	Reason for assignment to priority category			Effective control
	Prevalence	Morbidity	Mortality	
1. *High*				
Diarrhoeal disease	high	high	high	available
Measles	high	high	high	available
Malaria	high	high	high	available
Whooping cough	high	high	high	available
Schistosomiasis	high	high	high	available
Neo-natal tetanus	high	high	high	available
2. *Medium*				
Respiratory infections	high		high	none
Poliomyelitis	high		low	available
Tuberculosis	high		high	difficult
Onchocerciasis	medium	high	low	difficult
Meningitis	medium		high	difficult
Typhoid fever	medium		high	difficult
Hookworm	high		low	difficult
Malnutrition	high	high		complex
3. *Low*				
S. American trypanosomiasis				difficult
African trypanosomiasis	low			difficult
Leprosy				difficult
Ascariasis		low	low	difficult
Diphtheria		low	low	
Amoebiasis				difficult
Leishmaniasis				difficult
Giardiasis				difficult
Filariasis				difficult
Dengue				difficult

Source: Walsh and Warren 1979.

Table 4.2. Number of deaths averted and years of life saved by Haiti clinic/surveillance services 1972

Age group X	Death rate per 1000 Programme	Death rate per 1000 National (1972)	Observed deaths N	Expected deaths N	Averted deaths	Life expectation at mean age of the group	Years of life saved
0	34	150	3	11	8	51.0	408
1–4	6	23	5	11	6	55.0	330
5–9	1	6	2	4	2	53.8	108
10–14	<1	4	0	1	1	50.2	50
15–39	2	11	1	5	4	39.5	158
40–64	9	20	3	3	0	21.4	0
>65	69	110	5	6	1	9.8	10
Total (N = 9,612)	8	18	19	41	22		1064*

*Years of life per 1,000 person-years = 111 = (1064/9612.1000).
Source: Berggren et al. 1981.

'control' areas raises ethical problems in the design of mortality studies. Health care with known and feasible methods of averting deaths should not be deliberately withheld from a population unless there are justifiable constraints of a logistic and financial nature. Alternatively, progress in a study area can be assessed by comparing results with the area's own baseline and with national population data, if available. An illustration is provided from a study done in Haiti (Berggren et al., 1981). Table 4.2 compares the reduced levels of mortality achieved by the programme with national (1972) rates.

These rates can be converted into 'number of deaths averted' and expressed as 'years of life saved', by multiplying the number of deaths averted in each group by the corresponding life expectancy at the mean age of the group. Table 4.2 shows that the averted 22 deaths are the equivalent of 1,064 years saved and the annual life saving accrued is 111 years of life per 1,000 person-years.

The indicator 'person-years of life saved' gives considerable weight to saving of children's lives. A discounting factor may be applied that decreases the input of each person-year with time (Ewbank, 1984).

Morrow et al. (1981) have developed a method of assessing quantitatively the relative importance of different diseases in developing countries. The impact of the disease on a community is measured by the number of healthy days of life which are lost through illness, disability, and death as a consequence of the disease. To obtain the measure, data are required on the incidence rate, the case fatality rate, and the duration of the disability. Sufficient information on the disease is necessary to establish the average age at death. A comparison of the number of healthy days saved by alternative health procedures and their costs provides criteria for the determination of which causes of death are, in fact, preventable within a realistic set of priorities and capability for a particular country.

Some Demographic Indicators Used: Mortality Levels

An early paper (Bourgeois-Pichat and Pan, 1956) listed some indicators that could be utilized to study mortality trends in developing countries. Some of these indicators have been used widely—for instance, the infant mortality rate and the expectation of life at birth. Others, whether due to lack of data or intrinsic problems, such as the age distibution effect on the crude death rate, have been utilized less, or only with caution.

Figure 4.1 presents data from the Matlab area of Bangladesh and shows the utilization of neo-natal, post-neonatal, infant, and child (1–4 years) mortality rates and the crude death rate as indicators of changes in mortality levels.

The data cover the period 1966–81, during which a fair number of upheavals took place in the country. The two major peaks in the infant

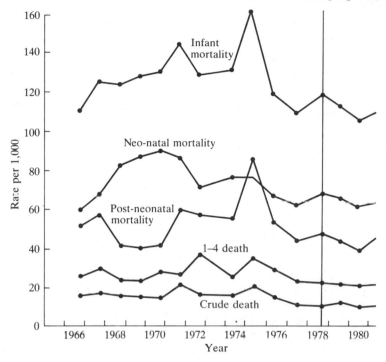

Figure 4.1. Infant (neo-natal and post-neonatal) mortality rate, child 1–4 death rate, and crude death rate in Matlab, Bangladesh, 1966–81
Source: D'Souza, 1986.

mortality rate correspond to periods of stress during the liberation struggle of 1970–1 and the famine during 1974–5. The neo-natal mortality rate is generally high, between 60 and 90 per 1,000, indicating high levels of tetanus and deaths classified as due to 'certain diseases of infancy'. The peak in the post-neonatal rate indicates a large number of deaths related to malnutrition during the period of food shortage of 1974–5. The child mortality rate also shows two peaks and is more sensitive as a mortality indicator than the crude death rate, which changes more slowly. Figure 4.2 shows the cause-of-death patterns of child mortality from some diseases in Matlab from 1975 to 1981. Apart from the higher mortality rates during the difficult period of 1975, the consistently higher female mortality in most categories is worth noting. Clearly, this differential belongs to the category of preventable mortality (D'Souza and Chen, 1980).

The infant mortality rate (IMR) has been extensively used as an indicator of the overall mortality level of a country. It is sensitive to changes in prevailing levels of public health. Modern medical technology—in particular immunization—can reduce infant mortality rates within relatively

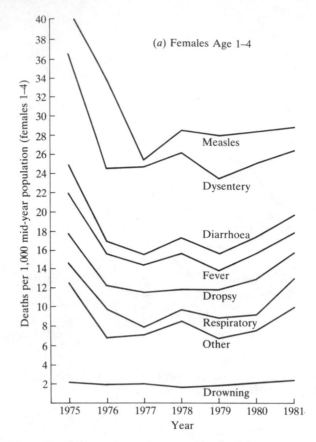

Figure 4.2.   Selected death rates by sex and cause of children aged 1–4 years in Matlab, 1975–81
Source: Zimicki *et al.*, 1985.

short periods of time. The expectation of life at birth is an overall indicator of mortality levels in a given country and has been used for comparison purposes between countries (cf. Arriaga and Davis, 1969; Preston, 1976). In addition to some technical problems associated with its use (Pollard, 1982), projections of $\overset{\circ}{e}_0$ over time have not met with uniform success. Coale (1982) examines some earlier projections made in the 1950s with actual results. A projection for Europe was not successful—life expectancies were set too low—as advances in health technology were not foreseen. A projection for India that assumed a rapid decline in death rates at first and a slackening of reduction when mortality was still rather high appears to have been successful, and a successful projection was also made for Mexico. In both these cases correct assumptions had been made about the future course of

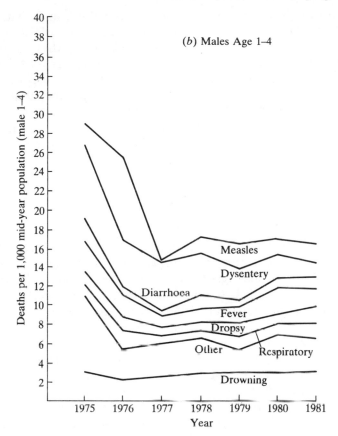

(b) Males Age 1–4

disease control. In the case of Egypt the exercise of projection 'failed' as developments in improvement of health were not correctly foreseen.

Problems of Classification of Cause of Death Data

The 'small area' studies referred to earlier include estimates of mortality rates by cause of death. In most developing countries, medical validation of cause of death is not practicable. 'Lay reporting' systems have been used to obtain information on causes of death (World Health Organization, 1978). Within the Matlab area data on causes of death have been collected through non-medical personnel. Problems related to classification have been found to be quite important. Three areas where errors of classification occur may be mentioned: respondent bias, interviewer bias, and local, as against medical, perception of disease (Zimicki *et al.*, 1985).

Conceptual problems are also inherent in classification of cause of death data. Death is rarely monocausal, and the selection of one underlying cause may not always be easy. Diseases with severe complications, such as malnutrition, measles, and malaria, may be overlooked in the classification process. The use of the concept 'death averted' may be fraught with problems. Averting a death from a particular cause may mean that the individual dies of an alternative cause within a short period of time. Oral therapy is known to be a low-cost therapy against dehydration and deaths from watery diarrhoea. To conclude that a death averted due to diarrhoea is necessarily a life saved may be incorrect. Malnourished children at high risk of death due to diarrhoea are also at high risk from a set of other causes.

Cause of Death Structure

The widely utilized Coale and Demeny tables, which were denoted as North, South, East, and West, assumed differing cause-of-death structures for children under 5 and at older ages (Coale and Demeny, 1966). The new UN life-tables also rely on implicit assumptions regarding the underlying cause-of-death structure (United Nations, 1982). Regional patterns have been discerned in mortality structures.

As vital registration in developing countries is often of poor quality or non-existent, demographic studies on mortality that include explicit analyses of cause-of-death structures are not numerous. The necessary link between mortality levels and causes of death was the subject of an early study by Bourgeois-Pichat (1952; cf. also 1978). He divided causes of death into two broad classes, exogenous and endogenous. Using the metaphor of 'hard rock' and 'soft rock' to describe these two classes, Bourgeois-Pichat argued that the exogenous causes of death could be controlled by public health measures, immunization, and antibiotics. This would be the metaphorical equivalent of erosion of the soft rock. The declining percentage of deaths from infectious diseases amongst deaths from all causes provided evidence of this phenomenon.

China succeeded in producing a dramatic drop in infant and child mortality rates during the period after 1949. Until then periodic epidemics, including plagues, cholera, and smallpox, raged across the country. Infectious and parasitic diseases such as tetanus and malaria, respiratory diseases like pneumonia and tuberculosis, and gastro-intestinal infections were widespread. As a result of a sustained health campaign that included preventive services—the renowned 'barefoot doctors' scheme—immunization, and nutrition improvement programmes, China has been able to register within the short period of thirty years an 'epidemiological revolution'. Unlike the situation in many developing countries at a similar level of development, some sources of cause-of-death data exist which document the changing pattern of mortality (Figure 4.3). Data from the Shingsan district of Beijing show that during the period 1956–9 respiratory and commu-

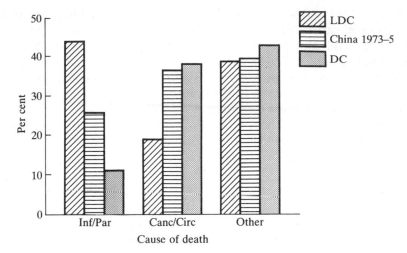

Int/Par: Infectious and parasitic diseases.
Canc/Circ: Cancer and circulatory diseases.

Figure 4.3.   China epidemiological transition
Source: World Bank, 1984.

nicable diseases ranked highest among the causes of death (over 40 per cent), whereas in the period 1974–8 cardiovascular diseases (over 51 per cent) were the most important reported causes of death (World Bank, 1984).

A more specific investigation of relationships between overall age-specific death rates and the cause-of-death structure has been provided by Preston *et al.* (1972). Cause-of-death rates from 165 populations were examined and tabulated. The populations stemmed from Northern and Western Europe (59), Southern and Eastern Europe (29), overseas European populations (36), and Africa, Asia, and Latin America (41). The set of tables provided includes, for each population, one which presents the 'number of persons surviving to age *x* if specified causes were eliminated'.

Death rates were age-standardized on the basis of two standard populations: West female stable populations with parameters $\mathring{e}_0$ 45.0, $r = 0.02$, and $\mathring{e}_0$ 65.0, $r = 0.01$, respectively.

A linear model was fitted to descibe the association between particular causes of death and the overall death rate (Preston, 1976). The causes of death were grouped into 11 broad categories. For each of the 11 causes, equations of the form $M = \Sigma a_i + b_i M_i$ were estimated through least-square regression techniques, where a_i and b_i are fitted for the *i*th cause, M_i is the death rate for all causes combined, and M the predicted death rate for the *i*th cause, under the conditions that $\Sigma a_i = 0$ and $\Sigma b_i = 1.0$. The technique is potentially of use for developing countries, since the pattern of causes of deaths can be estimated from the crude death rates. If applied with caution it can be useful in situations where insufficient national data on causes of death exist.

The standard tables have been utilized to assess available cause of death data from a variety of sources in Kenya (Ewbank *et al.*, 1986). Thus, age–site-specific cancer rates are developed for Kenya using Norwegian rates. Assumptions include similarity of age pattern of incidence and case fatality rates in Kenya and Norway. Tuberculosis data are compared with respiratory tuberculosis rates in Hong Kong to establish plausibility of estimates made regarding the effectiveness of a BCG campaign.

Lopez and Hull (1982) have pointed out problems that arise from taking a population with an older age distribution as standard. Since the overall death rate is dependent on the age structure of the population and can be written as $M = \Sigma m_i p_i$, where m_i and p_i refer to the age-specific death rate and the age proportion respectively, it is clear that the use of an older population would imply more deaths from causes prevalent at older ages. Cardiovascular diseases and neoplasms would be emphasized as causes of death. Calculating a new set of a_i and b_i on the basis of the young age distribution which exists in Java, they have shown that a cause of death structure for Java 1972 was obtained that was closer to the existing patterns of cause of death than would have been the case had a model based on an older age structure been utilized.

Two parameters, $\mathring{e}_0$ and r (expectation of life at age zero and rate of population growth, respectively), have been used by Lopez and Hull to select the standard population. In view of the fact that the population age distribution changes at the younger ages are more sensitive to changes in r

Table 4.3. Crude and age-standardized (two standards) death rates (per 1,000) of females in Guatemala 1961 and Costa Rica 1960

1960	Guatemala 1961			Costa Rica		
	CDR	SR(1)	SR(2)	CDR	SR(1)	SR(2)
All causes	16.21	16.66	19.15	8.12	8.14	14.30
Respiratory tuberculosis	0.27	0.29	0.38	0.10	0.11	0.15
Other infections	3.99	3.93	3.67	0.88	0.72	0.61
Neoplasms	0.34	0.42	0.76	0.74	0.95	2.08
Cardiovascular diseases	0.49	0.59	1.21	1.03	1.41	3.90
Influenza/pneumonia/ bronchitis	2.58	2.62	2.88	0.89	0.77	1.06
Certain Degenerative diseases	0.16	0.20	0.34	0.24	0.30	0.68
Maternal mortality	0.24	0.24	0.24	0.13	0.14	0.14
Diseases of infancy	1.67	1.68	0.95	0.71	0.51	0.30
Motor vehicles	0.03	0.04	0.05	0.03	0.03	0.04
Other violence	0.14	0.15	0.15	0.15	0.17	0.37
Other and unknown	4.06	4.31	6.26	2.05	2.15	4.28

$$\mathring{e}_0 = 48.357 \qquad\qquad \mathring{e}_0 = 65.142$$

than in $\dot{e}_0$, it is important to ensure that the r of the standard model utilized does correspond closely enough to the r of the actual population. For developing countries the higher value of r would seem to be indicated in most cases, since it gives a broader base to the age pyramid where a large proportion of the deaths take place.

Table 4.3 provides data from Guatemala and Costa Rica. The standardized rates from the younger and older populations are taken from Preston *et al.* (1972). One notices that in both cases the crude rates from the countries correspond well with the standardized rates from the younger model life-table. This result is to be expected in the case of Guatemala since both parameters r and $\dot{e}_0$ are close to West Model parameters; however, in the case of Costa Rica it is clear that though the $\dot{e}_0$ value is close to that of the older standard life-table the results correspond better with the younger age distribution, due to a higher r level.

Development of an Index of Preventable Deaths (Infant and Child)

It is clear from the preceding sections that various indicators are required to estimate 'preventable' deaths. A single indicator would be totally insufficient to describe the complex process as a result of which deaths can be classified as preventable. In the report prepared for the World Health Organization (D'Souza, 1983) two approaches were suggested. In both approaches a transformation of the usual mortality indicators is recommended. The problems involved with the use of the infant mortality rate have been mentioned earlier. Large drops in the IMR are related to control of infectious diseases, requiring small changes in the public health environment. A logistic transformation is proposed (cf. Mosteller and Tukey, 1977) and an infant mortality index (IMI) is defined with a scale from zero (IMR = 5 per 1,000) to 100 (IMR = 300 per 1,000):

$$IMI = 100 - A.(\ln (q_0/(1 - q_0) + B)$$

where A and B are constants defined by the high and low points of the scale. It should be noted that values of the IMR higher than 300 known to have existed historically would appear after transformation as an IMI greater than 100; IMR values lower than 5 would become negative IMI values. The transformed scale spreads the difficulty involved in mortality control more uniformly along the scale.

First Approach

In this approach it is assumed that data on cause of death and cost-feasibility of intervention are not available. It has been shown that a transformation of mortality measures can portray better the difficulty involved in preventive disease control. Hence an appropriate first approximation of a preventable death index (PDI) would be:

PDI (study population) = IMI (study population) − IMI (standard population)

If we assume in the case of infant mortality that IMI = 30 represents the hard rock of mortality, then as an appropriate indication of the elimination of most preventable diseases of infectious and parasitic origin:

PDI (study population) = IMI (study population) − 30

The values of the PDI would range from zero to 70 for developing countries. Negative values of the PDI could mean erosion of the hard rock, and can be utilized for measures of mortality control in developed countries. Clearly, other standards can be selected, depending on what may be considered feasible for particular regions.

Second Approach

In this case it is assumed that data on mortality patterns are available, and that there is information on the cost-feasibility structure. Some elements need definition:

M_i = death rate due to cause i;

M = death rate due to all causes;

CF_i = cost-feasibility factor (taking values between 0 and 1) for preventing cause of death i. (This factor may be a complex function assuming the role of quantifier of the elements of cost, feasibility, acceptability, and so on of mortality control mentioned earlier. It is assumed that prohibitive costs and logistics make preventive measures unfeasible and $CFi = 0$; where low-cost feasible approaches to prevention of death are available, $CFi = 1$.)

PDI (study population) = IMI * Σ((Mi/M) * CFi).

A simple example may illustrate the construction of the PDI. Let us assume that there are only two types of causes of death: type a due to causes of infectious and parasitic origin, and type b due to congenital defects. Also let us assume that

$$CF_i = IMI * (Ma/M * 1 + Mb/M * 0)$$

$$= IMI * Ma/M$$

that is, the IMI multiplied by the proportion of deaths due to infectious and parasitic diseases to all deaths. In this simplified case the PDI definition used in Approach 2 can be related to that of Approach 1.

The last equation may be written:

$$
\begin{aligned}
IMI − PDI &= IMI − IMI * Ma/M \\
&= IMI(1 − Ma/M) \\
&= IMI * Mb/M \text{ since } Ma/M + Mb/M = 1 \\
&= \text{the proportion of the IMI due to congenital defects}
\end{aligned}
$$

$$\text{(hard rock level)}$$
$$= \text{IMI (standard population)}$$
i.e. PDI (Approach 2) = IMI − IMI (standard population)
$$= \text{PDI (Approach 1)}$$

If one does not have all the elements of the cause-of-death structure one may utilize the indirect estimates of Mi/M obtained from the cause-of-death tabulations of Preston *et al.* (1972). When detailed CFi information is not available, one can utilize, with suitable adjustments, values provided by Walsh and Warren (1979).

Table 4.4 presents values of q_0 and corresponding values of the IMI. Rounded-off values of q_0 to the nearest 0.005 can be used, with the exception of q_0 = 0.012 where the approximation of 0.010 would not be appropriate since index values are very sensitive to changes in q_0 at that stage. A line to denote a possible distinction between 'hard' and 'soft' rock of mortality is set below q_0 = 0.030, assuming that where an infant mortality rate is below 30 per 1,000 there are few deaths of infectious and parasitic origin. A second dotted line has been set below q_0 = 0.100, since in developing countries infant mortality levels below 100 per 1,000 are unlikely without some improvements in social structures and environmental health. The tentative term 'intermediate rock' has been utilized for levels of q_0 between 0.30 and 0.100. Diarrhoeal diseases still require control at this stage. At IMR levels higher than 100 per 1,000 immunization programmes are effective, particularly if malnutrition problems are under control. All these settings are somewhat different for various regions of the developing world and should be suitably adjusted.

Table 4.4. Values denoting levels of infant mortality index and preventable death index

q_0 (rounded)	Actual q_0 value	IMI	PDI	Bourgeois-Pichat classification
0.300	(0.300)	100	70	Soft rock (large percentage of deaths of
0.215	(0.216)	90	60	infectious origin)
0.150	(0.150)	80	50	
0.100	(0.100)	70	40	
0.070	(0.068)	60	30	Social change necessary (intermediate rock?)
0.045	(0.044)	50	20	
0.030	(0.029)	40	10	
0.020	(0.019)	30	0	Hard rock
0.010	(0.012)	20		(large percentage of deaths due to
0.008	(0.077)	10		congenital defects and other neo-natal
0.005	(0.005)	0		causes)

Table 4.5.   Values denoting levels of child mortality index and preventable death index

$_4q_1$ (rounded)	Actual $_4q_1$ value	Index value		Bourgeois-Pichat classification
		IMI	PDI	
0.150	(0.150)	100	70	Soft rock
0.100	(0.100)	90	60	(large percentage of
0.070	(0.068)	80	50	deaths of infectious
0.045	(0.044)	70	40	origin)
0.030	(0.029)	60	30	
0.020	(0.019)	50	20	
0.010	(0.012)	40	10	
0.008	(0.008)	30	0	Hard rock
0.005	(0.005)	20		(congenital defects)
0.003	(0.003)	10		
0.002	(0.002)	0		

Similar transformations of other mortality measures are also possible. Table 4.5 presents transformation of the child mortality measure $(_4q_1)$. Here the high point for $_4q_1$ has been set at 0.150 and the low point at 0.002. The division between hard and soft rock is put below $_4q_1 = 0.008$. Most preventable deaths are in infant and child mortality groups just dealt with.

Some Applications

Demographic data on China have been relatively scarce till recent years, when a flood of data have been released. Several demographic studies have confirmed the high quality of the data (Coale, 1982; Hill, 1984). In the area of mortality, however, incomplete registration has been estimated at a level of 38 per cent during the period 1953–64 and 16 per cent for the period 1964–82. The data are still, though, sufficient to provide, through indirect estimation techniques, a fairly adequate picture of the mortality and epidemiological transition that has taken place. These data provide a valuable instance of testing the use of the PDI in a concrete case.

The epidemiological transition began in China's cities and then progressed through the rural areas. Before 1949, apart from infectious diseases, malnutrition and high fertility made for extremely high infant mortality rates. Table 4.6 provides IMR values from 1950 to 1982. The initial value of 252 per 1,000 in 1950 decreased to 200 per 1,000 by the year 1959. However, the gains made prior to the Great Leap Forward of 1958 were followed by a period of famine and disorder resulting in a sharp rise in infant mortality rates. The IMR rose to 330 per 1,000 in 1960 before falling back to 193 in 1962. After that year the IMR fell rapidly to 100 per 1,000 in 1972 to reach a level of 45 per 1,000 in 1982. As an indicator the weakness of the IMR is clear. Thus, during the decade of the fifties the IMR fell around 50

Table 4.6. Comparative IMR and IMI values for China 1952–82

Year	IMR value	IMI value
1950	252	94.6
1952	240	93.1
1954	225	91.2
1955	216	90.1
1957	200	87.9
1959	252	94.6
1960	330	103.1
1962	193	86.9
1964	180	85.0
1965	165	82.6
1967	139	78.0
1969	122	74.7
1970	109	71.8
1972	100	69.6
1974	87	66.2
1975	84	65.3
1977	64	58.7
1979	57	55.9
1980	53	54.2
1982	45	50.3

points if one excludes the difficult years around 1960. During the next decade the fall in the IMR was about 100 points, and in the decade 1972–82 the fall in the IMR was again about 50 points.

If one now reviews the performance of the IMI as an indicator one notices that during the fifties the fall in the IMI was about 6 points only, from about 93 to 87. During the next decade, 1962–72, the fall in the IMI was about 17 points, from around 87 to around 70. Finally, during the decade 1972–82 the IMI fell 20 points, from 70 to about 50. Clearly, in terms of reflecting improvements in the health status of the country, the IMI does much better than the IMR. If, as suggested in Approach 1, and IMI of 30 is considered the standard level for the eradication of most preventable deaths of infectious and parasitic origin, China has a PDI value of 20.

The value of using the IMI instead of the IMR for policy issues is illustrated further by two examples. In Table 4.7 a comparison is made between infant mortality levels in Bangladesh and Sri Lanka for the five-year periods 1950–5 and 1980–5, utilizing both the IMR and the IMI. If one uses the IMR as a measure of mortality decline in preventable deaths the performance of both countries is quite similar: a decline of 46.9 points for Bangladesh as against 50.1 points for Sri Lanka. If one uses IMI values, however, the difference in performance is quite different. Sri Lanka

Table 4.7. Comparative IMR and IMI values for some countries 1950 and 1980

Country	IMR value			IMI value		
	1950	1980	Difference	1950	1980	Difference
Bangladesh	179.5	132.6	46.9	84.9	76.8	8.1
Sri Lanka	90.7	40.6	50.1	67.2	47.9	19.3
Netherlands	24.2	8.4	15.8	35.9	11.7	24.2
Canada	35.9	10.4	25.5	45.0	16.6	28.4
United States	27.8	12.1	15.7	39.0	20.0	19.0
Japan	50.6	7.4	43.2	53.1	9.0	42.1

*Source: United Nations secretariat 1982.

does nearly twice as well in mortality control over the period 1950–80 as Bangladesh.

Using the IMI instead of the IMR for developed countries also produces interesting results. The Netherlands and the USA show similar IMR decline from 1950–80, whereas the decline in IMR for Canada is much superior. If the IMI is utilized the Canadian advantage over the Netherlands is greatly reduced and the USA is shown to have the smallest drop in mortality levels. Japan's mortality control measured by the IMR represents 43.2 points and by the IMI 42.1 points. By both measures Japan's achievement is much superior to the set of countries considered.

Table 4.8 provides projected or estimated values of the IMR and corresponding IMI values for Africa from 1950 and 2025. If one glances down the difference columns for the IMR values one notices that these values

Table 4.8.   Index values for infant mortality rates in Africa 1950–2025

Years	IMR*	Difference	Index value	Difference
1950–55	184.3		85.6	
1955–60	172.3	12.0	83.7	1.9
1960–65	160.3	12.0	81.8	1.9
1965–70	149.4	11.9	79.9	1.9
1970–75	138.5	11.9	77.9	2.0
1975–80	127.1	11.4	75.7	2.2
1980–85	116.4	10.7	73.5	2.2
1985–90	106.0	10.4	71.1	2.4
1990–95	96.2	10.2	68.7	2.4
1995–2000	87.0	9.2	66.2	2.5
2000–05	78.3	8.7	63.6	2.6
2005–10	70.2	8.1	60.9	2.7
2010–15	62.7	7.5	58.2	2.7
2015–20	55.8	6.9	55.4	2.8
2020–25	49.4	6.4	52.5	2.9

*Source: United Nations secretariat 1982.

diminish with time. At face value this would indicate that the mortality decline is slowly tapering off. If one reviews the differences in IMI values over time one notices that these values slowly increase, indicating that if the countries were to maintain the schedule proposed over time increasing efforts would be required.

Discussion

The preceding sections have briefly reviewed some measures demographers and epidemiologists have used to assess preventable deaths. Some conceptual problems have been noted in cost allocation and cause-of-death classification. A major focus of the chapter has been the standardization of a mortality index that would indicate changes in mortality levels in a manner which would consider the difficulty involved in mortality control. Once appropriate assumptions have been made regarding local and country settings with regard to what is considered preventable, the formulation of a PDI follows from the standardized mortality index.

The mortality indices used here have been derivations of q_x values, since it is assumed that such estimates exist—at least from the variety of indirect estimation procedures now available. It has been pointed out that the knowledge of cause-of-death structures is basic to a more precise understanding of the future course of mortality. The existing tabulated data on causes of death, from the historical experience of—mostly—developed countries, have been shown to be useful. It would appear from the illustrations provided that tabulations with various levels of r would be quite useful. Age-specific cause of death data have been tabulated for broad groupings of $\overset{\circ}{e}_0$ (Preston, 1976). Similar tabulations for specific r values (say between 1.0 and 3.00) could provide a grid within which broad groups of cause-of-death rates would be selected for particular developing countries. Such information does not usually exist in registered data on a nationwide scale.

Studies from 'small areas' can be used to validate the indirect estimates of cause-of-death structure obtained from the above tabulations. More importantly, such study areas can provide information on the various parameters relating to the selection of health strategies—efficacy of treatment, cost, and so on. Standardized approaches should be developed to ensure meaningful comparison between projects and countries. In this connection the role of the National Household Survey Capability Program (NHSCP), conducted with UN support, may also prove useful (United Nations, 1983).

Apart from being easy to construct, the mortality index has been set on a scale from zero to 100 to provide simple percentiles which can be useful for policy. Thus 'hard rock' is considered to be less than 30. The particular setting of the 'low' and 'high' points can appear arbitrary. However, available experience in the Matlab area of Bangladesh, as well as work elsewhere (Kermani *et al.*, 1984), show that levels of mortality are related to the elimination of various diseases. The analogy of types of rock corresponds to such a process. Historical data provide similar support for such a belief (Preston *et al.*, 1972). A reference to the actual death rates involved can be made by an inverse transformation from the index values.

It is important to note that the mortality index has been developed for policy-makers, and integrates the idea of 'difficulty' of control, which is wider than the straightforward notion of 'death'. The use of the Richter scale for earth tremors has meaning even to lay persons in the area of seismology. Readings of 6 or 7 arc considered very severe earthquakes. Similarly, PDI values over 50 can be taken to imply very little mortality control in a country. Indices are important because of the relative nature of the information they provide. Falls or rises in the Cost of Living Index have a policy impact, even though they do not directly designate what constituent has fallen or risen, or what absolute value has been used as a baseline. Differences in IMI have been shown to provide more significant information than the use of the IMR alone.

More complex formulations of indices related to health exist (Chiang, 1965). However, the objective of the PDI formulation here has been to develop a tool that may be useful in developing countries where reliable data are not easily available. Apart from better information on the cause-of-death structure, the knowledge of the dynamics of epidemic spread within a population would assist a more precise PDI formulation. Specific models have been developed for the understanding of individual infectious diseases (Anderson, 1982). This material, though important, is beyond the scope of this chapter, which has remained with more general issues.

The use of logistic transformation can be justified for more than mere statistical nicety. Apart from the illustrations on possible use for policy already provided, it should not be forgotten that standardization procedures are commonplace in demography. However, standardizations of underlying distributions have been used infrequently. The particular choice of distribution—logistic, Cauchy, or Gaussian—has been shown to make little difference (cf. Mosteller and Tukey, 1977). The use of logarithmic transformations is frequent in demographic literature. Multiplicative models become additive, and this property is clearly of great relevance, since causes of death are associated and the use of associated multiple decrement is often indicated. The Brass African model uses the logit transformation. A similar use is found in the new UN model life-tables. It should also be noted that the particular transformation utilized is basically the logarithm of the 'odds' of dying. In fact, since it is 'differences' in IMI that are mainly used, the transformation consists of the logarithm of the 'odds ratio' commonly used in epidemiology.

Applications of the IMI to the case of China, where the fall in the infant mortality rate and the resulting epidemiological transition has been well documented, show the value of the IMI as a useful policy tool.

References

Anderson, R. M. (ed.) (1982), *Population Dynamics of Infectious Diseases*, Chapman & Hall, New York.

Arriaga, E. E. and K. Davis (1969), 'The Pattern of Mortality Change in Latin America', *Demography* 6(3), 223–41.

Berggren, W., D. Ewbank, and G. Berggren (1981), 'Reduction of Mortality in Rural Haiti through a Primary Health Care Program', *New England Journal of Medicine* 304, 1324–30.

Bourgeois-Pichat, J. (1952), 'Essai sur la mortalité biologique de l'homme', *Population*, Jul.–Sept.

—— (1978), 'Future Outlook of Mortality Decline in the World', *Population Bulletin of the United Nations* 11, 12–41.

—— and C. L. Pan (1956), 'Trends and Determinants of Mortality in Underdeveloped Areas', *Millbank Memorial Fund 1956*, 11–25.

Castillo, B., F. Solis, and G. Mardonis (1983), 'Influencia del Sector Salud en Los Niveles de la Mortalidad Infantil Chilena' in *Infant and Child Mortality in the Third World*, CICRED, Paris.

Chiang, C. L. (1965), *An Index of Health: Mathematical Models*, National Centre for Health Statistics, series 2, no. 5, Washington.

Coale, A. J. (1982), 'A Reassessment of World Population Trends', *Population Bulletin of the United Nations* 14, 1–6.

—— (1984), 'Rapid Population Change in China, 1952–1982', Committee on Population and Demography, report no. 27, National Academy Press, Washington, DC.

—— and P. Demeny (1966), *Regional Model Life Tables and Stable Populations*, Princeton University Press, Princeton, NJ.

D'Souza, S. (1983), 'Development of an Index of Preventable Deaths', report prepared for the WHO mortality project.

—— (1984), 'Small Area Intensive Studies for Understanding Mortality and Morbidity Processes: Two Models from Bangladesh—the Matlab Project and the Companiganj Project', paper presented at the UN/WHO working group on Data Bases and Measurement of Levels, Trends and Differentials in Mortality, Bangkok, 1981, in *Data Bases for Mortality Measurement*, ST/ESA/SER.A/84, United Nations, New York.

—— (1986), 'Mortality Structure in Matlab (Bangladesh) and the Effect of Selected Health Interventions' in United Nations, *Determinants of Mortality Change and Differentials in Developing Countries*, New York, 117–44.

—— and L. C. Chen (1980), 'Sex Differentials in Mortality in Rural Bangladesh', *Population and Development Review* 6 (2), 257–70.

Evans, J. R., K. L. Hall, and J. Warford (1981), 'Health Care in the Developing World: Problems of Scarcity and Choice', *New England Journal of Medicine* 305 (19), 117–1127.

Ewbank, D. (1984), 'The Use of Mortality Data for Evaluating the Success of Specific Health and Development Programs' in *Data Bases for Mortality Measurement*, ST/ESA/SER.A/84, United Nations, New York.

—— , R. Henin, and J. Kekovole (1986), 'An Integration of Demographic and Epidemiologic Research on Mortality in Kenya' in United Nations, *Determinants of Mortality Change and Differentials in Developing Countries*, New York, 33–85.

Foege, W. H. (1983), 'Social Policy, Health Policy and Mortality Prospects in the Developing World: Immunization Programs', IUSSP seminar on Social Policy, Health Policy, and Mortality Prospects, INED, Paris.

Foster, S. (1983), *Immunizable and Respiratory Diseases and Infant and Child Mortality*, paper prepared for workship on Child Survival, Bellagio, Italy.

Gordon, J. (1956), discussion of paper by M. Balfour, *Some Considerations regarding the Permanence of Recent Declines in Mortality in Underdeveloped Areas*, Millbank Memorial Fund, New York.

Hill, K. (1984), 'Demographic Trends in China, 1951–1981', supplementary paper no. 1 to World Bank Country Study, *China: The Health Sector*, World Bank, Washington, DC.

Kermani, S., A. Laraba, T. Anane, S. Laaloui, Z. Belhocine, and J. -P. Grangaud (1984), *Evolution de la mortalite infantile dans le secteur sanitaire et universitaire de Cherage (Alger) de 1976–82*, 3e Congrès de l'UNAS PA, ● Abidjan.

Lopez, A. D., and T. H. Hull (1982), 'A Note on Estimating the Cause of Death Structure in High Mortality Populations', *Population Bulletin of the United Nations* 14, 66–70.

Morris, M. D. (1978), *Measuring the Condition of the World's Poor*, Overseas Development Council, Pergamon Press, New York.

Morrow, R. H., P. G. Smith, and K. P. Nimo (1981), 'Quantitive Method of Assessing the Health Impact of Different Diseases in Less Developed Countries', *International Journal of Epidemiology* 10, 73–82.

Mosley, W. H. (1983), 'Will Primary Health Care Reduce Infant and Child Mortality? A Critique of Some Current Strategies, with Special Reference to Africa and Asia, IUSSP seminar on Social Policy, Health Policy, and Mortality Prospects, INED, Paris.

Mosteller, F., and J. Tukey (1977), *Data Analysis and Regression*, Addison Wesley. Reading, Mass.

Pollard, J. (1982), 'Methodological Issues in the Measurement of Inequality of Death' in WHO, *Mortality in South and East Asia: A Review of Changing Trends and Patterns, 1950–1975*, Manila, 531–58.

Preston, S. H. (1976), *Mortality Patterns in National Populations: With Special Reference to Recorded Causes of Death*, Academic Press, New York.

—— (1980), 'Causes and Consequences of Mortality Declines in Less Developed Countries during the 20th Century' in R. A. Easterlin (ed.), *Population and Economic Change in Developing Countries*, University Press, Chicago, 289–360.

—— N. Keyfitz, and R. Schoen (1972), *Causes of Death: Life Tables for National Populations*, Seminar Press, New York.

Taucher, E. (1981), *Chile: Mortalidad de 1 â 4 años de edad. Tendencias y causas*, Notas de Poblacion Ano IX no. 26, Chile, 27–54.

United Nations (1983), *Indirect Techniques for Demographic Estimation*, Manual X, New York.

—— , Secretariat (1980), 'Concise Report on the Monitoring of Population Trends', *Population Bulletin of the United Nations* 12, 1–19.

—— —— (1982), 'Infant Mortality: World Estimates and Projections 1950–2025', 31–53, 'Construction of the New UN Model Life Table System', 54–66, *Population Bulletin of the United Nations* 14.

—— , Statistical Office (1981), *The Role of the NHSCP in providing Health Information in Developing Countries*.

——/World Health Organization (1982), *Levels and Trends of Mortality since 1950*, United Nations, New York.

Walsh, J., and K. Warren (1979), 'Selective Primary Health Care: An Interim Strategy for Disease Control in Developing Countries', *New England Journal of Medicine* 301, 967–74.

World Bank (1984), Country Study, *China: The Health Sector*, Washington, DC.

World Health Organization (1978), *Lay Reporting of Health Information*, Geneva.

Wyon, J. B., and J. C. Gordon (1971), *The Khanna Study*, Harvard University Press.

Zimicki, S., L. Nahar, A. M. Sardar, and E. D'Souza (1985), *Cause of Death Reporting in Matlab: A Source Book of Cause Specific Mortality rates*, Matlab 1975–1981, ICDDR, B. Bangladesh.

Part III

Biological and Social Factors

5 Changing Trends in Mortality Decline during the Last Decades

EDUARDO E. ARRIAGA

US Bureau of the Census

There has been a general concern about recent trends of mortality in developing countries. This concern emerged because in most of the developing countries for which there is information, mortality decline slowed down during the 1960s (as it also did in some developed countries). Data from most of these countries had shown significant gains in life expectation at birth during the 1950s; hence, optimistic predictions of future trends of mortality were made. However, life-tables for some developing countries in the early 1970s showed that the expected fast pace of mortality decline had not continued during the 1960s. Those populations for which information was available had mortality rates during the 1950s which declined rapidly at practically all ages, but during the 1960s most of the gain in life expectation was due to the reduction of infant mortality. At adult ages male mortality rates were only slightly reduced, or, in some countries, even tended to increase (Arriaga, 1981; Sivamurthy, 1981).

As a result of massive programmes for reducing 'excess' mortality during the 1950s, the age pattern of mortality decline in most developing countries was rather similar. Public health programmes were focused on infectious and contagious diseases. Consequently, the number of deaths from those were reduced in most of the countries, and hence the pattern of mortality change by age was also similar. Such similarities in the pattern of mortality decline did not continue during the 1960s. This situation generated several questions. For instance, was the slowing down of mortality decline a real phenomenon, or was it the consequence of the indices used for measuring the change of mortality? Do those developing countries with available information (the only ones than can be analysed) represent the 'developing countries' of the world? If there was indeed a slowing down of mortality decline in developing countries, was this an inevitable mortality trend? Since more information is now available for some countries, this chapter reviews mortality trends in a few developing countries. First, an attempt is made to

The author wishes to thank staff members of the Center for International Research who made valuable comments; Janet Sales, who typed several drafts; and Vivian Cash, who prepared the input data for the computer runs and prepared some of the tables in this chapter.

answer the previous three questions. Second, such data as are available for the middle or late 1970s are analysed so as to clarify as far as possible recent trends of mortality, including an analysis of the causes of death. Third, developing countries for which recent information is available will be compared with the United States in 1980, to determine the age patterns and causes of death that contribute to the differentials in life expectation between them.

Mortality Change during the 1950s and 1960s

Since crude death rates (actual or standardized) and life expectation at birth are not good indices for measuring the change of mortality, the index used here is the relative change of *temporary life expectation* (Arriaga, 1981, 1984). This index measures the annual change in temporary life expectation between any specific ages, in relation to the possible maximum change in temporary life expectation. The greater the value of the index, the faster the mortality decline. (A brief explanation is given in Appendix 5.I.)

This index of annual relative change of temporary life expectation shows that although, in most countries, the pace of mortality decline was reduced in the 1960s in relation to the 1950s, mortality decline accelerated during the 1960s in 5 out of 19 countries for males and in 6 out of 19 countries for females (Arriaga, 1981). The countries in which the mortality decline accelerated were Chile, Colombia, Costa Rica, Malaysia, Paraguay, and Taiwan.[1] The analysis was also conducted by causes of death for a few countries with such information. It was found that in almost all countries (*a*) the mortality decline during the 1960s was due mainly to a reduction of mortality from infectious, contagious, and parasitic diseases; and (*b*) the decline of these diseases was not as fast as in the previous decade.

The question is whether or not those countries for which there is information can be accepted as representing all developing countries. No statistical answer can be given, since most developing countries do not have comparable information. Nevertheless, those countries with reliable information not only seem to be better-off economically, but also have a higher proportion of literate persons (Bureau of the Census, 1983). Although there are some exceptions, most of those countries for which the analysis can be made are probably those 'more developed' within the group known as developing countries. Hence, whatever conclusions are drawn from the available information may not hold true for 'most of the developing countries of the world'.

Finally, it was pointed out earlier that the 1950s was a special decade in which several developing countries implemented massive public health pro-

---

[1] The countries analysed were: Argentina, Belize, Brazil, Chile, Colombia, Costa Rica, Guatemala, Honduras, Malaysia, Mauritius, Mexico, Panama, Paraguay, Peru, Puerto Rico, Singapore, Sri Lanka, Taiwan, and Venezuela.

grammes (Arriaga and Davis, 1969). Such programmes brought fast declines in infectious, contagious, and parasitic diseases, resulting in a mortality reduction that can be labelled as the fastest in the history of those countries. Unfortunately, mortality decline is not only dependent upon public health programmes but also upon a number of other societal characteristics that are related to development, such as nutrition, education, water supply, housing, communications, and so forth. Public health programmes without development can reduce mortality, but only down to certain levels. The opposite is also true—development without a proper public health system and social programmes cannot reduces mortality efficiently. During the 1950s, some developing countries improved public health programmes without a similar improvement in economic conditions, producing a rapid increase in life expectation.

Although from 1960 to 1970 some countries in which the pace of mortality decline slowed had a substantial increase in per capita income, the increase was a result of sudden large investments (mostly foreign) that require time for the benefits to spread to most of society. The increase in per capita income observed during the early 1960s would have had its effect, in large sectors of the population, only during the late 1960s or 1970s.

It seems that the slowing down of mortality decline observed in most countries during the 1960s was due mainly to the extremely rapid mortality decline during the 1950s. This is supported by the fact that the annual pace of mortality decline during the two decades (from about 1950 to 1970) was higher for those countries which experienced a slowing down of the mortality decline during the 1960s than for those countries in which the mortality decline accelerated during the 1960s (Arriaga, 1981). In simple words, the slowing down of the pace of mortality decline in most of the countries was a logical consequence after a decade of astonishingly fast reduction of mortality. This statement refers only to those countries with available information, which, as has already been pointed out, may not represent the majority of the developing countries of the world.

Mortality Change during the 1970s

There are recent reliable life-tables for dates between 1970 and 1980 for nine developing countries: Argentina, Cost Rica, Cuba, Hong Kong, India, Korea, Singapore, Taiwan, and Venezuela (Table 5.1). When the pace of mortality decline in these countries between birth and age 75 years is analysed, four show an acceleration of the mortality decline during the 1970s relative to the 1960s (Table 5.2). There are three interesting cases: (*a*) India, where after a long experience of rather slow mortality decline, there was a considerable increase in mortality reduction during the late 1970s; (*b*) Argentina, which had increased male mortality during the 1960s, has reduced mortality during the 1970s at a faster rate even than during the

Table 5.1.   Life expectancy at birth and temporary life expectancy from birth to age 75 years, selected countries and years

Country	Year	Life expectancy, at birth		Temporary life expectancy from birth to age 75 years	
		Male	Female	Male	Female
Argentina	1947	58.68	62.95	56.71	59.49
	1960	63.16	68.88	60.41	63.77
	1970	61.82	69.19	59.58	64.40
	1978	65.43	72.12	62.35	66.51
Chile	1952	50.80	53.53	49.12	51.30
	1960	54.18	58.71	52.42	56.58
	1970	58.50	64.68	56.11	60.73
Costa Rica	1950	53.96	56.97	51.96	54.33
	1963	62.15	65.03	59.82	61.15
	1973	65.18	70.15	61.78	65.40
	1980	70.30	75.04	66.27	69.19
Cuba	1953	56.69	61.01	55.05	58.65
	1970	68.55	71.81	64.56	66.47
	1980	71.15	74.57	66.26	68.19
Hong Kong	1961	63.64	70.51	61.51	65.60
	1971	67.36	75.01	64.36	68.65
	1976	69.57	76.42	65.87	69.58
India	1956	41.89	40.55	39.50*	38.03*
	1966	46.37	44.65	41.57*	41.04*
	1977	50.84	49.99	46.21*	44.25*
	1980	54.08	54.73	48.32*	47.50*
Mexico	1950	46.16	49.00	44.44	46.80
	1960	56.38	59.58	53.52	56.08
	1970	58.39	62.38	55.68	58.78
Panama	1950	48.83	51.05	47.34	49.12
	1960	59.75	63.18	57.14	59.70
	1970	63.54	66.28	60.34	62.01
Singapore	1947	47.36	51.20	46.46	49.78
	1957	60.25	65.22	59.25	63.21
	1970	65.11	69.98	63.70	67.48
	1980	68.84	74.10	65.95	68.97
Taiwan	1951	53.10	57.34	51.96	54.91
	1961	61.32	65.59	59.36	62.03
	1971	66.43	71.45	63.69	66.83
	1981	67.43	72.55	64.49	68.38
United States	1940	61.60	65.89	59.30	62.49
	1950	65.47	70.96	62.59	66.30
	1960	66.80	73.24	63.69	67.80
	1970	67.04	74.64	63.89	68.38
	1980	69.96	77.48	65.91	69.80

* From birth to age 65 years.
Source: Appendices.

Table 5.2. Annual percentage relative change[a] of temporary life expectancies from birth to age 75 years for selected countries, period, and ages, by sex

Country	Period	Male	Female	Country	Period	Male	Female
Argentina	1947–60	1.72	2.45	Korea	1966–70	3.00	2.84
	1960–70	−0.55	0.61		1970–9	1.42	1.31
	1970–8	2.60	2.73				
				Singapore	1947–57	5.77	7.32
Costa Rica	1950–63	2.81	3.03		1957–70	2.52	3.40
	1963–73	2.60	3.60		1970–80	2.09	2.08
	1973–80	4.69	6.93				
				Taiwan	1951–61	3.80	4.28
Cuba	1953–70	3.74	3.76		1961–71	3.19	4.52
	1970–8	2.34	2.95		1971–81	0.73	2.08
Hong Kong	1961–1	2.37	3.84	United States	1940–50	1.72	2.43
	1971–6	3.39	3.12		1950–60	0.65	1.15
					1960–70	0.13	0.49
India	1956–66[b]	0.88	1.17		1970–80	1.33	1.30
	1966–77[b]	1.67	1.36				
	1977–80[b]	3.35	4.75	Venezuela	1950–61	3.87	4.50
					1961–71	0.85	1.56
					1971–5	2.06	3.66

[a] The annual relative change of temporary life expectancy refers to the observed change of the temporary life expectancy during the period of time in relation to the total possible change, estimated annually (Arriaga, 1981).
[b] From birth to age 65 years.

1950s; and (*c*) Costa Rica, the most unusual case, has during the three decades continuously accelerated its mortality decline, achieving, together with Cuba, the lowest level of mortality in 1980 in the Latin American region. Hong Kong, on the other hand, has an accelerated mortality decline for males, but the opposite occurred for females during the 1970s. The remaining three countries show a slowing down of the mortality decline during the 1970s. For Singapore and Taiwan, the pace of the mortality decline during the 1970s was the slowest of the last three decades.

Changes in mortality by age groups in most of the countries during the 1950s produced a rather similar pattern of contributed life years to the life expectations from birth to age 75. The reduction of infant mortality, from the 1950s up to the most recent years for which there is information, has invariably been the largest single-age contributor to the change of temporary life expectation. Although most of the age groupings span ten years, the reduction of infant mortality contributed a larger number of life years than any other age group, in most cases (Tables 5.3 and 5.4). The exception is India, where females, according to the intercensal life-tables 1951–61 and 1961–71, had an increase of infant and child mortality.

The magnitude of the contribution of infant and child mortality to the

Table 5.3. Years contributed by the mortality change at each age group to the total change of temporary life expectancy from birth to age 75 years, selected countries and periods, males

Country	Period	Total change 0–75 years	Age groups Under 1 year	1–4 years	5–14 years	15–24 years	25–34 years	35–44 years	45–54 years	55–64 years	65–74 years
Argentina	1947–60	3.70	.90	.45	.23	.36	.31	.38	.49	.42	.16
	1960–70	−0.83	−.03	.09	.02	−.02	−.08	−.16	−.23	−.24	−.16
	1970–8	2.77	1.14	.33	.10	.12	.17	.17	.21	.32	.20
Chile	1952–60	3.30	.73	.69	1.13	.67	.32	−.01	−.10	−.09	−.04
	1960–70	3.69	1.55	1.23	.28	.18	.07	.13	.07	.08	.09
Costa Rica	1950–63	7.14	2.14	.61	.90	.85	.75	.57	.61	.53	.16
	1963–73	3.68	1.67	1.22	.26	.06	.07	.14	.14	.06	.05
	1973–80	3.49	2.11	.49	.15	.05	.12	.08	.11	.21	.15
Cuba	1953–70	9.51	2.79	1.82	.52	.69	.82	.90	.97	.68	.25
	1970–8	1.70	1.50	.08	.02	.04	.01	.01	−.05	−.01	.09
Hong Kong	1961–71	2.88	1.14	.71	.17	.04	−.03	.10	.29	.38	.08
	1971–6	1.68	.50	.13	.04	.01	.13	.13	.22	.34	.18
India*	1956–66	3.36	1.13	.67	−.39	−.00	.21	.72	.53	.50	.13
	1966–77	3.66	.19	.29	1.18	.80	.77	.59	.37	.07	−.00
	1977–80	2.40	.73	−.35	.22	.14	.12	.14	.26	.44	
Mexico	1950–60	9.08	2.15	3.15	.88	.62	.66	.60	.51	.36	.13
	1960–70	2.17	.19	.82	.30	.19	.25	.19	.18	.05	−.00
Panama	1950–60	10.59	3.38	1.68	1.36	1.10	1.04	.79	.60	.45	.19
	1960–70	2.30	1.51	−.33	.22	.25	.24	.10	.07	.14	.11
Singapore	1947–57	12.79	5.55	2.09	.56	1.13	1.49	1.23	.63	.12	−.02
	1957–70	4.45	1.45	.75	.35	.01	.18	.35	.51	.64	.21
	1970–80	2.25	.72	.15	.14	.08	.05	.25	.27	.36	.23
Taiwan	1951–61	7.40	2.50	.96	.84	.40	.71	.73	.72	.41	.13
	1961–71	4.33	1.57	1.05	.20	.16	.12	.24	.38	.45	.16
	1971–81	0.80	.28	.08	.03	−.09	.05	−.05	.03	.26	.21
United States	1940–50	3.29	1.23	.36	.24	.27	.39	.36	.25	.13	.07
	1950–60	1.09	.28	.09	.10	.05	.11	.16	.15	.12	.02
	1960–70	0.20	.43	.05	.03	.17	−.11	.07	.04	.01	−.01
	1970–80	2.02	.56	.05	.08	.10	.07	.24	.34	.40	.17
Venezuela	1950–61	9.00	4.15	1.26	1.11	.83	.69	.41	.27	.19	.09
	1961–71	1.34	.24	.46	.16	.04	.12	.25	.16	−.06	−.03
	1971–5	1.06	.26	.23	.16	.01	−.02	.02	.17	.16	.07

* For ages 0–65 years.

Table 5.4. Years contributed by the mortality change at each age group to the total change of temporary life expectancy from birth to age 75 years, selected countries and periods, females

Country	Period	Total change 0–75 years	Under 1 year	1–4 years	5–14 years	15–24 years	25–34 years	35–44 years	45–54 years	55–64 years	65–74 years
Argentina	1947–60	4.28	.91	.47	.27	.57	.47	.43	.48	.46	.22
	1960–70	0.64	.10	.16	.05	.09	.08	.00	.04	.08	.03
	1970–8	2.10	1.06	.32	.07	.08	.08	.07	.10	.20	.13
Chile	1952–60	4.54	.50	.24	1.26	.96	.71	.37	.22	.14	.06
	1960–70	4.89	1.68	1.80	.29	.27	.34	.18	.15	.08	.09
Costa Rica	1950–63	6.82	2.00	.49	1.03	.97	.91	.54	.42	.33	.13
	1963–73	4.25	1.55	1.24	.27	.11	.16	.26	.26	.28	.13
	1973–80	3.79	1.84	.58	.15	.14	.18	.18	.24	.25	.23
Cuba	1953–70	7.83	2.15	1.76	.52	.57	.75	.70	.57	.37	.23
	1970–8	1.72	1.20	.07	.05	.22	.05	.10	.03	.06	.09
Hong Kong	1961–71	3.05	1.21	.85	.17	.06	.18	.17	.16	.21	.03
	1971–6	0.93	.35	.06	.02	.05	.01	.10	.17	.04	.11
India*	1956–66	3.24	.47	1.05	−.72	.33	.51	.76	.44	.42	
	1966–77	3.41	−.32	−1.50	1.68	.15	.83	1.37	.78	.39	
	1977–80	3.48	1.05	1.34	.32	.08	.22	.03	.12	.32	
Mexico	1950–60	9.80	2.00	3.56	.93	.59	.63	.59	.48	.36	.14
	1960–70	2.70	.35	.90	.32	.28	.28	.21	.19	.12	.04
Panama	1950–60	9.80	3.60	1.53	1.09	.85	.85	.71	.59	.42	.16
	1960–70	3.20	1.56	−.23	.23	.25	.30	.26	.35	.38	.10
Singapore	1947–57	13.43	5.30	2.48	.62	.99	1.36	1.00	.73	.68	.26
	1957–70	4.27	1.23	.85	.32	.21	.28	.42	.45	.36	.16
	1970–80	1.50	.46	.15	.06	.04	.14	.21	.22	.13	.09
Taiwan	1951–61	7.12	1.68	.81	.86	.51	.83	.92	.77	.54	.21
	1961–71	4.81	2.05	1.34	.23	.27	.30	.12	.17	.25	.07
	1971–81	1.55	.42	.13	.06	.04	.11	.33	.18	.16	.12
United States	1940–50	3.81	1.06	.34	.22	.41	.47	.41	.37	.34	.19
	1950–60	1.50	.23	.08	.07	.13	.15	.19	.23	.28	.14
	1960–70	0.58	.35	.05	.02	−.03	.01	−.01	.02	.08	.08
	1970–80	1.42	.44	.06	.05	.06	.11	.20	.21	.18	.12
Venezuela	1950–61	9.26	3.72	1.20	1.34	1.35	.88	.49	.29	.18	.11
	1961–71	2.04	.35	.38	.21	.22	.30	.26	.22	.04	.06
	1971–5	1.47	.26	.39	.05	.06	.13	.14	.18	.20	.06

* For ages 0–65 years.

increase of life years varies considerably among countries and between periods of time—from a contribution of 93 per cent made by ages 0–4 years to the total change of temporary life expectancy for Cuban males, to negative contributions in Argentina and India during the 1960s. The contribution was more uniform, or similar by age, during periods of fast mortality decline than during periods of slow decline, although during the latter the contribution made by infant mortality became more dominant.

Countries with the same mortality level in the late 1960s had different trends of mortality during the 1970s. Information for these countries supports the hypothesis that generalizations about recent trends of mortality in developing countries are almost impossible to make. Each country seems to be a separate case due to the unique combination of the mortality level already achieved and the socio-economic characteristics of the population. Thus, the similarity of the pace and pattern of mortality decline observed in many developing countries during the 1950s was apparently a unique phenomenon. Whether or not that phenomenon will be repeated in other developing countries is uncertain.

The Change of Causes of Death

A study of causes of death permits analysis of the change of mortality from two different points of view. The first is a calculation of the contribution of each cause of death to the change of mortality within each age group. The second is a calculation of the contribution made by any change of each cause of death to life expectation, or years of life.

Relatively few developing countries have reliable information on causes of death. Among countries for which the change of mortality has been analysed, only 8 present information on causes of death by age and sex that allows determination of the main causes responsible for the reduction of mortality during different periods of time. Only 5 countries have information on causes of death which reaches the late 1970s.

The analysis of mortality change by age and causes of death does, however, permit some generalization. The reduction of mortality from infectious, contagious, and parasitic diseases, and diseases of the respiratory system, made the largest contribution to the reduction of mortality in most of the developing countries during the 1960s. Mortality from accidents, degenerative diseases, and diseases of the circulatory system did not change significantly during the same period (Arriaga, 1981).

Although the countries for which analysis by causes of death is possible have different levels of mortality, and the observations pertain to different periods, there are some similarities with respect to the causes of death which contributed the most to mortality decline. This similarity is more pronounced at the younger ages. In the 12 periods studied for 8 countries (Tables 5.5 and 5.6), for males in every period and for females in all but one, the reduction of deaths from infectious, contagious, and parasitic diseases was one of the three main groups of causes contributing most to the decline of infant mortality. A very similar situation was observed at ages 1–4 years. (It should be mentioned here that the group of 'other' diseases includes deaths of early infancy, those connected with complications of delivery, and puerperal infections.) At older ages (over 45 years), the reduction in deaths due to circulatory diseases and degenerative diseases had a significant effect on mortality decline in all countries. Nevertheless, it seems that there was a different pattern of causes of death between some Latin American and Asian populations. In Hong Kong, Singapore, and Taiwan the reduction of mortality from diseases of the respiratory system in old age seems to be more important than it was in Latin American countries. Although Chile has some resemblance to the Asian countries, in Costa Rica and Argentina the reduction of mortality from diseases of the circulatory system and degenerative diseases were significant contributors to the decline of mortality. It seems that mortality related to diseases of the respiratory system in some Asian countries was 'excessively' high in the past. Their rather recently observed economic development may have had an important impact on reducing deaths from diseases related to the respiratory system.

The contribution of the change in each cause of death within each age group to the change of life expectancies can be estimated by using a new technique which does not require the construction of multi-decrement life-tables (see Appendix 5.I). Although nine groups of causes of death were analysed, they were reduced to five specific groups, with a sixth for 'other' causes.

For all ages, the specific contribution, in number of life years added to life expectation, made by the mortality reduction in each group of causes of death can be seen in Table 5.7. In the Latin American countries, except Chile and Argentina, the largest contributors were infectious, contagious, and parasitic diseases, while in Asian countries diseases of the respiratory system were the largest contributors. Since it is practically impossible to make further generalizations for all countries, the most important features of the experience of each country during the latest period for which there is information are indicated below.

Argentina—1970–8: The reductions in diseases of the respiratory system and of infectious, contagious, and parasitic diseases were the first and second most important contributors to the increase of years of life between birth and age 75. The contribution of the reduction of accidents, diseases of the circulatory system, and degenerative diseases was greater for males than females, although males still had higher mortality from such diseases than females. The reduction of diseases of the respiratory system among infants made the largest contribution of life years of all groups of causes to any age group.

Table 5.5.   Causes of death contributing most to the mortality change in specified ages, selected countries, *circa* 1950 to 1960, males

Country, period, and life expectancy at birth (E_0)		Age groups			
		Under 1 year	1–4 years	5–14 years	15–24 years
Argentina					
Period 1970 to 1978	E_0 61.82 65.43	Respiratory system Infectious and parasitic Others	Infectious and parasitic Respiratory system Others	Accidents Infectious and parasitic Others	Accidents Respiratory system Degenerative Diseases
Chile					
Period 1960 to 1970	E_0 54.20 58.50	Infectious and parasitic Others Respiratory system	Infectious and parasitic Respiratory system Others	Infectious and parasitic Respiratory system Others	Respiratory system Other Infectious and parasitic
Costa Rica					
Period 1963 to 1973	E_0 62.15 66.18	Infectious and parasitic Others Respiratory system	Infectious and parasitic Others Respiratory system	Infectious and parasitic Others Accidents	Others Infectious and parasitic Degenerative diseases
1973 to 1980	66.18 70.30	Infectious and parasitic Respiratory system Others	Infectious and parasitic Respiratory system Anaemia and avitaminosis	Infectious and parasitic Respiratory system Circulatory system	Circulatory system Infectious and parasitic Others
Hong Kong					
Period 1961 to 1971	E_0 63.64 67.36	Infectious and parasitic Respiratory system Degenerative diseases	Infectious and parasitic Respiratory system Accidents	Infectious and parasitic Accidents Others	Respiratory system Infectious and parasitic
1971 to 1976	67.36 69.57	Others Infectious and parasitic Respiratory system	Infectious and parasitic Respiratory system Others	Infectious and parasitic Respiratory system Degenerative diseases	Others Respiratory system Infectious and parasitic
Mexico					
Period 1960 to 1970	E_0 56.38 58.39	Infectious and parasitic Others	Infectious and parasitic Others Respiratory system	Infectious and parasitic Others Respiratory system	Others Infectious and parasitic Respiratory system
Panama					
Period 1960 to 1970	E_0 59.75 63.55	Infectious and parasitic Others Respiratory system	Others	Accidents Others Infectious and parasitic	Others Accidents Respiratory system
Singapore					
Period 1957 to 1970	E_0 60.25 65.11	Infectious and parasitic Others Respiratory system	Infectious and parasitic Respiratory system Others	Infectious and parasitic Others Respiratory system	Others Infectious and parasitic Respiratory system
1970 1980	65.11 68.84	Infectious and parasitic Others Respiratory system	Infectious and parasitic Respiratory system Others	Others Infectious and parasitic Accidents	Others Infectious and parasitic Respiratory system
Taiwan					
Period 1956 to 1961	E_0 59.68 61.32	Infectious and parasitic Circulatory system Degenerative diseases	Infectious and parasitic Accidents Others	Others Respiratory system Infectious and parasitic	Others Respiratory system Infectious and parasitic
1961 1971	61.32 66.43	Infectious and parasitic Others Respiratory system	Infectious and parasitic Respiratory system Others	Infectious and parasitic Others Respiratory system	Others Accidents Infectious and parasitic

Note: See Appendix Table 5.A for groups of causes of death

25–34 years	35–44 years	45–54 years	55–64 years	65–74 years
Accidents Others Respiratory system	Accidents Respiratory system Circulatory system	Degenerative diseases Accidents Respiratory system	Circulatory system Degenerative diseases Respiratory system	Circulatory system Degenerative diseases Respiratory system
Respiratory system Other Circulatory system	Respiratory system Circulatory system Infectious and parasitic	Respiratory system Degenerative diseases Circulatory system	Others Respiratory system Circulatory system	na
Infectious and parasitic Degenerative diseases Others	Degenerative diseases Others Infectious and parasitic	Others Degenerative diseases Infectious and parasitic	Degenerative diseases Others Infectious and parasitic	Others Degenerative diseases Infectious and parasitic
Others Infectious and parasitic Respiratory system	Degenerative diseases Infectious and parasitic Anaemia and avitaminosis	Infectious and parasitic Circulatory system Respiratory system	Circulatory system Other Degenerative diseases	Circulatory system Infectious and parasitic Respiratory system
Respiratory system Infectious and parasitic Circulatory system	Respiratory system Circulatory system Infectious and parasitic	Respiratory system Circulatory system Infectious and parasitic	Circulatory system Respiratory system Infectious and parasitic	Circulatory system Infectious and parasitic Accidents
Respiratory system Others Infectious and parasitic	Respiratory system Others Infectious and parasitic	Respiratory system Others Infectious and parasitic	Respiratory system Others Infectious and parasitic	Others Respiratory system Infectious and parasitic
Others Infectious and parasitic Accidents	Others Infectious and parasitic Accidents	Others Infectious and parasitic Accidents	Others Infectious and parasitic	Others Infectious and parasitic
Others Respiratory system Infectious and	Others Respiratory system Accidents	Respiratory system Others Accidents	Others Respiratory system Circulatory system	Others Degenerative diseases Circulatory system
Respiratory system Others Infectious and parasitic	Respiratory system Others Infectious and parasitic	Respiratory system Others Infectious and parasitic	Others Respiratory system Infectious and parasitic	Others Infectious and parasitic
Respiratory system Others Circulatory system	Respiratory system Others Degenerative diseases	Respiratory system Others Infectious and parasitic	Respiratory system Others Infectious and parasitic	Others Infectious and parasitic Respiratory system
Respiratory system Others Infectious and parasitic	Respiratory system Others Infectious and parasitic	Others Respiratory system Infectious and parasitic	Respiratory system Others Infectious and parasitic	Others Circulatory system Respiratory system
Others Respiratory system Infectious and	Others Respiratory system Circulatory system	Others Respiratory system Circulatory system	Others Circulatory system Respiratory system	Others Infectious and parasitic

Table 5.6.   Causes of death contributing most to the mortality change in specified ages, selected countries, *circa* 1950 to 1960, females

Country, period, and life expectancy at birth (E_0)		Age groups			
		Under 1 year	1–4 years	5–14 years	15–24 years
Argentina					
Period 1970 *to* 1978	E_0 69.19 72.12	Respiratory system Infectious and parasitic Others	Infectious and parasitic Respiratory system Others	Infectious and parasitic Others Respiratory system	Others Respiratory system Infectious and parasitic
Chile					
Period 1960 *to* 1970	E_0 58.71 64.68	Infectious and parasitic Others Respiratory system	Infectious and parasitic Respiratory system Others	Infectious and parasitic Respiratory system Others	Respiratory system Others Infectious and parasitic
Costa Rica					
Period 1963 *to* 1973	E_0 65.03 70.15	Infectious and parasitic Others Respiratory system	Infectious and parasitic Others Respiratory system	Infectious and parasitic Others Respiratory system	Others Circulatory system Infectious and parasitic
1973 *to* 1980	70.15 75.04	Infectious and parasitic Respiratory system Anaemia and avitaminosis	Infectious and parasitic Respiratory system Anaemia and avitaminosis	Infectious and parasitic Respiratory system Circulatory system	Others Infectious and parasitic Respiratory system
Hong Kong					
Period 1961 *to* 1971	E_0 70.51 75.01	Infectious and parasitic Respiratory system Others	Respiratory system Infectious and parasitic Accidents	Infectious and parasitic Accidents Respiratory system	Respiratory system Infectious and parasitic Others
1971 *to* 1976	75.01 76.42	Others Respiratory system Infectious and parasitic	Infectious and parasitic Respiratory system Anaemia and avitaminosis	Infectious and parasitic Respiratory system Others	Circulatory system Infectious and parasitic Others
Mexico					
Period 1960 *to* 1970	E_0 59.58 62.32	Infectious and parasitic Others	Infectious and parasitic Others Respiratory system	Infectious and parasitic Others Respiratory system	Others Infectious and parasitic Respiratory system
Panama					
Period 1960 *to* 1970	E_0 63.18 66.28	Infectious and parasitic Others Respiratory system	Accidents	Others Respiratory system Accidents	Others Accidents Respiratory system
Singapore					
Period 1957 *to* 1970	E_0 65.22 69.98	Infectious and parasitic Respiratory system Others	Infectious and parasitic Respiratory system Others	Respiratory system Infectious and parasitic Others	Others Respiratory system Infectious and parasitic
1970 *to* 1980	69.98 74.10	Infectious and parasitic Others Respiratory system	Respiratory system Infectious and parasitic Others	Others Infectious and parasitic Respiratory system	Others Infectious and parasitic Respiratory system
Taiwan					
Period 1956 *to* 1961	E_0 63.54 65.59	Circulatory system Degenerative diseases	(All diseases increased)	Infectious and parasitic Respiratory system Others	Others Respiratory system Circulatory system
1961 *to* 1971	65.59 71.54	Infectious and parasitic Others Respiratory system	Infectious and parasitic Respiratory system Others	Infectious and parasitic Others Respiratory system	Accidents Others Circulatory system

Note: See Appendix Table 5.A for groups of causes of death

25–34 years	35–44 years	45–54 years	55–64 years	65–74 years
Others	Others	Degenerative diseases	Circulatory system	Circulatory system
Respiratory system	Respiratory system	Respiratory system	Degenerative diseases	Degenerative diseases
Infectious and parasitic	Degenerative diseases	Others	Others	Others
Others	Respiratory system	Respiratory system	Others	
Respiratory system	Others	Others	Respiratory system	na
Infectious and parasitic	Circulatory system	Degenerative diseases		
Others	Others	Degenerative diseases	Degenerative diseases	Others
Respiratory system	Degenerative diseases	Others	Others	Degenerative diseases
Infectious and parasitic	Infectious and parasitic	Circulatory system	Infectious and parasitic	Infectious and parasitic
Others	Circulatory system	Circulatory system	Circulatory system	Circulatory system
Circulatory system	Others	Others	Degenerative diseases	Respiratory system
Respiratory system	Infectious and parasitic	Infectious and parasitic	Respiratory system	Infectious and parasitic
Respiratory system	Respiratory system	Respiratory system	Circulatory system	Circulatory system
Others	Circulatory system	Circulatory system	Respiratory system	Respiratory system
Circulatory system	Accidents	Degenerative diseases	Infectious and parasitic	Infectious and parasitic
Respiratory system	Others	Others	Others	Others
Others	Respiratory system	Respiratory system	Respiratory system	Respiratory system
Infectious and parasitic	Degenerative diseases	Degenerative diseases	Anaemia and avitaminosis	Anaemia and avitaminosis
Others	Others	Others	Others	Others
Infectious and parasitic	Infectious and parasitic	Infectious and parasitic	Infectious and parasitic	Infectious and parasitic
Respiratory system	Respiratory system	Degenerative diseases		
Others	Others	Others	Others	Others
Respiratory system	Respiratory system	Degenerative diseases	Degenerative diseases	Degenerative diseases
	Degenerative diseases	Respiratory system	Circulatory system	Circulatory system
Others	Others	Others	Others	Others
Respiratory system	Respiratory system	Respiratory system	Respiratory system	Infectious and parasitic
Infectious and parasitic	Infectious and parasitic	Infectious and parasitic	Infectious and parasitic	
Others	Others	Others	Others	Others
Respiratory system	Respiratory system	Respiratory system	Respiratory system	Infectious and parasitic
Circulatory system	Circulatory system	Circulatory system	Infectious and parasitic	
Others	Others	Others	Others	Circulatory system
Respiratory system	Respiratory system	Respiratory system	Respiratory system	Others
Circulatory system	Infectious and parasitic	Circulatory system	Infectious and parasitic	Respiratory system
Others	Others	Others	Others	Others
Respiratory system	Respiratory system	Respiratory system	Infectious and parasitic	Infectious and parasitic
Circulatory system	Infectious and parasitic	Infectious and parasitic	Respiratory system	

Table 5.7.   Contribution of specific causes of death to the change of temporary life expectancy from birth to age 75 years, all ages and under 1 year, selected countries and periods, males and females

	Argentina 1970-8		Chile 1960-70		Costa Rica 1963-73		1973-80	
	Male	Female	Male	Female	Male	Female	Male	Female
Total change (in years) of the temporary life expectancy from birth to age 75 years	2.77	2.10	3.60	4.80	3.68	4.25	3.49	3.79
Total contribution of selected causes (all ages)	1.92	1.34	2.27	2.92	2.10	2.32	2.79	3.06
Respiratory system	.65	.56	1.28	1.51	.22	.33	.58	.68
Degenerative diseases	.25	.13	.02	.00	.31	.39	.11	.11
Accidents	.24	.12	− .31	− .09	− .06	− .06	− .15	.08
Circulatory system	.20	.08	.10	.06	− .16	− .06	.31	.50
Infective and parasitic	.51	.50	1.41	1.63	1.79	1.72	1.74	1.64
Anaemias and avitaminosis	.07	.05	n.a.	n.a.	n.a.	n.a.	.20	.21
Per cent of total contribution due to selected causes	70	64	63	61	57	55	80	81
Contribution of infant mortality rate change	1.14	1.06	1.55	1.68	1.67	1.55	2.24	2.00
Contribution of selected causes	.99	.89	1.65	1.74	1.40	1.29	1.86	1.64
Respiratory system	.41	.37	.29	.35	.13	.18	.40	.41
Infective and parasitic	.34	.33	.75	.75	.91	.87	1.22	1.10
Other	.17	.14	.61	.64	.36	.24	.13	.03
Anaemias and avitaminosis	.07	.05	n.a.	n.a.	n.a.	n.a.	.11	.10
Per cent of the total infant mortality contribution due to selected causes	87	84	106	104	84	83	83	82

Note: See Appendix Table 5.A. for groups of causes of death.

Chile—1960-70: The reduction of infectious, contagious, and parasitic diseases produced a gain of one and a half years of life expectation between ages 0 and 65. The decline of diseases of the respiratory system also made a significant contribution. Most of the contribution of reductions in infant mortality to the increase of life years was due to the reduction of infectious, contagious, and parasitic diseases and diseases of early infancy (which are included in the group of 'others').

Costa Rica—1963-73, 1973-80: The contribution of the groups of causes of deaths to the increase of years of life was astonishingly similar during the two periods of time. Infectious, contagious, and parasitic diseases contributed around 1.7 years of life in both periods (the largest contribution). However, while a change (an increase) in mortality from diseases of the circulatory system tended to reduce life expectation during the first period, a change in the opposite direction added 0.3 and 0.5 years among males and females, respectively, during the second period. Among infants, the reductions of infectious, contagious, and parasitic diseases added about one year of life in each period.

Hong Kong—1961-71, 1971-6: Each period presents a completely different pattern. While the reduction of infectious, contagious, and parasitic diseases contributed more than one year of life during the first period, the contribution during the second period was almost insignificant; during that second period the reduction of mortality from diseases of the respiratory

Hong Kong 1961–71		Hong Kong 1971–76		Mexico 1960–79		Panama 1960–70		Singapore 1957–70		Singapore 1970–80		Taiwan 1961–72	
Male	Female	Male	Female	Male	Female	Male	Female	Male	Female	Male	Female	Male	Female
2.85	3.04	1.71	.93	2.17	2.70	3.20	2.30	4.45	4.27	2.25	1.50	4.33	4.81
2.61	2.71	.60	.28	1.30	1.28	.96	.68	1.88	1.63	1.32	.85	2.94	3.15
1.05	1.11	.79	.35	− .16	− .15	.40	.20	1.12	.91	.61	.36	.86	.96
− .26	− .01	− .11	.02	− .02	− .00	.12	.06	− .17	− .11	.09	− .05	− .13	− .17
.09	.14	.12	− .07	.11	− .03	.19	.01	− .12	− .00	.28	.09	− .10	.13
.49	.29	− .17	− .21	− .14	− .12	.08	− .07	− .16	− .13	.13	.19	.32	.10
1.24	1.17	.19	.17	1.51	1.60	.93	.47	1.20	.96	.16	.19	1.98	2.13
n.a.	n.a.	02	.01	n.a.	n.a.	n.a.	n.a.	n.a.	n.a.	.06	.08	n.a.	n.a.
91	89	35	30	60	57	30	30	42	38	59	57	68	66
1.14	1.21	.50	.35	.19	.35	1.56	1.51	1.45	1.23	.72	.46	1.57	2.05
1.05	1.13	.51	.34	.66	.78	1.32	1.24	1.00	.85	.65	.39	1.60	2.04
.38	.40	.11	.11	− .37	− .27	.16	.23	.20	.19	.14	.12	.13	.31
.75	.67	.02	.02	.60	.57	.91	.67	.59	.49	.08	.08	1.08	1.14
− .08	.06	.38	.21	.43	.48	.25	.34	.21	.17	.43	.18	.39	.59
n.a.	n.a.	.00	.00	n.a.	n.a.	n.a.	n.a.	n.a.	.00	.00	.01	n.a.	n.a.
92	93	100	97	347	223	85	82	69	69	90	85	102	100

system was the largest contributor of years of life. In addition, the increase of accidents, diseases of the circulatory system, and degenerative diseases during the second period acted to reduce life by 0.4 of a year.

Mexico—1960–70: Although mortality was still high in 1960, it did not decline very much during the next decade. The only diseases whose reduction contributed significantly to the increase of life were infectious, contagious, and parasitic diseases, and their contribution was only 1.5 years. The contribution of life years made by the change in infant mortality was the lowest among the countries analysed.

Panama—1960–70: Declines in the five groups of causes of death listed in Table 5.7 made a relatively small contribution to increase in life expectation in this country (only 30 per cent). But nevertheless the reduction of deaths from infectious, contagious, and parasitic diseases added almost 1 year to the life expectation of males and 0.5 years to that of females.

Singapore—1957–70, 1970–80: The reduction of deaths from respiratory and infectious, contagious, and parasitic diseases in this country from 1957–70 made a contribution of life years which exceeded 2.3 years and 1.9 years for males and females, respectively. However, during the same period the increase of mortality from degenerative diseases, accidents, and diseases of the circulatory system reduced the number of life years (0.45 and 0.24 for males and females, respectively). The total decline in infant mortality added more than a year of life, of which half a year was due to the decline of infectious, contagious, and parasitic diseases among infants. During the later period, 1970–80 (when Singapore had already achieved low mortality), the main contributor to the increase of life years was the reduction of mortality from respiratory diseases; for infants, the group of causes with the largest contribution was 'other' (mainly because of the reduction of deaths from diseases of early infancy such as puerperal infections and complications during delivery).

Taiwan—1961–72: Taiwan's experience resembled that of Singapore during a similar period. The reduction of mortality from infectious, contagious, and parasitic diseases and diseases of the respiratory system added 2.8 and 3.1 years of life among males and females, respectively. Mortality from degenerative diseases and accidents increased, and tended to reduce the life of the population. Among infants, the reduction of mortality from infectious, contagious, and parasitic diseases contributed an additional year of life to each sex.

The Gap between Developing Countries and the United States

The United States has achieved low mortality levels (particularly for females) when compared with the rest of the world. The comparison of the United States with the countries considered in this article has the purpose of identifying (*a*) the causes of death that may be reduced in developing countries; (*b*) possible gains in life expectation if mortality differentials for each cause of death are reduced; and (*c*) the differences among developing countries (since all are compared with the United States as standard). (See Tables 5.8 and 5.9.)

For males, Costa Rica and Hong Kong have the lowest mortality between birth and age 75, even lower than the United States. The difference in mortality from diseases of the circulatory system between the United States and Costa Rica gives to the latter 1.1 more years of life than the former (Table 5.9). Similarly, a half year in favour of Costa Rica is due to mortality differentials for accidents and degenerative diseases. On the other hand, if Costa Ricans wish to reduce male mortality further, efforts should be concentrated on diseases of the respiratory system and infectious, contagious, and parasitic diseases. If the mortality level from these two groups were reduced to the level of the United States, males in Costa Rica would, on the average, add another half year of life from birth to age 75. Life among Costa Ricans could also be increased by further reduction of infant mortality.

Hong Kong and Singapore are not so different from Costa Rica. These three countries have achieved low mortality levels and are no longer representative of the mortality conditions in developing countries. However, some attention should be given to such situations as the case of Chile, Mexico, and Panama in 1970. Although these three countries continued to

Table 5.8. Comparison of the United States temporary life expectancy from brith to age 75 years with selected countries, contribution of the mortality differential at each particular age group to total difference of temporary life expectancy, by sex

Country and year	Sex	Total	Contribution of age groups									
			Under 1 year	1–4 years	5–14 years	15–24 years	25–34 years	35–44 years	45–54 years	55–64 years	65–74 years
Argentina 1978	Male	3.56	2.01	.30	.14	– .12	.06	.34	.43	.29	.11
	Female	3.29	1.79	.34	.13	.16	.25	.27	.16	.06	.13
Chile 1970	Male	9.80	5.01	.73	.29	.77	.86	1.00	.93	.62	.20
	Female	9.07	4.51	.73	.25	.72	.58	.76	.71	.77	.43
Costa Rica 1980	Male	– 0.36	.67	.08	.12	– .23	– .05	– .01	– .31	– .45	– .18
	Female	0.60	.42	.09	.07	– .01	.04	.03	– .09	– .05	.09
Hong Kong 1976	Male	– 0.16	.11	.03	.03	– .38	– .14	.00	– .01	.09	.11
	Female	0.22	.06	.08	.04	– .04	.06	.02	– .05	.03	.02
Mexico 1970	Male	10.23	4.37	2.18	.66	.38	.81	.94	.60	.26	.04
	Female	11.02	3.92	2.48	.69	.51	.85	.87	.67	.65	.38
Panama 1970	Male	5.58	2.84	1.86	.64	.28	.18	.17	– .05	– .17	.02
	Female	7.79	2.37	1.96	.66	.45	.58	.54	.47	.44	.32
Singapore 1980	Male	– 0.04	– .15	.01	– .06	– .30	– .23	– .13	.15	.37	.29
	Female	0.82	.02	.03	.04	– .03	– .02	– .03	.04	.42	.34
Taiwan 1972	Male	2.22	1.20	.23	.15	– .15	.09	.16	.06	.22	.25
	Female	2.97	.94	.21	.12	.08	.18	.40	.26	.38	.40

Table 5.9. Difference in temporary life expectancy from birth to age 75 years between the United States (1980) and selected countries and the contribution to such differential by selected causes of death, all ages and age under 1 year, male and female

	Argentina 1978		Chile 1970		Costa Rica 1980		Hong Kong 1976		Mexico 1970		Panama 1970		Singapore 1980		Taiwan 1972	
	Male	Female	Male	Female	Male	Female	Male	Female	Male	Female	Male	Female	Male	Female	Male	Female
Total difference (in years) of the temporary life expectancy from birth to age 75 years (US–country)	3.56	3.29	9.80	9.07	– .36	.60	– .16	.22	10.23	11.02	5.58	7.79	.09	.82	2.22	2.97
Total difference due to selected causes:	3.22	2.96	9.43	8.64	– .67	.45	– .20	.22	8.64	9.40	3.64	5.72	.16	.89	2.02	2.82
Respiratory system	.54	.47	3.10	2.67	.34	.31	.76	.37	3.11	2.87	1.40	1.59	.68	.43	1.52	1.24
Degenerative diseases	.14	– .01	.17	.49	– .31	– .14	.45	.03	– .69	.11	– .40	– .01	.31	.10	.06	– .02
Accidents	– .14	– .03	1.44	.32	– .21	– .13	– .91	– .17	.80	.08	.01	– .07	– .88	– .32	– .12	.11
Circulatory system	.59	.54	– .14	.69	– 1.12	– .16	– .65	– .09	– .73	.54	– .62	.36	.05	.37	– .49	.56
Infectious and parasitic	.82	.78	1.86	1.82	.20	.18	.08	.04	3.84	3.91	2.12	2.32	.09	.08	.45	.39
Other[a]	1.27	1.21	3.00	2.65	.43	.39	.07	.04	2.31	2.11	1.13	1.51	– .09	.23	.60	.54
Per cent of total difference due to selected causes	90	90	96	95	186	75	125	100	84	85	65	73	177	109	91	95
Total difference due to different infant mortality rates:	2.01	1.79	5.01	4.51	.67	.42	.11	.06	4.37	3.92	2.84	– 2.37	– .15	.02	1.20	.94
Difference due to selected causes:	1.80	1.58	4.81	4.32	.67	.45	.25	.17	3.96	3.53	2.17	1.77	– .01	.11	1.21	.94
Respiratory system	.32	.30	1.82	1.70	.18	.11	.11	.08	1.56	1.41	.55	.49	.06	.05	.70	.61
Infectious and parasitic	.59	.54	1.44	1.34	.15	.12	.03	.02	1.71	1.61	.92	.86	.02	.03	.31	.25
Other[b,a]	.89	.74	1.55	1.28	.34	.22	.11	.07	.69	.51	.70	.42	– .09	.03	.20	.08
Per cent of total difference due to infant mortality made by selected causes	90	88	96	96	100	107	225	283	91	90	76	75	7	550	101	100

[a] Includes anaemia and avitaminosis.
[b] Most of deaths pertain to early infancy causes.

Notes: See Appendix Table 5.A for groups of causes of death.

reduce mortality (mainly infant mortality) after 1970 their comparison with the United States gives a picture of mortality improvements that 'developing countries' could make. More than 3 years of life between birth and age 75 could be added to populations like those of Chile and Mexico in 1970, if only infant mortality from respiratory diseases and infectious, contagious, and parasitic diseases were reduced to levels similar to the United States (Table 5.9). Among males, almost another one and a half years of life could be added if mortality rates from accidents were reduced from levels found in Chile in 1970 to the levels of the United States. (For Mexico, it would be 0.8 of a year.) Countries with situations similar to that of Mexico in 1970 could increase the average life of their populations by almost 7 years if they reduced mortality from diseases of the respiratory system and infectious, contagious, and parasitic diseases at all ages.

Conclusions

The similarity of massive public health programmes applied in some developing countries in the 1950s or earlier produced not only a fast mortality decline but also a similar decline by age and causes of death. Diseases of the respiratory system and infectious, contagious, and parasitic diseases were significantly reduced from very high levels. The reductions in these causes of death were the main contributors to the increase of life expectancy.

During the 1960s, the patterns of mortality reduction in these countries presented fewer similarities than previously. Some countries, because of particular characteristics (education, nutrition, and area of the territory) and the concern of their planners in improving health conditions, were able to continue a fast reduction of mortality. Hong Kong, Costa Rica, Cuba, Singapore, Paraguay, and Malaysia, among others, are examples. Other developing countries suffered a stagnation of the mortality decline. Argentina, Mexico, and Sri Lanka are typical documented cases (Arriaga, 1981, Meegama, 1981). During the 1960s, infant and child mortality was reduced much more than adult mortality, and in some populations adult males suffered an increase in mortality. In general, during the decade of the 1960s there was a slowing down of the mortality decline, but it was in relation to the pace during the previous decade, which was one without precedent. In addition, the reduction of mortality during the 1960s depended, more than before, upon the social and economic characteristics of each population, and since those differ from country to country, generalizations become more difficult to make.

The mortality trends in developing countries during the 1970s have become even more distinct in each country. The available information pertains to countries which have already achieved rather low mortality levels, and further reduction will be more dependent than before upon the characteristics of each country. Generalizations are almost impossible to make concerning the pace and pattern of the mortality trend in the 1970s. For those developing countries which have achieved low mortality, further reduction could be achieved by concentrating efforts on reducing deaths from diseases of the respiratory system and those related to infectious, contagious, and parasitic diseases. However, mortality reduction from these causes of death would only increase life expectation by a fraction of a year. If these countries with low mortality can afford to have expensive equipment for further reducing early infant mortality, another fraction of a year could be added to life.

In those countries where life expectations at birth still range between 60 and 65 years, a significant increase of life years could be achieved by concentrating efforts on reducing mortality from respiratory and infectious, contagious, and parasitic diseases.

The question remains of the situation in countries where no information is available. The registration sample system of India has provided some mortality data for that country. Mortality in India appears to have declined slowly during the 1950s and 1960s. However, information for the latter part of the 1970s shows a more rapid mortality decline. Other countries may soon follow the trend of India, with a faster mortality decline during a rather short period of time. Although no reliable information exists on causes of death, it is likely that the reduction will be made possible by combating infectious, contagious, and parasitic diseases, and diseases of the respiratory system. In other words, the experience of countries such as Sri Lanka, Costa Rica, Cuba, and even China, where mortality was rapidly reduced during the 1950s and 1960s without substantial economic development, can be repeated in other developing countries. Programmes for reducing mortality which have been conducted in those countries may serve as examples of what can be done in other developing countries to extend life expectation.

APPENDIX 5.1

Measuring the Change of Mortality

In this chapter, the change of mortality has been measured by using the index of relative annual change of temporary life expectations. The index is:

$$\text{ARC} = 1 - (1 - \text{RC})^{1/n}$$

where

$$\text{RC} = \frac{{}_i e_x^{t+w} - {}_i e_x^{t}}{i - {}_i e_x^{t}}$$

and

$$_i e^t = \frac{T_x^t - T_{x+i}^t}{1_x}$$

The RC index measures the change in the average number of years lived between ages x and $x + i$ by those alive at age x from year t to $t + n$, in relation to the maximum possible change. The latter is the difference between the length of the age group (i) under study and the average number of years lived between age x and $x + i$ by those alive at age x in year t.

Estimation of the Contribution of the Mortality Change by Age and Causes of Death to the Life Expectation

A recent article (Arriaga, 1984) gives a simple procedure for measuring the contribution to life expectation made by the change of mortality at each particular age group. The procedure estimates the number of years added to or removed from life expectation because of the decrease or increase (respectively) of the central mortality rates of life-tables. The contribution of mortality change by causes of death to the life expectations was estimated under the assumption that the contribution to the life expectation by the mortality change by causes of death in each age group was proportional to the contribution to the change of the total central mortality rate made by the mortality change in each cause of death in the same age group. In symbols, for each age group, the contribution to the life expectation made by the change of mortality in a specific age group ($SAC_j(e_x)$) is a function of the mortality change in each age group ($m_j^1 - m_j^0$) from year 0 to 1.

$$SAC_j(e_x) = F(m_j^1 - m_j^0)$$

If we write $C_j = m_j^1 \quad m_j^0$ for the total change of mortality in the age group j, the change of mortality for each cause of death would be

$$_cC_j = {}_cm_j^1 - {}_cm_j^0$$

and consequently

$$C_j = \Sigma_{c=1}^s {}_cC_j$$

for the s groups of causes of death. In other words, the change of mortality in a given age group equals the sum of the changes of mortality in each cause of death within the same age group. Therefore, it is assumed that the contribution to the life expectation made by the change of each cause of death will be (proportional):

$$_cSAC_j(e_x) = SAC_j(e_x) \frac{_cC_j}{C_j}$$

This procedure gives results which are similar to those produced by using multiple-decrement life-tables. The advantage is that this procedure does not require the construction of as many multiple-decrement life-tables as the product of the number of age groups by the number of causes of death being analysed for each sex.

APPENDIX 5.2. SOURCES OF DATA

Causes of Death

For all countries except the United States and Taiwan 1971–3, these were obtained from various years of World Health Organization, *World Health Statistics Annual*,

Geneva. For the United States 1979 and 1980, they were obtained from the US Department of Health and Human Services, *Vital Statistics of the United States (1979 and 1980)*, vol. 2, *Mortality*, Washington, DC, 1983 and 1984. For Taiwan 1971, 1972, and 1973, the figures came from National Health Administration, *Health Statistics, Vital Statistics*, 1971, 1972, 1973, Taipei, Taiwan.

Sources of Life-tables

Argentina	1946–8	Camisa, Zulma, *Tabla Abreviada de Mortalidad. Republica Argentina, 1946–48*, CELADE, Santiago, Chile, 1964.
	1959–61	Ortega, Antonio, *Tablas Completas de Mortalidad Para la Republica Argentina, 1959–61*, CELADE, Santiago, Chile, 1967.
	1969–70	US Bureau of the Census, unpublished life-table, Washington, DC, 1979.
	1975–80	Instituto Nacional de Estadistica y Censos, and UN CELADE, *Estimaciones y Proyecciones de Poblacion 1950–2025*, Buenos Aires, 1982.
Chile	1952 1960	Arriaga, Eduardo, *New Life Tables for Latin America Populations in the Nineteenth and Twentieth Centuries*, Institute of International Studies, University of California, Berkeley, 1968.
	1969–70	US Bureau of the Census, *Country Demographic Profiles: Chile*, Washington, DC, 1978.
Costa Rica	1950	Arriaga, Eduardo, op. cit.
	1963	Ibid.
	1972–4	US Bureau of the Census, *Country Demographic Profiles: Costa Rica*, Washington, DC, 1977
	1980	Rosero, Luis and Caamano, Hernan, 'Tablas de vida de Costa Rica 1900–1980' in *Mortalidad y Fecundidad en Costa Rica*, Asociacion Demografica Costarricense, San Jose, March 1984.
Cuba	1952–4	Gonzalez, Fernando and Debasa, Jorge, 'Cuba: Evolucion y adjuste del censo de 1953 y las estadisticas de nacimientos y defunciones entre 1943 y 1958. Tabla de Mortalidad por Sexo 1952–54', CELADE, Santiago, Chile, 1970.
	1969–71	Bureau of the Census, Rowe, Patricia, and O'Connor, Susan, 'Detailed Statistics on the Urban and Rural Population of Cuba: 1950 to 2010', Center for International Research, Washington, DC, March 1984.
	1977–8	Ibid.
Hong Kong	1961	Commissioner of Census and Statistical Planning, 'Hong Kong Life Tables 1961–68', Hong Kong, 1963.

	1971	Census and Statistical Department, 'Hong Kong Life Tables 1971–1991', Hong Kong, 1973.
	1976	Census and Statistical Department, 'Hong Kong Life Tables', Hong Kong, March 1978.
India	1951–61	Jain, S. P., Office of the Registrar General, 'Actuarial Report and Life Tables 1951–1961', New Delhi.
	1961–70	Chari, R B., Registrar General and Census Commissioner, *Life Tables: Census of India 1971. Series I, India*. Paper 1 of 1977, New Delhi, 1977.
	1976–7	Registrar General, *Sample Registration Bulletin*, vol. 14, no. 2, December 1980.
	1980	Registrar General, *Census of India 1981: Series I, India*. Paper 1 of 1984. Population Projections for India 1981–2001, New Delhi, 1984.
Mexico	1950	Arriaga, Eduardo, op. cit.
	1960	Ibid.
	1969–70	Rowe, Patricia, *Country Demographic Profiles: Mexico*. US Bureau of the Census, Washington, DC, 1979.
Panama	1950	Arriaga, Eduardo, op. cit.
	1960	Ibid.
	1969 70	US Bureau of the Census, *Country Demographic Profiles: Panama*. Washington, DC, 1977
Singapore	1947	US Bureau of the Census, unpublished life-tables.
	1957	Chua, S. C., State of Singapore, *Report on the Census of Population 1957*, Singapore, no date.
	1980	US Bureau of the Census, unpublished life-tables.
Taiwan	1951	Lu Liang Chinn, Chu Yihui, and Wei Shou Pen, 'Abridged Life Tables for Residents of Taiwan 1950–1969' (no date or name of institution).
	1961	Ministry of Interior, 'Abridged Life Tables for Taiwan 1961–70', Taipei, March 1972.
	1971	Ministry of Interior, *1971 Taiwan Demographic Fact Book*, Taiwan, 1972.
	1981	Ministry of Interior, *1981 Taiwan–Fukien Demographic Fact Book*, Taipei, December 1982.
United States	1980	US Department of Health and Human Services, National Center for Health Statistics, *Monthly Vital Statistical Report*, vol. 33, no. 3, supplement, 22 June 1984.
Venezuela	1950	Arriaga, Eduardo, op. cit.
	1961	Ibid.
	1971	US Bureau of the Census, unpublished life-table.

Table 5.A.   Groups of causes of death

Cause group	Diseases 1960[a]	1970[b]	1980[c]
Certain respiratory diseases	B1	A6	020–1
	B31–2	A89, A91–6	310–15
			319–21
			323–7
			329
Certain degenerative disease	B18–19	A45–61	080–170
	B33	A98	341, 360
	B39	A109	
Accidents and violence	BE45–50	AE138–50	E470–560
Certain circulatory diseases	B22	A80–8	250–300
	B25–9		
Other parasitic and	B2–17	A1–5	010–019
infectious diseases	B30	A7–44	022–070
	B36	A90	
	B43	A99	
Anaemias	B21	A67	200
Avitaminosis	Included in next section	A65	190–3
Other causes	All diseases not mentioned elsewhere.		
Senility and unknown causes	B45	A136–7	465–9

[a] Diseases were grouped according to the Abbreviated List of 50 Causes for Tabulation of Mortality (see World Health Organization, *International Classification of Diseases*, 1955 revision, volume 1, Geneva, 1957).
[b] Diseases were grouped according to the List of 150 Groups of Causes for Tabulations of Morbidity and Mortality (see World Health organization, *International Classification of Diseases*, 1965 revision, volume 1, Geneva, 1968).
[c] Diseases were grouped according to the list of ICD-9 of 1979, which includes the causes of death (see World Health Organization, *International Classification of Diseases*, 1979 revision, Geneva, 1979).

References

Arriaga, E. E. (1981), 'The Deceleration of the Decline of Mortality in LDCs: The Case of Latin America', *IUSSP International Population Conference, Manila 1981*, vol. 2, International Union for the Scientific Study of Population, Liège, 21–50.

—— (1984), 'Measuring and Explaining the Change of Life Expectancies', *Demography* 21(1), 83–96.

—— and Kingsley Davis (1969), 'The Pattern of Mortality Change in Latin America', *Demography* 6(3), 223–42.

Bureau of the Census (1983), *World Population 1983: Recent Demographic Estimates for the Countries and Regions of the World*, Washington, DC.

Meegama, S. (1981), 'The Decline of Mortality in Sri Lanka in Historical Perspective', *IUSSP International Population Conference, Manila 1981*, vol. 2,

International Union for the Scientific Study of Population, Liège, 143–64.

Sivamurthy, M. (1981), 'The Deceleration of Mortality Decline in Asian Countries', *IUSSP International Population Conference, Manila 1981*, vol. 2, International Union for the Scientific Study of Population, Liège, 51–78.

6 Trends in Socio-economic Differentials in Infant Mortality in Selected Latin American Countries

JOSÉ MIGUEL GUZMAN
CELADE, Santiago, Chile

At the beginning of the 1950s, Latin American countries presented very high infant mortality rates, although there were great differences between them. Nevertheless, in the period 1950–80 infant mortality experienced very important reductions, and at the same time expectation of life at birth increased in all Latin American countries. This reduction of infant mortality in Latin America occurred within a context of sustained economic growth. Between 1950 and 1978 the regional gross national product per capita grew by 2.6 per cent a year, producing an increase of social wealth in these countries. Although this economic growth did not contribute directly to improving the distribution of the social product (CEPAL, 1979), there is no doubt that the effect of this maintained economic growth was an improvement in certain aspects of the population's living conditions, at least in some sectors.

In spite of this great decrease in mortality it is not possible to conclude that infant mortality levels of the individual countries are now closer to each other. While it is true that in 1975–80 the absolute difference between the highest and the lowest mortality rate declined to 112 points, which compares favourably with the 163-point difference in 1950–5, in relative terms the difference between the extremes increased from four to five times.

The objective of this work is both to study how the situation has changed within each country, in different socio-economic and geographical groups, and to examine if the pattern of descent of mortality has contributed to reductions or increases in the social differences. To reach these objectives we study the decrease of infant mortality in selected countries of Latin America and especially infant mortality trends for groups classified by geographic residence, the education of the mothers, and—in the cases where data exists—also by social class.

Methodology and Data

In this study a method developed by Coale and Trussell is used (United Nations, 1983), that permits the estimation of probabilities of dying from birth until age x ($x = 1, 2, 3, 5, 10, 15, 20$), based on the proportion of children who died in relation to the total number of children ever born of mothers classified by quinquennial groups of ages. This technique, furthermore, permits the estimation of the moment in the past in which each estimate is located. Therefore, it is possible to get a set of infant mortality rates for a period 10 to 15 years before a census or survey, by transforming each $q(x)$ into $q(1)$ (for practical ends equivalent to infant mortality rate) and using for this purpose the Coale–Demeny model life-tables.

In a recent paper (Guzman, 1985) it has been demonstrated that the levels and trends of these estimates are affected by the model life-table used. In all the countries examined here West model life-tables have been used because the examination of additional information for each country has proven that this model approximates best the age pattern of mortality. However, because the correspondence between the model and reality cannot be exact and because the model could not represent all the studied subgroups of the population, the results of the application of this method must be interpreted with caution.

The infant mortality estimates in this study have been made for Honduras, Paraguay, Peru, Guatemala, and Panama. These five countries were selected taking into account that the infant mortality rate estimated from two or more different sources showed a consistent tendency.[1] The Panama and Guatemala data were taken from two works recently published by CELADE (Behm and Modes, 1983; Behm and Vargas, 1984).[2]

Trends and Differentials of Infant Mortality

Countries studied are at different stages of the infant mortality transition (see Table 6.1). For the most recent period, 1975–80, we have a range going from more than 100 per 1,000 (Peru) to around 30 per 1,000 (Panama). The decline in the infant mortality rate was more important in the case of Panama, which already had low infant mortality rates. Peru and Paraguay show the lowest decline. Paraguay started at the same level as Panama, but in the last period (1975–80) it had a rate 65 per cent higher.

---

[1] The sources used in each country are: *Honduras*: 1974 and Second National Demographic Survey, 1983, (EDENH-II). *Peru*: 1978 census and National Fertility Survey 1977–8 (ENAF-78). *Paraguay*: 1972 census and National Demographic Survey (EDENPAR-77). *Panama*: 1980 census. *Guatemala*: 1973 and 1981 censuses.

[2] In some cases for Paraguay the results of a very recent study incorporating information from 1972 and 1982 censuses will be used (CELADE, 1986).

Table 6.1. Infant mortality rates in selected countries, 1950–55, 1975–80

Country	1950–55	1975–80	Decline (per cent)
Peru	136	105	23
Honduras	131	83	37
Guatemala	119	82	31
Paraguay	66	53	20
Panama	66	32	52
Latin America	102	71	31

Source: Honduras; CELADE, 1987, Paraguay: CELADE, 1986. Other countries: population projections, CELADE. Latin America (including Caribbean countries): Naciones Unidas, 1984.

Geographic Levels and Trends of Infant Mortality

Hugo Behm and collaborators, using census and survey data of 1970 in many countries of the area, pointed out that in two-thirds of the countries the risk of mortality in the first two years of life in rural areas was 30–60 per cent higher than in urban areas. The authors associated these differences with different degrees of modernization and development of rural and urban sectors in Latin America, and disparities of living-standards generated by these factors (Behm and Primante, 1978, 32).

What are the urban–rural differences in infant mortality in the countries studied and how have these differences changed in the last two decades? The infant mortality rates by urban and rural areas for selected years between 1960 and 1980 are shown in Table 6.2. This information leads to the conclusion that the decline of infant mortality rates has occurred in all countries, and not only in urban but also in rural areas. However, the magnitude of this decline has been different in both areas, periods considered, and also varied by country. First, rural areas have been incorporated later to the decline. Second, it can be observed that in countries with the highest infant mortality (like Peru and Honduras) the decline was greater in the urban areas than in the rural ones. This contributes to increase the absolute and relative differences between the two areas.

In Guatemala, the decline in the 1970s was more important in rural areas, leading to a minor reduction of differences in the infant mortality rate between areas. This pattern is clearer in the case of Panama, the more advanced country in the reduction of infant mortality, where the process of decline in infant mortality rates was more important in the rural areas, contributing to a notable reduction in the relative differences between areas.

In Paraguay, the urban and rural differences are less than those found in other countries studied; also, the reduction of infant mortality has been slower and seems to follow a similar trend in both urban and rural areas.

Table 6.2.   Infant mortality rate according to area of residence in selected countries, 1960–80

Country and year	Infant mortality rate		Rural over-mortality (2)/(1)
	Urban (1)	Rural (2)	
Peru			
1960	133	180	1.35
1965	115	170	1.48
1975	80	150	1.88
Decline (per cent) 1960–75	40	17	—
Honduras			
1960	122	135	1.11
1970	92	119	1.29
1980	67	92	1.37
Decline (per cent) 1960–80	45	32	—
Guatemala			
1960	116	149	1.28
1966	103	138	1.34
1976	77	101	1.31
Decline (per cent) 1960–76	34	32	—
Paraguay			
1960	65	73	1.12
1965	59	66	1.10
1975	50	56	1.12
Decline (per cent) 1960–75	23	23	—
Panama			
1968	34	60	1.76
1976	28*	38	1.36
Decline (per cent) 1968–76	18	37	—

* For this year, this rate comes from Vital Statistics.
Source: See text.

However, in a recent study, higher infant mortality rates have been found for the rural areas than those used in this study. These new calculations, using the 1972 and 1982 censuses, show a faster decline in urban areas than in the rural ones. Hence the tendency towards an amplification of differences would be even higher than detected with our data.

In conclusion, according to the way the decline of infant mortality has occurred in the different areas, it seems possible to distinguish three steps. There is an initial one of high infant mortality rates, with differentials, by countries which were relatively constant: this could be the situation for some countries before 1960. Subsequently, urban infant mortality (mainly in metropolitan areas) falls faster than that in rural areas, contributing to amplify the differences by area of residence. Finally, the third step is distinguished by more rapid decline of infant mortality in rural areas, sometimes even faster than in urban areas, which leads to a reduction of the area differences.

The complete disappearance of differences by areas does not seem to be imminent in most of the countries. In Panama, in 1975, the rural infant mortality rate was still 22 per cent higher than that in the urban areas; however, it is easy to see that in those countries with low infant mortality the absolute differences are minimal.

Socio-economic Differences in Infant Mortality

In spite of the operative importance for health policy of the urban–rural differential of infant mortality, it has been found that this difference tends to disappear when social class and mother's education are controlled (Behm and Vargas, 1984; United Nations, 1985). This implies that residence has no effect *per se* on infant mortality, but that the differences can be explained by the different composition of each area in terms of the social and cultural characteristics of people involved.

Infant Mortality Differences by Social Class

The unequal mortality conditions faced by individuals in a society have been shown to be a consequence of social differences as indicated by different living conditions (such as work conditions, food, health, hygienic conditions, personal hygiene care, and so forth), besides the differences in access to medical knowledge and its benefits. Most of the less developed countries are characterized by an enormous economic and social inequality due to the unequal distribution of wealth. Social class reflects the insertion of the individual in the productive structure, the ownership and/or control of means of production and working conditions in general. In consequence, it determines the form and magnitude of how different social actors take possession of the social surplus. This refers not only to material wealth but also to the product of science and culture. Breilh and Granda (1983) maintain that this way of working and consuming in their dialectic unit determines living conditions. Consumption is divided into two parts: personal consumption—obtained through salary or profit—and collective consumption, which refers to that part of the surplus which is socialized through the State or other institutions.

It has been possible to study infant mortality trends and differentials for some countries by social groups. These are used in this study as a proxy for social class. The countries with available information are Honduras (1970–80), Guatemala (1968–76), and Paraguay (1966–75). The data have permitted classification of women in five different social groups, in function of the occupation and the occupational category of the head of the household. These groups are: (1) agricultural workers (salaried); (2) farmers (non-salaried); (3) non-agricultural salaried workers; (4) non-agricultural non-salaried workers (*petite bourgeoisie*); and (5) middle-class (mainly salaried).

The infant mortality estimates show substantial consistency with the conditions associated a priori with each class (Table 6.3). In three of the countries studied there are important differences in infant mortality by social groups whose extremes are defined by the middle class and the salaried agricultural workers, the infant mortality rate in the latter being twice

Table 6.3. Infant mortality rates according to social class, Honduras 1970–80, Guatemala 1960–76, and Paraguay, 1966–75

Social group	Infant mortality rate		Decline (per cent)
(*a*) Honduras	1970	1980	1970–80
Agricultural sector			
(1) Salaried workers	125	100	21
(2) Farmers	120	95	25
Non-agricultural sector			
(3) Non-salaried workers	102	69	32
(4) Salaried workers	100	68	32
(5) Middle class	59	49	16
Ratio(1)/(5)	2.1	2.0	—
(*b*) Guatemala	1968	1976	1968–1976
Agricultural sector	128	103	20
(1) Salaried workers	122	97	20
(2) Farmers	138	112	19
Non-agricultural sector	102	84	18
(3) Non-salaried workers	107	90	16
(4) Salaried worker	100	82	18
(5) Middle class	53	49	8
Ratio (1)/(5)	2.4	2.1	—
(*c*) Paraguay	1966	1975	1966–75
Agricultural sector			
(1) Salaried workers	74	74	0
(2) Farmers	64	61	5
Non-agricultural sector	59	52	12
(3) Non-salaried workers	—	—	—
(4) Salaried workers	—	—	—
(5) Middle class	49	38	22
Ratio (1)/(5)	1.5	1.8	—

Sources: Honduras: EDENH-II, 1983. Guatemala: Behm and Vargas, 1984. Paraguay: CELADE, 1986.

as high as in the first group. Three social groups, clearly differentiated by their infant mortality, can be distinguished:

(1) The first group is formed of farmers and agricultural workers; not only does it present the highest infant mortality rate but at the same time in this group there occur between 50 and 60 per cent of total births of these countries. Children born in this sector are exposed to a high infant mortality even after there have been substantial declines in overall mortality (about 100 per 1,000 in Honduras and Guatemala and 74 in Paraguay). In general the differences between salaried and non-salaried workers are quite small, with a slightly higher mortality among the salaried. Similar results have been found in other countries (Chackiel, 1982). In the context of Latin American agricultural structures, there is a certain homogeneity of poverty conditions for the whole agricultural sector—excluding a minority sector of major land owners. On the other hand, health policies implemented by the state in the form of primary health care are directed towards the total rural sector and thus probably do not favour one class over the other.

(2) The second group is formed of non-agricultural workers, basically linked to industrial and service activities, and by the *petite bourgeoisie*, composed of small non-agricultural owners and the self-employed. It shows infant mortality rates 15–20 per cent below those of the first group. As in the agricultural sector, there is no important difference between salaried and non-salaried. This can be explained because included in both groups is the poorest urban population sector, whose members are living principally in shanty towns with great instability in employment and the worst living conditions of the urban sector.

(3) Finally, the middle class is characterized by a relatively low infant mortality rate, implying that it was already in a process of advanced decline. But even in Paraguay, with the lowest infant mortality rates of the three countries studied, this rate is near 40 per 1,000. That means that in these countries the middle class, formed of non-manual workers with high formal education levels who therefore receive the highest income among the working sectors, has not yet benefited from all the advantages associated with this status in other countries. It must be said that in Honduras and Guatemala only one of twenty births occurs to women of this class; in Paraguay, where this class is more important in relative terms, only one of ten births occurs in this group.

The information available, for the 1970s or some earlier years, shows that infant mortality declined in all social groups in the three countries studied. In the case of Honduras and especially in Guatemala, the decline among agricultural workers was slightly higher than occurred in the middle class, leading to a slight decrease in the differences between the extremes. Contrary to the case of Guatemala, where the decline was almost the same in all social groups—excepting the middle class—in Honduras the greatest decline occurred in non-agricultural sectors. In both countries, the important decline in these sectors leads to a decrease in the differences between the middle class and other urban sectors.

The case of Paraguay is a special one. In this country, we have already seen that there has not been an important decline in infant mortality. When information is analysed by social class it is clear that this results from the stagnation of infant mortality in high infant mortality groups (especially in the agricultural sector); the decline in the infant mortality rate has been inversely related to its level. In this country the greatest decline of the infant mortality rate has been observed in the middle class. In the other two countries this rate tends to stagnate in this class.

Education and Trends in Infant Mortality

As for other social characteristics of the population, differences in infant mortality by education must be explained in two ways:

(1) By the effects of this variable on some proximate determinants of mortality. It is recognized that a better education should improve the willingness of the population to accept improvements of modern preventive and curative medicine at such times as pregnancy and giving birth; moreover, it enables them to improve nutritional habits, hygiene, and child care. Some studies have shown that the importance of maternal education remains after controlling for other socio-economic variables; that would mean that education has an independent effect on infant mortality (United Nations, 1985).

(2) On the other hand, the infant mortality differences by education could be the result of the effect of other socio-economic variables which are associated with education: for example, higher education is linked to industrial and service sectors which are almost exclusively urban, as well as to high-income groups. In consequence, a higher level of education is associated with better living and nutrition conditions and greater access to efficient health care.

The strength of the empirical relationship between maternal education and infant mortality is already well known. Around 1970 in most of the Latin American countries except Cuba the risk of death for children less than two years old of illiterate mothers was between three and five times higher than for children of mothers with more than ten years of schooling (Behm and Primante, 1978). The results of the current study once more confirm the magnitude of these differences (Table 6.4). Some other important facts can also be observed: first, at least in some countries, even children of mothers in the lower education level show declining risks of dying in infancy; the decline of infant mortality, especially during the 1970s, occurred in the highest mortality groups, that is, with lower education

Table 6.4. Infant mortality rate according to education of mother (years) in selected countries, 1960–80

Country and year	Infant mortality rate				
	No schooling (1)	1–3 (2)	4–6 (3)	7 and more (4)	Relation (1)/(4)
Peru[a]					
1965	165	110	85	55	3.0
1975	158	100	73	44	3.6
Decline (per cent) 1965–75	4	9	14	20	—
Honduras					
1960	141	119	96	47	3.0
1970	132	102	83	43	3.1
1980	115	89	74	40	2.9
Decline (per cent) 1960–80	18	25	23	15	—
Guatemala					
1960	154	113	74	41	3.8
1968	144	108	75	40	3.6
1976	106	86	65	36	2.9
Decline (per cent) 1960–76	31	24	12	12	—
Paraguay					
1960	74[b]		56	42	1.8
1965	72[b]		52	38	1.9
1975	69[b]		46	30	2.3
Decline (per cent) 1960–75	7[b]		18	29	—
Panama					
1967	80	58	40	22	3.6
1974	64	45	29	19	3.4
Decline (per cent) 1967–74	20	22	28	14	—

[a] Refers to the following educational groups: 0–2, 3–4, 5, and 6 and more.
[b] Refers to the group 0–3 years of schooling.
Source: See text.

levels, except in Paraguay and Peru, where it was minimal.

On the other hand, for children of women with high education (seven or more years) this decline has been slower in Honduras, Guatemala, and Panama. This may suggest a certain tendency of infant mortality rates to stagnate, and is similar to what has been observed in the analysis by social class. Peru and Paraguay, however, show the greatest decline in higher education groups. As a result, the relative difference between less and most educated groups decreased in the former, but not in the latter, countries. Even there, however, children of women with no schooling have an infant mortality rate three times higher than children of women with seven or more years of education.

Some Factors Affecting Infant Mortality Differentials and Trends

Differences in infant mortality between socio-economic and geographical groups can be explained by the specific characteristics of each group in terms of three kinds of factors or proximate determinants: (1) the 'ecological risks' associated with living conditions (especially habitat conditions); (2) conduct, attitudes, and practices related to maternal and child care and nutrition and to the fertility patterns; and (3) the level and quality of the medical and sanitary attention received (see Mosley, 1985). A decline in infant mortality within the different social groups means changes in one or more of these factors.

Without pretending to be exhaustive, the importance of these factors will be analysed for some of the countries under study. It is well known that the environment where the children live and grow up affects the incidence and persistence of sickness. Unfavourable conditions include deplorable habitat (inadequate housing, overcrowding, and suchlike), non-availability of potable water or sewerage systems, a deficient communication network, lack of electrical energy, and so on. In most countries there has been great progress in improving these conditions in the last decades, basically as a response to the expanding needs of the productive process; but this has taken place especially in the cities, and has benefited basically the middle and upper social classes, which have the resources to finance better housing and habitat conditions. Excepting Panama, where important programmes for rural sanitary services were developed, very poor rural habitat conditions prevail.

In Peru, in 1972, only 25 per cent of households had potable water, this percentage being almost nil in rural areas. The same percentages apply to the availability of sanitary services. In Guatemala, the situation is very similar. In Paraguay, more than 90 per cent of houses have sanitary services of some sort in urban as well as rural areas, although a high percentage of these dwellings only have access to a common latrine (a situation almost like having no sanitary service). The availability of potable water between 1960 and 1975 was near to 30 per cent in urban areas and only 6 per cent in rural areas. By 1979, this percentage had increased, but especially in urban areas (59 compared to 10 per cent).

In Honduras, there was no change in access to potable water in urban and rural areas between 1962 and 1983, the percentage of dwellings covered being near 40 and 4 per cent, respectively. But at the same time, the percentage of housing without sanitary services was reduced by 50 per cent in both urban and rural areas, this reduction being more important in absolute terms in rural areas. In Panama, changes in access to basic services were greater in rural areas, rural dwellings without sanitary services being reduced by 60 per cent between 1961 and 1980 (36 per cent in 1960 and 12 per cent in 1980). The percentage of houses with potable water was multiplied by six during the same period, reaching in 1980 50 per cent in the whole

Table 6.5.   Percentage of deliveries by place, and of children by medical care in urban and rural area

	Peru 1977–78		Honduras 1984		Paraguay 1977	
	Urban	Rural	Urban	Rural	Urban	Rural
Non-institutional delivery	40	92	22	78	25	70
Children without medical attention*	24	66	10	20	9	44
Children not vaccinated	18	53	—	—	20	58

* First medical control.
Sources: Fernandez, 1984, and MSP *u* ASHOPLANFA, 1986.

country and 71 per cent and 26 per cent in urban and rural areas, respectively. From these figures it may be noted that the recent narrowing of the gap between rural and urban infant mortality goes simultaneously with the change in access to services.

The second factor analysed relates to medical attention. For Peru, Paraguay, and Honduras the available information shows very great differences between urban and rural areas and within social class and education groups in terms of delivery and postnatal attention and vaccination. Table 6.5 shows clearly the situation prevailing in both areas. Similar results have been found for socio-economic and maternal education groups.

Experience in Costa Rica demonstrates that the only way to make possible a sustained reduction in infant mortality is to change this situation by delivering medical and sanitary attention to the less favoured sector (Rosero, 1985). This has also been the case in Panama, where low infant mortality in rural areas has been achieved through the implementation of health policies and sanitation measures, especially primary health care introduced due to improvements in the communications network and because of a certain integration of the community to health care systems (Guerra, 1981).

In Honduras, where more information is available, some interesting events have occurred in the last two decades in terms of health care. Hospital attention given by the state had not improved by the beginning of the seventies and may even have deteriorated. These health services, which are basically curative, were accessible to the poor in urban areas, principally metropolitan areas, and to those persons coming from rural areas near the cities. However, the medical attention through social insurance increased rapidly. The parts of the population which benefited most were the salaried urban sectors. In general, all urban sectors with medium and high incomes (salaried and non-salaried) benefited, as well, from the increase of private medical attention. However, the major impact in the rural areas was the establishment of rural health centres, through which primary attention has been increased in the entire country. This is clearly demonstrated by the fact that 80 per cent of births which occurred between 1979 and 1984 in rural areas were attended in these centres.

It is very important to note the increase of vaccinations in most countries. In Honduras, these campaigns have benefited residents of the cities as well as dwellers in rural areas. For example, the vaccines administrated by the health ministry (polio, tetanus, measles, and others), reached 1.4 million vaccines in 1980, compared to 120,000 in 1960 (CELADE, 1987).

Data on health policy in Paraguay show that health expenditure declined in the last decade, with a drop in the numbers of visits to doctors in hospitals and no evidence of a major programme of primary health care (CELADE, 1986).

Finally, consider the last set of proximate determinants. Available data on breast-feeding patterns show that the average duration of breast-feeding is higher in high infant mortality groups (Ferry and Smith, 1983). Thus, mortality differentials are not as great as they might become were breast-feeding to be reduced among these high-risk groups. In terms of nutrition, at least for Honduras there is no evidence of an amelioration of nutritional status; in fact it even seems that the proportion of malnourished children has increased (CELADE, 1987). In Paraguay, there is evidence of an increase in consumption of calories and proteins between 1965 and 1976, but the same data also show great differences between social groups (CELADE, 1986).

There is not much information on patterns of child and maternal care. However, not only has formal education increased but important gains have also occurred in health education, linked to primary health care and family planning programmes, and in general to an important development of the communication network. These changes have also affected cultural patterns, such as the acceptance of child health care as a 'right' and/or 'duty' of the family.

Fertility declines should probably have had some impact on infant mortality declines because of the relative decrease of children in high-risk groups. In all the countries studied fertility has been declining, but at the same time there remain differences between social groups in terms of both levels and trends of fertility. In some cases, like rural Honduran families which have maintained a stable level of fertility in the last two decades, the impact of this variable is probably minimal.

Conclusions

In most Latin American countries a great decline in infant mortality occurred during the last two decades, especially during the seventies. Infant mortality trends estimated in this work for different socio-economic and geographic groups permit the conclusion that the decline has been almost universal, with reductions in rural areas, in less educated groups, and in the agricultural salaried classes and farmers. In Peru and Paraguay, however, the reduction in these groups has been very small.

The tendencies observed show two kinds of situation. The first is a tendency to decrease—or at least not to increase—of social differences in mortality risks. This is the case of Panama, Guatemala, and, to some extent, Honduras. The second is the situation prevailing in Peru and Paraguay, where infant mortality differentials are clearly increasing. The case of Peru can be understood as a characteristic of the relatively delayed mortality transition in this country. This is not so in Paraguay, which was already considered a country of relatively low infant mortality in the sixties.

Although in the urban context decline in infant mortality has generally been faster than in other areas, in more highly educated groups, or in other words in middle-class sectors, the reduction tends to be increasingly slow, and in some sectors a tendency to stagnate can already be observed, with rates around 40–50 per thousand. While it is important to obtain more recent estimates to prove this phenomenon, one explanation of it could be the economic stagnation these privileged groups experienced, expressed via a decline in real incomes.

Although in some cases the above-mentioned trends contributed to the reduction of relative differences among infant mortality rates, important differences still remain. It clearly appears that the disappearance of the said differences will depend on a more equal distribution of the social surplus, including better access to medical care.

References

Behm, H., and D. Primante (1978), 'Mortalidad en los primeros años de vida en la América Latina', *Notas de Población* 6(16), 23–44.

—— and L. Modes (1983), *Panamá: la mortalidad infantil según variables socioeconómicas y geográficas 1966–1976*, ser. A, no. 1043, San José, Costa Rica.

—— and E. Vargas (1984), *Guatemala: diferencias socioeconómicas de la mortalidad de los menores de dos años 1968–1976*, ser. A, no. 1044, San José, Costa Rica.

Breilh, J., and E. Granda (1983), 'Un marco teórico sobre los determinantes de la mortalidad', document presented at the Congreso Latinoamericano de Población y Desarrollo, México City, November 1983.

CELADE (1986), *Paraguay: La mortalidad infantil según variables demográficas y socioeconómicas y geográficas, 1955–1980*, ser. A, no. 172, Santiago, Chile.

—— (1987), *La mortalidad infantil en Honduras 1960–1982*, Santiago, Chile.

CEPAL (1979), *América Latina en el umbral de los años 80*, Santiago, Chile.

Chackiel, J. (1983), 'La mortalidad infantil en América Latina: Niveles, tendencias y determinantes', paper presented at the Congreso Latinoamericano de Población y Desarrollo, México City, November 1983.

Fernández, R. (1984), *Análisis de la información sobre atención materno-infantil de las Encuestas de Fecundidad de América Latina*, World Fertility Survey, TECH 2296 (draft), London.

Ferry, B., and D. P. Smith (1983), *Breastfeeding differentials*, Comparative Studies, Cross-national Summaries, World Fertility Survey no. 23, London.

Guerra, F. (1981), *Determinantes de la mortalidad infantil en Panamá (1940–1974)*, CELADE, ser. D, no. 99, Santiago, Chile.

Guzmán, J. M. (1985), 'Infant Mortality Trends from Retrospective Information: Problems in the Selection of the Mortality Models', paper presented at the International Population Conference, Florence, 1985.

Mosley, H. (1985), 'Les Soins de santé primaires peuvent-ils réduire la mortalité infantile? Bilan de quelques programmes africains et asiatiques' in J. Vallin *et al.* (eds.), *La Lutte contre la mort*, INED, IUSSP, Paris, 105–36.

MSP (Ministerio de Salud Pública) y ASHOPLANFA (Asociación Hondureña de Planificación Familiar) (1986), *Encuesta nacional de salud materno infantil de Honduras, 1984 (ENSMI 1984), Tegucigalpa, Honduras.*

Naciones Unidas (1984), Mortalidad infantil: Estimaciones y proyecciones mundiales, 1950–2025, Boletín de Población, no. 14, New York.

Rosero, L. (1985), 'L'Influence des politiques économiques et sociales: Le Costa Rica' in J. Vallin *et al.* (eds.), *La Lutte contre la mort*, INED, IUSSP, Paris, 331–56.

United Nations (1983), *Indirect Techniques for Demographic Estimates*, Manual X, ST/ESA/SER,A/81, New York.

—— (1985), *Socioeconomic Differentials in Child Mortality in Developing Countries*, ser. A, no. 97, New York.

7 Socio-economic Differentials in Infant and Child Mortality in Indonesia in the 1970s: Trends, Causes, and Implications

BUDI UTOMO and MEIWITA BUDIHARSANA ISKANDAR

Department of Population and Biostatistics, Faculty of Public Health,
University of Indonesia, Jakarta, Indonesia

Infant and Child Mortality Trends

In Indonesia, data on infant and child mortality are almost invariably based on indirect techniques of measurement. Soemantri (1983) has shown that estimates from different censuses and surveys provide evidence of a general decline in infant and child mortality levels, though there is a 10 per cent gap between the trends obtained from the 1971 population census and from the 1976 intercensal population survey (Figure 7.1). Hull and Sunaryo (1978) suggested that this was due partly to age misstatements and partly to the design of the questions.

Indonesia's infant mortality rate (IMR) declined from 150 in 1961 to 135 in 1971, representing an average annual reduction rate of 1.5 per cent.

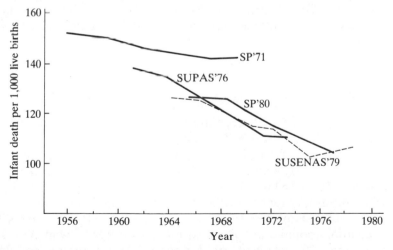

Figure 7.1. Time trend of infant mortality rate in Indonesia
Source: Soemantri, 1983.

Table 7.1.   Infant mortality rates for recent census years,[a] Indonesia

	1961	1971	1980
Urban	—	106	79
Rural	—	141	106
Total	150[b]	135	98

[a] Derived from Central Bureau of Statistics, *Perkiraan Angka Kelahiran dan Kematian: Hasil Sensus Penduduk 1971 dan 1980*. The figures given in this chapter use data from the 1971 and 1980 censuses, but due to the method of estimation the time reference is actually about two years prior to the census year (i.e., 1969 and 1978). The IMR figures reported in the table above have been extrapolated, using the average annual reduction rate for the 1971–80 period of about 3.2 per cent per year. The total IMR obtained in this way corresponds to the figure given in the Central Bureau of Statistics publication, *Statistical Profile of Children and Mothers in Indonesia 1982*.
[b] World Bank, 1982*b*.

During the 1970s, the annual decrease was more than twice as fast at about 3.2 per cent, resulting in an infant mortality rate of 98 per 1,000 live births in 1980 (Hapsara, 1983). Dasvarma (1983) confirmed this finding with an estimation of 97 per 1,000 live births by using data on last live birth survivorship (Table 7.1).

Infants have experienced more rapid mortality decline than children. Drawing on the 1971 and 1978 censuses, Adioetomo (1983) estimated that the probability of dying between birth and the second birthday, q_2, has been reduced from 0.179 at the end of the sixties to 0.141 at the end of the seventies. This represents an annual reduction of 2.4 per cent compared to an infant mortality decline of 3.2 per cent during that same period. According to the Central Bureau of Statistics (1982), the latest estimate of the death rate among Indonesian children aged 1–4 years is about 18 per 1,000 children.

Spatial Variations

In a country as large and geographically fragmented as Indonesia, a considerable variation in IMR among regions and provinces is not surprising. Table 7.2 shows a wide gap in both IMR and annual IMR decline between Yogyakarta (in Java) and West Nusa Tenggara. Yogyakarta's IMR of 62 is one-third of West Nusa Tenggara's 187. Except for Nusa Tenggara, among the other five bigger islands variation does not appear to be large. However, the country's highest IMR only affects 2 per cent of the infant population. The next highest IMR, of 129 in West Java, affects another 20 per cent of Indonesia's total infant population (UNICEF, 1984).

Table 7.2. Infant mortality rate (IMR), and annual IMR decline, 1969–78, by province*

Province	Infant mortality rate			
	Urban	Rural	Total	Decline 1969–78 (per cent)
Sumatera				
DI Aceh	65	93	91	−4.8
North Sumatera	70	94	89	−3.2
West Sumatera	89	125	121	−2.4
Riau	69	126	113	−2.4
Jambi	79	123	118	−2.9
South Sumatera	75	104	98	−4.8
Bengkulu	65	110	106	−5.0
Lampung	91	98	97	−4.5
Java				
DKI Jakarta	79	92	80	−4.9
West Java	105	134	129	−2.7
Central Java	78	100	96	−4.4
DI Yogyakarta	50	66	62	−5.1
East Java	84	102	99	−2.0
Nusa Tenggara				
Bali	69	90	88	−4.0
West Nusa Tenggara	142	194	187	−1.7
East Nusa Tenggara	56	129	124	−2.2
Kalimantan				
West Kalimantan	66	122	116	−2.3
Central Kalimantan	72	103	100	−2.7
South Kalimantan	101	124	121	−3.3
East Kalimantan	75	110	99	−0.7
Sulawesi				
North Sulawesi	80	96	94	−2.1
Central Sulawesi	85	131	128	−1.4
South Sulawesi	107	109	108	−4.2
Southeast Sulawesi	88	116	114	−5.6
Maluku & Irian Jaya				
Maluku	78	128	124	−1.7
Irian Jaya	89	110	106	−0.8
Indonesia	86	113	107	−3.2

* These estimates are based on the 1971 and 1980 censuses (see note to Table 7.1). IMR decline is the average annual rate of reduction (in %).
Source: Soemantri, 1983.

Overall, there are 12 provinces (including West Java) that show a higher level of infant mortality than the national average. Together, these provinces contained 40 per cent of Indonesia's infant population in 1980. In the other 14 provinces IMRs were lower than the national average.

The annual decline of IMR during 1969–78 was most impressive in South-East Sulawesi (−5.6 per cent), Yogyakarta (−5.1 per cent), and Bengkulu (−5.0 per cent). On the other hand, several provinces in the eastern part had annual rates of decline of less than 2 per cent, namely, East Kalimantan (−0.7 per cent), Irian Jaya (−0.8 per cent), and West Nusa

Table 7.3.   Infant mortality rate and per capita income by province, 1980

Province	Infant Mortality Rate, 1980[a]	Income 1980 (thousands Rp)[b]
DKI Jakarta	81	264.3
West Java	131	97.3
Central Java	108	68.2
D.I. Yogyakarta	63	69.0
East Java	113	89.4
Subtotal Java	104	n.a.
DI Aceh	91	259.7
North Sumatera	89	131.3
West Sumatera	122	83.0
Riau	113	108.5
Jambi	120	n.a.
South Sumatera	98	153.8
Bengkulu	107	91.1
Lampung	98	74.8
Subtotal Sumatera	93	n.a.
West Kalimantan	117	106.8
Central Kalimantan	100	134.2
South Kalimantan	122	121.2
East Kalimantan	100	298.1
Subtotal Kalimantan	106	n.a.
North Sulawesi	96	115.5
Central Sulawesi	129	71.5
South Sulawesi	108	91.3
South East Sulawesi	117	75.4
Subtotal Sulawesi	108	n.a.
Bali	89	112.5
West Nusa Tenggara	188	53.4
East Nusa Tenggara	125	56.9
Maluku	125	121.1
Irian Jaya	125	123.9
East Timor	n.a.	n.a.
Subtotal E. Islands	n.a.	n.a.
Total Indonesia	105	n.a.
Indonesia Urban	87	n.a.
Indonesia Rural	114	n.a.

Sources: [a] World Bank staff estimates (1984*b*, 136).
       [b] Central Bureau of Statistics, *The 1980 Population Census.*

Tenggara and Maluku (− 1.7 per cent).

Infants born in urban areas have a much better chance of survival than those in rural areas: the overall rate of infant mortality in urban areas was 86 as against 113 in rural areas in 1968–78. The widest urban–rural gap exists in East Nusa Tenggara (73 deaths per 1,000 live births), Riau (57/1,000), West Kalimantan (56/1,000), West Nusa Tenggara (52/1,000), and Maluku (50/1,000). With the exception of Riau, all these provinces are located in the eastern part of the archipelago, where health care and education in rural areas are not as developed as in the western part. In Java, urban–rural differentials vary only from 11 to 29 deaths per 1,000 live births. Provinces with the lowest urban–rural differential include South Sulawesi and Lampung, with differentials of only 2 and 7 deaths per 1,000 live births, respectively.

Socio-economic Differentials

Data on mortality differentials are far from adequate, especially by provinces. Only two socio-economic factors will be discussed here, namely per capita income and mother's level of education.

Looking at infant mortality by province, per capita income does not have a consistent correlation with IMR. For example, Yogyakarta has the lowest IMR in the country, while its per capita income is lower than in most other provinces. Lampung is another example of a low per capita income with low IMR. But the provinces of West Nusa Tenggara, East Nusa Tenggara, Central Java, East Java, and West Sumatera have obviously low per capita income as well as high IMR.

The inequality in the mortality rate is, however, due not only to different levels of per capital income but also to geographical variations in water supply and sanitation, education (which will be discussed later on), health care, and other services. These factors influence the differences in IMR between, for instance, Yogyakarta and West/East Nusa Tenggara, which show a similar low level of income but unusually large mortality differences.

One of the strongest determinants of infant and child mortality is mother's educational status. To some extent this is because education may provide her with knowledge about health and nutrition. According to a World Bank study (1984*b*), there is little doubt that the achievements in the provision of primary education have facilitated Indonesia's rapid economic growth over the last decade. Between 1971 and 1980 the proportion of females aged 10 and over who never attended school declined from 51 to 30 per cent, and among males it decreased from 29 to 19 per cent. Furthermore, while the proportion of males completing primary school apparently declined by about 4 per cent, the comparable figure for females rose by 12 per cent. A significant amount of progress is also evident at the secondary level, where the proportion of females who had completed secondary school

Table 7.4. Infant mortality rate by education of mother and by place of residence, 1971 and 1980 censuses

	1971 census[a]			1980 census[b]		
Education of mother	Urban	Rural	All	Urban	Rural	All
No schooling	0.160	0.155	0.171	0.127	0.127	0.127
Incompleted primary school	0.129	0.142	0.160	0.102	0.117	0.113
Completed primary school	0.091	0.106	0.113	0.074	0.090	0.087
Completed secondary school	0.061	0.082	0.071	0.052	0.074	0.063
Completed higher school	0.047	0.068	0.057	0.043	0.073	0.053
Index						
No schooling	100	100	100	100	100	100
Incompleted primary school	81	92	94	80	92	89
Completed primary school	57	68	66	58	71	69
Completed secondary school	57	53	42	41	58	50
Completed higher school	29	44	33	34	57	42

Sources: [a] Hull and Sunaryo, 1978.
          [b] Adioetomo, 1983.

doubled from 4 per cent (1971) to 8 per cent (1980).

Estimates from 1971 and 1980 censuses in Table 7.4 show that children born to mothers with higher educational attainment tended to have lower IMR. Infant mortality of children born to women with completed primary school was 25 per cent less than of those whose mothers had not completed primary schooling. Mortality among infants born to women with at least a completed secondary school education was 50 per cent lower than among those born to women with no education. The usual urban–rural difference in IMR was found to be more pronounced at the higher levels of female educational attainment.

Principal Causes of Infant and Child Mortality

The National Household Health Survey conducted in 1980 covered a population of 121,266 in 6 provinces located in Java, Sumatera, Kalimantan, and Sulawesi. It found that infant and child deaths under five years of age accounted for 45.7 per cent of total deaths. Of the deaths occurring during the first five years of life, 61 per cent took place within the first year (Table 7.5). About 40 per cent of deceased infants died in the first month, and 45 per cent of these neo-natal deaths occurred within the first week of life. Between 85 and 90 per cent of all infant and child deaths were caused by a very limited range of diseases, shown in Table 7.6 (Puffer, 1983). About half of them were due to immunizable diseases and diarrhoea.

Within the neo-natal period, tetanus alone causes more than 40 per cent of total mortality, while among older infants and young children the principal cause is dehydration due to diarrhoea. The most important

Table 7.5. Number of infants deaths by age in days and months

Age in days	Number	Percentage
1	15	14.7
2–6	31	30.4
7–13	32	31.4
14–20	17	16.7
21–9	7	6.8
Total	102	100.0

Age in months	Number	Percentage
<1	102	40.3
1	22	8.7
2	20	7.9
3–5	48	19.0
6–8	34	13.4
9–11	27	10.7
Total	253	100.0

Source: Boediarso, 1983.

implication of these facts is, therefore, that health intervention programmes can achieve a substantial reduction in the mortality rates.

Unfortunately, there is no information available on the mortality pattern among provinces. A more recent prospective survey carried out in West Java (Boediarso, 1984) tends to confirm the above mortality pattern: 30 per cent of the deaths in the first five years occurred within the neo-natal period (as compared with 25 per cent in the National Health Survey), and another 30 per cent in the remainder of the first year (37 per cent in NHS). It was also noted that 47 per cent of all deaths among children under five were due to infections and parasitic diseases, and 41 per cent of neo-natal deaths were caused by tetanus (47 and 43 per cent in NHS, respectively).

Malnutrition and low birth-weight are considered as underlying causes of high infant and child mortality. Nutritional deficiency was identified as an associated cause in 16 per cent of the deaths among children aged 1–4 (UNICEF, 1984, 37). There is typically a secondary mortality peak during the weaning period, around ages 1–2 years, when malnourishment often occurs during the transition between breast milk and a solid food diet.

Among children under five, UNICEF (1984) reports that 30 per cent are suffering from some degree of protein calorie malnutrition (PCM), of which 3 per cent are classified as severe. Vitamin A deficiency attacks about 375,000 under-fives annually, and about a third of these become blind as a result. Iodine deficiency in certain areas of the country was the cause of goitre in an estimated 12 million children and adults in 1979 and of about 100,000 cases of childhood cretinism in the endemic areas.

The incidence of low birth weight (less than 2,500 grams) was estimated at

Table 7.6. Principal causes of infant and child deaths in Indonesia, 1980

	Neonatal (<1 month)		Post-neonatal (1–11 months)		Child (1–4 years)		Total (under 5)	
	Percentage of cause	Percentage of age group	Percentage of cause	Percentage of age group	Percentage of cause	Percentage of age group	Percentage of cause	Percentage of age group
Infectious and parasitic diseases	54	28	45	35	46	37	47	100
Typhoid fever	(1)	14	(1)	14	(3)	71	(2)	100
Dysentery, diarrhoea, etc.	(9)	8	(33)	44	(34)	48	(28)	100
Diphtheria	—	—	(1)	33	(2)	67	(1)	100
Tetanus	(43)	80	(5)	13	(2)	7	(13)	100
Measles	—	—	(1)	33	(1)	67	(1)	100
Other	(1)	9	(5)	64	(2)	27	(3)	100
Nutritional deficiency	—	—	1	50	1	50	0.5	100
Meningitis	2	5	11	41	14	54	10	100
Influenza and pneumonia	11	11	29	44	28	45	24	100
Birth injuries and other perinatal	23	100	—	—	—	—	6	100
Subtotal	90	25	86	36	89	39	88	100
All other causes	10	22	14	41	11	37	12	100
Total	100	25	100	37	100	39	100	100

Source: Department of Health Household Health Survey 1980. Data found in Puffer, 1983.

around 14 per cent of all live births in Indonesia in 1983 (UNICEF, 1984, 37). This condition leads to a higher risk of infection and death in infancy and early childhood. Puffer (1983) found that mortality rates for those weighing less than 2,500 grams at birth are 5 to 9 times higher than for those in the 2,500–999 grams weight group, and 7 to 13 times higher than among those weighing 3,000–999 grams. Other factors related to the rate of still birth and low birth-weight include birth spacing, maternal education, the general health and nutritional status of the mother, and the frequency of pre-natal visits to a health centre (Puffer, 1983, 23).

Conclusions

In terms of economic performance, Indonesia has been quite successful in increasing its GDP at an average annual rate of 8 per cent (1971–6) and 8.1 per cent (1976–81). The rapid economic growth of the 1970s had a great impact on domestic investments in agriculture, manufacturing, and so forth. The provision of health facilities also improved dramatically in those years. The substantial changes in infant mortality and life expectation indicate a large measure of success. None the less, during the 1970s health efforts were still more concentrated on the development of basic infrastructure for service delivery and rehabilitation of the elements of the system that had deteriorated during the previous years.

Beginning with Repelita I in 1968, the Government's policy has been to achieve the widest possible coverage of basic health services in both urban and rural areas in all major regions of the country. It is important to note that, at the same time, family-planning services were available throughout most of the country. Since the formation of the National Family Planning Co-ordinating Board (BKKBN) in 1970, more than 6,000 family-planning service outlets in health centres and hospitals have been established, and Indonesia's population planning and control programme has become recognized as one of the most effective in Asia (Suyono, 1982).

On the whole, poverty declined between 1971 and 1980, a greater reduction occurring in the urban areas. Relating the above developments to causes of infant and child mortality, the following implications may be suggested.

Because 45 per cent of all deaths in the first five years of life are due to immunizable diseases and diarrhoea, proper health intervention programmes should be able to reduce dramatically infant and child mortality. In addition, factors that may prevent water-borne and other infectious diseases, such as access to clean water and sanitation facilities, should be given attention.

Changing the literacy situation for both the male and female population aged ten and above will benefit the health programmes in the reduction of infant and child mortality. Adult education programmes may be developed to reach the illiterate and semi-literate outside the formal school system.

In conclusion, while very substantial achievements have been made to reduce infant and child mortality rates, there is a general agreement that the health status of Indonesia's infants and children under five is still lower than in many other Asian countries.

References

Adioetomo, S. M. (1983), 'Infant and Child Mortality Differentials in Jakarta and Indonesia' in *An analysis based on the 1980 Population Census*, Central Bureau of Statistics and Demography Institute of the University of Indonesia, Jakarta.

Boediarso, L. R. (1983), 'The 1980 Household Survey' in *Proceedings of the Seminar on Infant Mortality Rate in Indonesia*, Jakarta, 84–5.

—— (1984), In-house seminar on Causes of Infant and Child Mortality, at UNICEF/Jakarta.

Central Bureau of Statistics (1978), *Indonesian Fertility Survey 1976: Principal Report*, vol. I, CBS, Jakarta.

—— (1979), *The Indonesian Child in Maps*, CBS, Jakarta.

—— (1980), *A Brief Note on 1980 Population Census*, CBS, Jakarta.

—— (1981), *Levels of Development of Public Welfare: 1970–1980*, CBS, Jakarta.

—— (1982), *The National Socio-Economic Survey 1980*, CBS, Jakarta, 9.

—— (1983), *Statistical Yearbook of Indonesia 1982*, CBS, Jakarta 45, 50, 51.

Dasvarma, G. L. (1983), 'Indonesian Infant Mortality Estimates for 1980 from Last Live Birth Data' in *Proceedings of the Seminar on Infant Mortality Rate in Indonesia*.

—— (1984), 'How Many Children Will Die in Indonesia', *Research Note No. 15, IPDP*, Dept. of Demography, The Australian National University, Canberra.

Government of Indonesia (1980), *Repelita IV* (the fourth five-year development plan), GOI, Jakarta ch. 23.

Hapsara (1983), 'The Long-term Development in Health' in *Proceedings of Seminar on Infant Mortality Level in Indonesia*, Jakarta, 25.

Hughes, G. A., and I. Islam (1981), 'Inequalities in Indonesia: A Decomposition Analysis', *Bulletin of Indonesian Economic Studies (BIES)*, March.

Hull, T., and Sunaryo (1978), 'Levels and Trends of Infant and Childhood Mortality in Indonesia', working paper no. 15, Indonesian Population Dynamic Project, Population Institute, University of Gajah Mada, Yogyakarta, 14–28.

Kadarusman, J. (1982), 'Infant and Childhood Mortality in Jawa and Bali', MA thesis, National Centre for Development Studies, Australian National University, Canberra.

Kasto (1983), *Estimation of Infant Mortality Rate in Indonesia based on the 1980 Census*, CBS, Jakarta.

Puffer, R. (1983), 'Infant and Childhood Mortality in Indonesia', paper presented at Seminar at the National Institute for Health Research and Development, Jakarta, 6–9.

Rutstein, S. O. (1983), 'Infant and childhood Mortality: Levels, Trends and Demographic Differentials', *WFS Comparative Studies* 24, World Fertility Survey, London.

Ruzicka, L. T. (1984), 'Birth Spacing and Child Survival, Some Methodological Issues', Research Note 11 (mimeo), International Population Dynamics Programme, Department of Demography, Australian National University.

Soemantri, S. (1983), 'Trend and Regional Differentials In Infant Mortality Rates' in *Proceedings of the Seminar on Infant Mortality Rate in Indonesia*, Jakarta.

Suyono, H. (1982), 'Explosion of Family Planning Users in Indonesia', BKKBN working paper.

UNICEF (1984), *An Analysis of the Situation of Children and Women in Indonesia*, UNICEF draft, Jakarta.

US Department of Agriculture (1971), *FAO Production Yearbook 1971*, FAO, Washington, DC.

World Bank (1982*a*), *Financial Resources and Human Development in the Eighties*, 107–8.

—— (1982*b*), *World Development Report 1982*.

—— (1983*a*), *Policies for Growth with Lower Oil Prices*, 170.

—— (1983*b*), *World Development Report 1983*.

—— (1984*a*), *Indonesia: Policies and Prospects for Economic Growth and Transformation*, East Asia and Pacific Regional Office.

—— (1984*b*), 'Indonesia: Urban Services Sector Report', *World Bank Report No. 4800—IND*.

World Health Organization (1979), *Proceedings of the Meeting on Socio-economic Determinants and Consequences of Mortality*, Mexico City, June 1979, Geneva.

—— (1980), *Rural Water Supply, East Java–Indonesia*, ch. 10.

—— (1983), *Decade Commencement Report*.

8 Determinants of Child Mortality in Turkey

NUSRET H. FISEK

Hacettepe University, Ankara, Turkey

Life expectancy at birth is considerably shorter in Turkey than in the developed countries, but this difference narrows considerably at ages beyond five years. Comparatively low adult mortality in Turkey is explicable by the similarity of the most frequent causes of death in Turkey and developed countries. These are diseases of the circulatory system, neoplasms, accidents, poisoning, and violence. The prevention and cure of these diseases and factors are quite difficult and have as yet been unsuccessful everywhere. Death rates from infectious diseases in Turkey are in the same range as those in the developed countries (World Health Organization, 1980; DIE, 1984).

The diseases which kill the great majority of children are, in contrast, easily preventable, or curable, or both. It should be noted that there are physicians in every town and city, and there is at least one hospital in every city in Turkey (SSYB, 1980, 39). The ratios of members of population to hospital beds and members of population to physicians are 394 and 1,739 respectively (SSYB, 1980, 60). Therefore, high child mortality cannot be attributed to the unavailability of health services. It might be due to poor utilization of health care facilities. The findings of the second Turkish Demographic Survey (TDS) support this hypothesis: quite a high percentage of the deceased were not examined or treated by a physician before they died. This is true even in the urban areas, as seen in Table 8.1.

In the respect of infant and child mortality, in addition to pneumonia and diarrhoea, malnutrition is also among the factors to be considered. According to the results of a nationwide sample survey, 17 per cent of infants and toddlers suffer from mild malnutrition and 2.4 per cent from marasmus (Koksal, 1977, 48).

In 1965, Etitmesgut Health District was established by the Institute of Community Medicine (ICM) at Hacettepe University as a field training and research area (ICM, 1970, 1973, 1977, 1981). The district is located to the north-west of the city of Ankara, and covers 83 villages and two towns. Its population reached about 90,000 in 1980 because of high immigration. The district has seven health centres and one 50-bed hospital with four specialist

Table 8.1. Percentage of deceased persons examined and treated by a physician during sickness or injury

Place of residence	Age groups			
	0–1	1–4	5 and over	Total
Metropolitan	94.9	50.0	88.4	98.3
Over 100,000	83.9	100.0	76.9	81.3
50,000–100,000	50.1	57.6	88.7	76.4
10,000–50,000	82.8	67.9	74.3	75.5
2,000–10,000	58.9	68.3	73.1	67.7
Rural				
Most developed	45.9	66.2	63.9	58.1
Middle	38.4	59.3	51.5	48.0
Less developed	20.6	30.0	47.7	33.1
Total	45.7	55.7	65.6	57.3

Source: Yener, 1981.

physicians and x-ray and laboratory facilities. There are one or two physicians, two public health nurses, between three and six auxiliary nurse-midwives, and one medical secretary in each health centre. Preventive and curative health care in the centres and hospital is provided free of charge to everyone living in the district.

Auxiliary nurse-midwives visit houses regularly and deliver their services to each family. They are responsible for antenatal care, delivery, postpartum care, child care, family planning, and person-to-person health education. In addition, they report births, deaths, and migration in their area. The population of the district and its major demographic characteristics are recorded on household forms, which are kept in the office of the health centres under the care of a medical secretary.

The major health problem of the district has been high child mortality. Fifty-nine per cent of deaths were of children under five years of age, and the infant mortality rate was 142 per 1,000 live births in 1967. The major causes of child death were pneumonia and diarrhoea.

Table 8.2. Infant mortality (IMR) and proportionate child (0–4) mortality (PMR) rates in Etimesgut Health District

Years	IMR (per 1,000)	PMR (per cent)	Years	IMR (per 1,000)	PMR (per cent)
1967	142	59.0	1977	72	37.3
1969	111	52.9	1979	62	34.1
1971	88	45.1	1981	62	33.8
1973	93	46.0	1983	47	26.0
1975	96	43.0			

Table 8.3.　Causes of death at age 0-4 in Etimesgut Health District

Causes of death	Infant N	Rate	Age 1-4 N	Rate
Pneumonia	107	65	17	4
Diarrhoea	33	20	1	0.2
Neonatal morbidity	23	14	—	—
Others	51	31	19	4
Total	214	130	37	8.2
PMR		44.2		8.1
Population		1,647		4,492

Rate: per 1,000 population.
PMR: Death at the given age over total deaths.
Source: ICM, 1970.

As seen in Tables 8.2 and 8.3, delivery of free health care in the district did not achieve the anticipated effect on child mortality. Therefore, a special investigation was started to study factors related to the utilization of health facilities.

The physicians of health centres were asked to visit the house of every person who had recently died, upon receiving a death report from an auxiliary nurse-midwife, and to interview family members and record their findings on a standard questionnaire. The following information is collected: age, sex, marital status, and profession of the deceased; date and place of death; causes of death (main, intermediate, and final cause); duration of sickness; was he/she seen by physician or health personnel during sickness? If not, why? Was it medically possible to cure him/her? Was it possible to cure him/her with the facilities available in the district?

Families of 487 deceased persons were interviewed in 1971, and 194 (39.8 per cent) of the dead were under five years of age. Fifty-six per cent of these children could have been treated with the available facilities in the district, had they been taken to health centre or hospital. The social aetiology of medically preventable deaths of those under and over five years of age is shown in Table 8.4. Parents' lack of concern and of belief in modern health care are more important factors for children than for adults. Transportation problems and economic factors were negligible factors.

These findings indicate that the provision of health services alone is not sufficient to control mortality. Cultural values and socio-economic conditions have to be changed.

Tezcan (1976, 86) studied the correlates of infant mortality in a district where acceptable medical care is available free of charge. He demonstrated that 34 per cent of infants were not taken to a physician when they were sick.

Toprak (1969, 57) investigated patient care in Etimesgut district and found that the utilization of available facilities is low and that the distance

Table 8.4. The effect of socio-cultural factors on mortality

| Social aetiology | Age groups | | | | Chi square |
| | 0–4 | | 5 and over | | |
	N	Per cent	N	Per cent	
Disinterest	61	31	61	21	7.01
Lack of belief	40	21	25	8.5	14.74
Transportation	6	3.1	4	1.4	2.26
Economic	3	1.5	5	1.7	—

Source: ICM, 1970.

to the health centre plays a crucial role in it. The average patient call to a health centre where medical care is free is around one per person per year. The frequency of patient calls in the villages which are more than 15 km from the health centre is only 10 per cent of the frequency of that in the villages with a health centre.

Disinterest on the part of the families in the care of sick children motivated Ebiri to study the reaction of the people to the death of a friend or relative (Ebiri, 1971). One of the groups he interviewed consisted of 50 married women of reproductive age. He asked them, Whose death would give you the most grief? Only 3 respondents out of 50 said that the death of a child would cause the most grief.

Çali interviewed 210 married women of reproductive age in Cavundur, a mountain village where the children of most of the women died before a health center was established. Her findings related to the utilization of medical care facilities and the reaction of the mothers to the death of the children. Table 8.5 shows that the value of the child increases with its age (Çali, 1978, 25–30).

Another observation about low utilization of services provided in Etimesgut and Cubuk Health Districts was reported by Oral *et al.*, based on a follow-up study of 2,364 infants and toddlers in 1978 to 1983. Auxiliary nurse-midwives visited mothers and children in their houses at least once a

Table 8.5. The age of the child when he/she died and the reaction of the mothers

Age	Did not grieve (per cent)	Not taken to physician (per cent)
0–28 days	43	93
1–12 months	46	87
1–2 years	33	86
3–6 years	18	70
7 and over	7	57

Source: Çali, 1978.

Table 8.6.   Non-compliance of women with recommendations for the care of their children

Recommendations by ANMs	Number	Complied (per cent)	Not complied (per cent)
As to care of the child	19,772	52.7	44.3
To go to physician	2,613	9.0	91.0
To go to hospital	73	34.2	65.8

Source: Oral *et al.*, 1983.

Table 8.7.   Infant mortality versus compliance

Mother	Total number of infants	IMR per 1,000 LB	Significance
Complied	608	36	13.331
Not complied*	1745	80	d.f. 1

* Complied with less than 90 per cent of recommendations.
Source: See Table 8.6.

Table 8.8.   Correlates of infant mortality

Correlates	Infant deaths per 1,000 LB		Chi square
	Yes	No	
Is the pregnancy wanted?	58	96	11.082
Are housing conditions good?	67	83	0.541
Have the women completed primary education?	60	82	4.544
Is the family poor?	88	68	0.579
Do the women have more than 4 children?	94	59	9.675
Is the child the first live birth of the mother?	56	77	2.337
Has the mother had a previous child death?	105	52	23.233
Is the age of the mother less than 30?	62	88	4.170

Source: see Table 8.6.

month, provided the necessary services, and made recommendations. They checked and recorded whether their recommendations were complied with or not during their subsequent visits. The women who complied with more than 90 per cent of the recommendations were recorded as complying in the analysis of the data and the remaining ones as the non-complying group. As seen in Table 8.6, non-compliance is quite frequent, with 66 per cent of women not complying with the recommendations. The occurrence of child

Table 8.9. Mother's compliance, socio-economic correlates, and infant mortality

Correlates		Complying mothers			Non-complying mothers		
		Population	IMR per 1,000	Probability	Population	IMR per 1,000	Chi square*
Primary	Yes	499	24	>0.05	528	100	0.321
education	No	132	83		485	111	
Housing	Good	603	32	>0.05	105	95	0.042
conditions	Poor	25	120		906	107	
Unwanted	Yes	106	85	>0.05	337	139	6.001
pregnancy	No	523	27		673	89	
First	Yes	198	15	>0.05	223	94	0.257
live birth	No	435	46		790	109	
Economic	Poor	24	83	>0.05	73	123	0.091
status	Good	608	34		937	104	
Age of	<30	634	36	>0.05	1,279	75	1.808
mother	30+	138	65		498	94	
Previous	Yes	117	94	>0.05	381	141	8.758
child death	No	515	23		628	82	
High	Yes	95	105	>0.05	352	125	2.178
parity	No	539	24		652	97	

* Fisher's exact chi square test.
Source: See Table 8.6.

deaths among the non-complying group was significantly higher than in the complying one (Oral, 1983).

The effect of eight variables shown in Table 8.8 on infant mortality was studied (Fisek, 1985). Five of these factors, pregnancy wanted or not, high parity, previous child death, education, and age have a significant effect on infant mortality.

Since compliance is a critical factor, the data were analysed using compliance as a control variable. As seen in Table 8.9 these correlates, except first live birth, no longer have a significant effect on infant mortality among the women who complied with the instructions on child care. Unwanted pregnancy, age of the mother, high parity, and previous child death have a significant effect on infant mortality among the mothers who did not comply with the advice.

Compliance of mothers with recommendations of health personnel is an index of deriving benefit from health care facilities. It modifies the effects of other social correlates on mortality as well. A comprehensive study of the correlates of mortality should include demographic, biological, medical, social, cultural, and administrative factors. Those related to health care delivery play a decisive role, especially in developing countries.

References

Çali, S. (1978), 'High Fertility and Value of Children in Cavundur', thesis for Diploma in Public Health, ICM, Hacettepe University, Ankara (in Turkish).

DIE (1984), 'Deaths in Provincial and District Centers in 1980 and 1981', State Institute of Statistics, Publication No. 1069, Ankara.

Ebiri, A. (1971), 'Social Characteristics and Cultural Behaviour of the People in Kazan', thesis for Diploma in Public Health, ICM, Hacettepe University, Ankara (in Turkish).

Fisek, N. H. (1985), 'Social Etiology of Child Mortality', unpublished data from research project on risk strategy.

Institute of Community Medicine (1970), 'Annual Report of Etimesgut Health District, 1967–1969' ICM, Hacettepe University, Ankara (in Turkish).

— (1973), 'Annual Report of Etimesgut Health District, 1970–1972', ICM, Hacettepe University, Ankara (in Turkish).

— (1977), 'Annual Report of Etimesgut Health District, 1973–1975', ICM, Hacettepe University, Ankara (in Turkish).

— (1981), 'Fifteen Years in Community Medicine in Hacettepe University', ICM, Hacettepe University, Ankara (in Turkish).

Koksal, O. (1977), 'Nutrition in Turkey', Hacettepe University, Ankara.

Oral, N. J., M. Bertan, N. H. Fisek, and A. Akin (1983), 'Report on the Evaluation of Risk Strategy in MCH Care in Turkey', ICM, HU.

SSYB (1980), 'Annual Report 1980', Ministry of Health and Social Assistance, Ankara (in Turkish).

Tezcan, S. (1976), 'Infant Mortality in the Cohort of the Last Five Years in Etimesgut District', dissertation submitted to Hacettepe University, Ankara.

Toprak, K. (1969), 'Factors Affecting Patient Care in the Rural Areas', thesis for Diploma in Public Health, ICM, Hacettepe University, Ankara (in Turkish).

World Health Organization (1980), '*World Health Statistics, Annual 1980*', WHO, Geneva.

Yener, S. (1981), '1974–1975 Turkish Demographic Survey: Mortality', doctoral dissertation, Hacettepe University, Ankara.

9 Effects of Inter-birth Intervals on Infant and Early Childhood Mortality

ALBERTO PALLONI

Center for Demography and Ecology, University of Wisconsin, Madison, Wisconsin, United States

The literature on the effects of pace of child-bearing on infant health and mortality has experienced a recent—and welcome—resurgence. On the one hand, several studies have addressed what turns out to be a not-so-trivial issue, namely that of establishing just what is known about the relationship in question and how such knowledge has been generated (Gray, 1981; Winikoff, 1983). On the other hand, other studies, while concentrating on more general issues, have pointedly remarked on the importance of the effects of inter-birth interval on mortality (Baldion, 1981; Martin *et al.*, 1983; Rutstein, 1983; Trussell and Hammerslough, 1983; Palloni, 1985). Some of the most controversial substantive issues and the intricacies of methodological difficulties are dealt with in two cross-national studies (Hobcraft *et al.*, 1983; Palloni and Millman, 1985) and in a few studies of single-country experiences (Palloni and Tienda, 1984; Knodel and Hermalin, 1984; Cleland and Sathar, 1984; DeSweemer, 1984). Some of these studies show that it is as difficult to specify the causal relationships of interest as it is to prepare and implement the design of the statistical procedures to estimate the effects of the variables contained therein.

This chapter aims at four targets. First, an effort is made to clarify the exact relationships involved and the types of mechanisms that operate. The result of such efforts is a set of well-defined hypotheses and completely specified models. Second, the most important technical difficulties are addressed and the solutions incorporated into an integrated procedure for the estimation of the models. Third, some of the most important hypotheses are tested on a sample of Latin American countries with available information. Finally, an effort is made to measure the effects of breast-feeding and pace of child-bearing, as should be done when the proper model specification is used. Some of the results are worth anticipating. Despite a

The research on which this chapter is based was partially supported by NICHD Grants No. HD18474 and NICHD No. HD15982. The computer facilities offered by the Centre for Demography and Ecology, University of Wisconsin, and supported by NICHD Grant No. HD05876 are gratefully acknowledged. Comments by John Marcotte and Stan D'Souza helped to improve the original version of the chapter.

series of precautions designed to prevent misleading inferences, the effects of pace of child-bearing on infant mortality and, to a lesser extent, on early childhood mortality are shown to be generalized and of considerable magnitude. This applies to both the effects of preceding and following birth interval. In only a few cases, and then too erratically, are these effects significantly altered by special contingencies, such as mother's education, levels of mortality and fertility, and patterns of breast-feeding. Finally, and perhaps surprisingly, it is verified that the main mechanisms through which the effects of inter-birth intervals operate do not, solely or mainly, involve the existence and variable duration of breast-feeding.

The Relations between Birth Intervals and Mortality

To avoid confusion it is important to clarify two basic concepts. First, when the effects of preceding and following birth interval are studied, they refer to the impact on the health status and death risks of the second and first of a pair of successive siblings, respectively. Second, unless otherwise stated, the length of an inter-birth interval refers to the length of the period elapsed between two successive *live births*. Adherence to this definition can and in fact does create some problems, to which we will refer later.

The Effects of the Preceding Birth Interval

In many studies, it has been shown that the death risks of index children whose birth closes a short birth interval are higher than those experienced by index children whose birth closes a longer birth interval (Wray, 1971; Federick and Adelstein, 1973; Wyon and Gordon, 1962; Wolfers and Scrimshaw, 1975; Wray and Aguirre, 1969; Hobcraft *et al.*, 1983; Palloni and Tienda, 1986). One mechanism involved in this relationship operates through the deterioration of the mother's capacities adequately to host a foetus and facilitate its normal growth process. A short birth interval may imply that the mother has not had sufficient time to regain her physiological capacities or her nutritional status. This may conduce to early termination of a pregnancy, premature live births, and low weight at birth for pregnancies terminated after a normal gestation period (Federick and Adelstein, 1973; Eastman, 1944; Jelliffe, 1966). Prematurity and low birth-weight lead to higher risks of death during the first month of life, but may also have negative health consequences throughout the first year of life (Puffer and Serrano, 1973). A second mechanism responsible for the deleterious effects of a short preceding birth interval is the likely impairment of the mother's capacity to produce milk. In turn, this is the outcome of either physiological weaknesses resulting from too closely spaced pregnancies or from nutritional depletion. It is highly likely that the operation of this mechanism may become more powerful as the birth order of the index child, and the age of the mother, increase. A third mechanism may operate when, as a consequence of norms of social interactions, there are restrictions in the distribution of scarce resources among the children in a household. One such resource which is fundamental for the child's health is maternal care. Deprivation of maternal care may be lethal for both the child who opens, as well as the one who closes, the birth interval.

The Effects of the Following Birth Interval

Numerous studies have documented the presence of negative effects on the health of the *first* child of a pair of children resulting from the birth of the second child of the pair (Wolfers and Scrimshaw, 1975; Wray and Aguirre, 1969; Wray, 1971; Hobcraft *et al.*, 1983; Palloni and Tienda, 1986). Three main mechanisms appear to be of considerable relevance. First, there is evidence suggesting that the occurrence of a conception shortly after a live birth curtails breast-feeding, if this is taking place at all. Curtailment may result from either the physiological impairment of the mechanisms leading to the production of milk and/or the cessation of breast-feeding in adherence to a cultural norm (Gray, 1981; Cantrelle and Leridon, 1971; Harfouche, 1970). A second mechanism is the increased competition for scarce resources: the allocation of material goods, time, and care is as relevant for the first child of a pair as it is for the second one. A third mechanism is the likely deterioration of the mother's capacity to attend the needs of other children throughout the duration of a pregnancy

The importance of the mechanisms sketched above may change over the period of infancy and early childhood and be heightened or diminished according to the existence of certain contingencies. In effect, one would expect that the mechanism operating through breast-feeding should produce higher effects during the first year of life, a period during which the nutritional and immunological properties of mother's milk are still well suited for the child's growth requirements. The effects that are due to lower birth-weight and prematurity ought to produce stronger effects during the first months of life, whereas those attributable to competition could vary during the first five years of life depending on what set of resources are subject to the harshest competition. The effects of preceding and following birth interval depend also on the existence of individual characteristics of the mother and the child, economic conditions affecting the access to material resources and services, and social and cultural conditions regulating the use of such resources. Thus, one would expect that the negative effects of a short birth interval would be stronger among children of higher birth order and among those born to mothers who are older at the time of the birth, since higher parity and older age at birth are known to produce significantly increased mortality risks (Federeci and Terrenato, 1980; Shapiro *et al.* 1968). By the same token, the negative effects of a short

Table 9.1. Hypothetical mechanisms relating pace of child-bearing and death risks at early ages

Birth interval	Mechanism	Contingencies
Preceding	(a) Weakening of milk production	Weaker as child ages
	(b) Prematurity Low birth-weight	Important only within first month of life
	(c) Sibling competition	Important through to age 5
Following	(a) Weaning of index child	Weaker as child ages
	(b) Maternal care during initial period of pregnancy	Relevant only during first nine months after conception
	(c) Sibling competition	Important through to age 5

Note: Access to services and availability of resources enhance (a), (b), and (c).

preceding birth interval could be expected to be exacerbated when the birth of the index child opens a short birth interval, and, on the other hand, the effects of a short following interval should be augmented when the birth closes a short birth interval. Similarly, in situations characterized by resource scarcity, it could be assumed that the negative impact of short birth intervals would be exaggerated. This is because under precarious material conditions the mechanisms operating through breast-feeding and resource competition become predominant (Palloni and Tienda, 1986). Table 9.1 displays, in a simple though somewhat incomplete and not entirely rigorous manner, the set of basic relations that have been briefly outlined.

Methodological Problems in the Estimation of Effects

The methodological difficulties that are encountered in any attempt to infer estimated magnitudes of effects have been described at length elsewhere (Palloni and Tienda, 1986; Winikoff, 1983). In this section of the chapter I will summarize only the most important ones and briefly describe what seem to be the optimum procedures for handling them.

Problems Generated by Failure to Control Confounding Influences

(a) The most trivial problem, but one which is not always resolved correctly, is that created by effects that covary with birth spacing. It is known, for example, that a higher age of the mother at the birth of the child is associated with higher neo-natal and, to a lesser extent, post-neonatal mortality. However, longer birth intervals that are a consequence of increased infecundity are also associated with higher age of the mother. Failure to control for age of the mother may lead to attenuation of the effects of birth intervals. The same argument applies to other attributes of the child, such as birth order, and attributes of the mother or household (such as mother's education, income, ethnicity, and residence).

(*b*) A more difficult problem is created by the association between health conditions of the household, child spacing, and the death risks of the index child. The death of the child initiating the birth interval may trigger the rapid closure of the interval either as a result of the shortening of the postpartum amenorrhoea period (in non-contraceptive societies) or as a deliberate strategy of replacement of the lost child (Knodel, 1968; Jain, 1969; Preston, 1978). However, since the health conditions of children born to the same mother are correlated, there will always be a gross association between the length of the preceding interval and the health conditions of the index child regardless of whether or not there are genuine effects of birth spacing on death risks.

(*c*) Finally, it is worth mentioning that erroneous inferences may result from the definitions used (Palloni and Tienda, 1986; Winikoff, 1983). Thus, the definition of birth interval used here overlooks the existence of conceptions that did not terminate in a live birth. Yet it is the existence of the conception itself that may be of relevance for health conditions. This is certainly the case when one studies the influence of the following birth interval: the mechanism operating through breast-feeding, for example, begins to act once a conception takes place, regardless of whether that conception is terminated by a live birth or by a spontaneous or induced abortion. Similarly, conceptions rather than births should be considered when studying the impact of preceding birth interval. In this case, a control for the existence (or number) of conceptions not terminated by a live birth would make it possible to avoid the attenuation of effects typically resulting from inter-birth intervals that are longer, as a consequence of higher rates of pregnancy losses or from higher mortality risks to which children are exposed. Of a different nature is the issue regarding a disproportionate number of premature births that are represented among those index children whose preceding birth interval is short (Winikoff, 1983). If one argues that prematurity itself is a result of a short birth-to-conception interval, the over-representation of premature births in the most unfavourable category is to be expected rather than to be controlled for. If, however, prematurity is thought to occur independently of the effects of rapid pace of child-bearing, then either the definition of birth interval given here ought to be changed or, if the definition is retained, a special control for prematurity should be introduced. In this chapter I have adhered to the first type of argument and will use, without control for prematurity, the stated definition of birth interval.

To resolve the first of the problems discussed earlier, it suffices to control for the appropriate characteristics: namely, age of the mother at birth, birth order, education of the mother, and so on. To resolve the second problem it is necessary to study the survival of the index child controlling for the survival status of the previous birth at the time of the *conception* of the index child. If the latter is not directly available, an estimate (subtracting 8.5 or 9 months from the date of birth) would suffice. Finally, the definitional problem has no solution as long as the only *reliable* information is a birth rather than a pregnancy history. This will create complications in the estimation of the effects of following interval and could lead to under-estimation of the effects of preceding birth intervals.

The Issue of Simultaneity: The Effects of the Following Birth Interval

A conception following too closely upon the birth of a child may be the result, rather than the cause, of the death of the earlier child. If, as is known to happen quite commonly in non-contraceptive societies, a couple engages in behaviour to replace a lost (index) child, the consequence will be a reduction in the expected time to a subsequent conception or live birth. Failure to recognize and appropriately deal with the consequent simultaneity bias results in a gross exaggeration of the negative effects of the following interval. Virtually the only way to deal with this problem is to study the survival of the index child over a period of time as a function of the occurrence of a conception before the beginning of such a period. This ensures that the event to which one imputes causal effects, namely the conception of the following child, does occur prior to the event which is taken as the outcome of the causal chain, that is the survival status of the index child.

An Integrated Model for the Estimation of Effects

To consolidate the preceding discussion, a survival model is now proposed. The model can be formally described as follows:

$$\ln \frac{_nq_x}{1 - {_nq_x}} = \alpha_0 Z + \alpha_1 PI1 + \alpha_2 PI2 + \alpha_3 PD + \alpha_4 FC_x$$

where $_nq_x$ is the probability of dying in the age interval $x, x+n$, and Z is a matrix of background variables including birth order of the index child, the age of the mother at birth, education of the mother, and region of residence (urban–rural). $PI1$ is a dummy variable taking on the value 1 if the birth of the index child occurred more than 18 but not more than 36 months after the birth of the preceding child; it assumes the value of zero otherwise. The variable $PI2$ takes on a value of 1 if the birth of the index child occurred after 36 months of the birth of the preceding child; it assumes a value of zero otherwise. These two dummy variables capture three categories. The residual category corresponds to those cases (index children) whose birth occurred 18 months or less after the birth of the preceding child. A first-born child is assigned a value of 1 in $PI2$ and zero in $PI1$. The variable PD takes on a value of 1 if the preceding child died prior to reaching age 1 and before the estimated conception date of the index child (date of birth minus 8.5 months). This variable allows control for spurious influences produced by the correlation of death risks among siblings and the replacement behaviour of parents. The variable FCX is designed to measure the effects of the following interval. It assumes a value of 1 if the estimated date of conception of the child born immediately after the index child occurred before the latter's xth month of life. A last-born child is assigned a value of zero on all FCX variables.

In this discussion I utilize the following age segments (in completed months): 0, 1–2, 3–5, 6–11, and 12–59. The variable FCX is defined only for $x = 3$, 6, and 12, since it is quite rare to find conceptions before the first month after a birth. Thus, $FC0$ and $FC1$ are not entered in the models.

The units of analysis are the index children who are observed alive at ages (in exact months), 0, 1, 3, 6, and 12. Such observations are utilized to estimate the parameters of model (1) for the age segments 0, 1–2, 3–5, 6–11, and 12–59, respectively. The dependent variable is the survival status of each child in an age segment: it assumes a value of 1 if the child dies within the segment and zero otherwise. The parameters are estimated using routine maximum-likelihood procedures for logit models with individual observations.

It is important to note that although model (1) resolves the technical difficulties examined above, it is insufficient to deal with certain problems that may have an effect on the final estimates. First, dates of conception are *estimated*, as dates of birth minus 8.5, rather than directly observed. This will introduce errors in the variables PD and FCX. Second, although the variables $FC3$ and $FC6$ may in fact adequately capture the consequences of a rapid following conception, it is less certain that $FC12$ will perform equally well. Note that if the next-youngest sibling is conceived, say, within 15 months of the date of birth of the index child, the latter will be classified together with all those whose mother never conceived another child at all. The most likely result is a downward bias in the estimate of X. Third, the nature of the definition of the variables $PI1$ and $PI2$ is such that first-order births are best treated by being classified together with those in the most favourable conditions ($PI = 1$). Yet, since first-order births may be exposed to higher mortality than second- and third-order births (Puffer and Serrano, 1973), the control for parity is imperative. Parity is introduced as two dummy variables representing, respectively, second-, third-, and higher-order births. This design increases the variance of the estimated

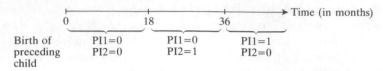

Figure 9.1. Representation of length of preceding interval

effects between parity and birth intervals. The same difficulty arises in the evaluation of FCX for last births, which, on average, are higher-order births.

Figures 9.1 and 9.2 graphically display the definitions of the variables measuring pace of child-bearing. Figure 9.1 represents the proposed categorization of length of preceding interval into three groups: those shorter than 18 months, those between 18 and 36 months, and those longer than 36 months. The two dummy variables defined here, $PI1$ and $PI2$, are sufficient to exhaust the categorization. Figure 9.2 illustrates the treatment given to the timing of the following conception for the age segment 3–5. In each age segment of interest one classifies the index children into those who enter the age segment *after* their mothers have conceived another child and those who do not. Only one dummy variable is required to represent such dichotomy.

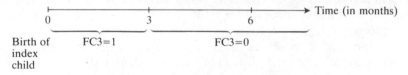

Figure 9.2. Representation of timing of following conception in the age segment 3–5

Application of the Model to Latin American Countries

The data on which the model will be estimated were collected as part of the World Fertility Survey Programme (WFS). They consist of country-specific birth (and in some cases pregnancy) histories elicited from women who, at the time of interview, were aged 15–49. In order to maximize consistency across countries, the analyses in this discussion are based only on birth histories. The consequences of this limitation are twofold: first, it is necessary to estimate the dates of conception of live births, and second, it is impossible to consider pregnancies which ended in non-live births. As a means of minimizing recall errors, the samples of births were limited to those occurring between one and fifteen years before the survey.

Elimination of those born the year preceding the survey permits avoidance of censoring problems without cumbersome solutions or assumptions.

Important Characteristics of the Data

Table 9.2 displays the total number of cases and the means of the variables $PI1$, $PI2$, and FCX ($x = 3, 6, 12$). The means of FCXs are equivalent to the proportions of cases who are in unfavourable positions, namely those who enter the corresponding age segment after their mothers have conceived another child. In Colombia, for example, 8 per cent of the children alive at age 3 months had a younger sibling conceived within the first 3 months of their birth, 18 per cent of those alive at age 6 months had a younger sibling conceived within the first 6 months of their birth, and 37 per cent of those alive at age 12 months had a younger sibling conceived within the first 12 months of their birth. Haiti shows the lowest values of FCX in all three segments (0.03, 0.07, and 0.19), whereas Colombia and Costa Rica show the highest values of FCX in all three segments (0.08, 0.18, and 0.37). The sum of the means of $PI1$ and $PI2$ represents the proportion of index children whose birth took place 19 or more months after the preceding birth. It reaches the highest values for Haiti (about 0.88 in all age segments) and the lowest in Colombia and Costa Rica (about 0.74 in all age segments). It is no coincidence that Haiti reveals indications of a slower pace of child-bearing. In fact, in contrast to the other countries, the pattern of breast-feeding in Haiti appears to be quite long and universal. It is known that longer breast-feeding leads, on average, to longer postpartum amenorrhoea and hence to longer birth intervals.

Table 9.3 presents some additional statistics of interest: the proportions of children who are never breast-fed, the mean duration of breast-feeding, the levels of infant and child mortality in the sample, estimated levels of fertility during a recent period, and a measure of current contraceptive prevalence.

The Magnitude and Significance of the Effects

Table 9.4 displays the estimated logit regression coefficients of the variables of interest and Table 9.5 the asymptotic t-ratios of the estimates. The first feature of interest is that, without exceptions, the coefficients are properly signed: a longer preceding birth interval implies lower mortality in the corresponding age segment, and a following conception taking place before a certain age implies higher death risks after that age. This finding is important even if some of the estimated effects are of small magnitudes or statistically insignificant or both. In fact, if one viewed each sign of the coefficients as a realization of an experiment with two possible results, a significance test would show that there is a very low probability that the

Table 9.2. Means of basic variables by age segments[a] (age segments in completed months)

Country	Number of cases	0		1-2		3-5			6-11			12-59		
		PI1	PI2	PI1	PI2	PI1	PI2	FC3	PI1	PI2	FC6	PI1	PI2	FC12
Colombia	9,428	.39	.35	.39	.36	.39	.36	.08	.39	.36	.18	.39	.36	.37
Costa Rica	8,528	.36	.38	.37	.38	.37	.38	.08	.37	.38	.17	.37	.39	.35
Ecuador	12,513	.42	.38	.42	.39	.42	.39	.06	.42	.39	.13	.42	.40	.29
Haiti	5,130	.44	.44	.44	.44	.44	.44	.03	.44	.45	.07	.44	.45	.19
Jamaica	6,544	.41	.40	.41	.40	.40	.40	.05	.41	.40	.12	.41	.40	.31
Mexico	19,159	.45	.34	.46	.34	.45	.34	.06	.46	.34	.14	.46	.34	.33
Panama	8,487	.40	.39	.40	.39	.40	.39	.06	.40	.39	.14	.40	.39	.31
Peru	16,604	.40	.39	.41	.39	.41	.39	.07	.41	.39	.14	.41	.40	.29
Trinidad	6,529	.34	.43	.34	.44	.34	.44	.07	.34	.44	.16	.34	.44	.32
Dominican Republic[b]	6,239	.40	.34	—	—	—	—	—	—	—	—	.40	.35	.37
Paraguay[b]	7,401	.42	.41	—	—	—	—	—	—	—	—	.43	.42	.24
Venezuela[b]	16,964	.34	.40	—	—	—	—	—	—	—	—	.34	.40	.36

[a] The definition of the variables is as follows:

PI1 = 1 if index child was born between 19 and 35 months after previous birth; 0 otherwise.

PI2 = 1 if index child was born after 35 months of previous birth; 0 otherwise.

FCX = 1 if the following living birth is conceived on or before the xth month of life of the index child.

[b] First age segment is 0–11.

Table 9.3. Proportions never breast-fed, mean duration or breast-feeding, levels of infant and child mortality, levels of fertility, and proportions contracepting

Country	Proportion never breast-fed	Mean duration of breast-feeding[a]	Infant mortality[b]	Child mortality[b]	Estimated total fertility rate[c]	Proportion of ever married women practising contraception[d]
Colombia	.11	7.4	.071	.046	4.7	.426
Costa Rica	.23	4.3	.070	.020	3.8	.734
Dominican Republic	.13	7.7	.090	.049	5.7	.407
Ecuador	.08	9.4	.111	.031	5.3	.388
Haiti	.05	10.8	.128	.091	5.3	.183
Jamaica	.07	7.1	.043	.019	5.0	.418
Mexico	.19	7.8	.086	.043	6.2	.325
Panama	.18	6.3	.044	.020	4.3	.649
Paraguay	.09	9.7	.056	.023	4.9	.367
Peru	.10	8.3	.114	.079	5.6	.324
Trinidad	.18	4.4	.041	.009	3.2	.570
Venezuela	.16	5.6	.045	.018	4.4[e]	.449[e]

[a] These values were calculated for the cohort born within the five years preceding the surveys. It is expressed in months.

[b] Infant and child mortality levels are calculated for the entire samples without regard for birth cohorts. Thus they do not represent current mortality in countries which have experienced mortality declines.

[c] These figures were directly calculated from the age-specific birth rates derived from birth histories and corresponding to the experience of five years before the interviews.

[d] These figures represent the porportions of ever married women who reported to be currently practising contraception regardless of method disclosed.

[e] In the case of Venezuela, the figures for Total Fertility Rate and Proportions Practising Contraception exclude the age group 45–9. In the case of Costa Rica and Panama the age group 15–19 is excluded.

Table 9.4. Logit regression coefficients of variables measuring length of inter-birth interval[a]

Country	Age segment (in completed months)												
	0		1–2		3–5		6–11			12–59			
	PI1	PI2	PI1	PI2	PI1	PI2	FC3	PI1	PI2	FC6	PI1	PI2	FC12
Colombia	−.4454	−.6712	−.2091	−.2099	−.8292	−1.293	.4410	−.5689	−1.503	.2463	−.2147	−.3140	.3924
Costa Rica	−.7949	−.7069	−.8967	−1.902	−.4458	−.9197	1.256	−.3242	−.7301	.8988	−.4931	−.6903	.5470
Ecuador	−.7164	−1.082	−.9482	−1.338	−.6337	−.7693	1.073	−.2230	−.7998	.7304	−.2651	−.6444	.3682
Haiti	−.6500	−1.101	−.2834	−1.248	−.0944	−1.528	.1637	−.5437	−.9076	.2858	−.0615	.2643	.3427
Jamaica	−.6015	−.5768	−.4595	−.6967	−.5199	−.7044	1.342	−.6845	−1.159	.5741	−.1386	.8638	.4139
Mexico	−.6753	−.7030	−.1185	.8485	−.6404	−.4538	1.318	−.7241	−.9244	.8033	−.3279	.4457	.4619
Panama	−.8109	−.9499	−.0876	−.4507	−.5343	−.6026	1.207	−.5578	−.3353	.4198	−.2761	.3061	.3026
Peru	−.6231	−1.252	−.3549	−1.053	−.9245	−1.498	.8329	−.3236	−1.238	.9075	−.3178	−1.011	.3915
Trinidad	−.6261	−.6644	−.7301	.6129	−.5637	−1.347	.7997	−.1021	−1.881	.1738	−.3611	−.4613	.3000
Dominican Republic[b]	−.5609	−.7849	—	—	—	—	—	—	—	—	.1328	.4013	.4454
Paraguay[b]	−1.050	−.8169	—	—	—	—	—	—	—	—	−.0971	.2589	.4692
Venezuela[b]	−.7055	−.7083	—	—	—	—	—	—	—	—	−.2845	.4795	.2560

[a] The definition of the variables is as indicated in footnote (a) of Table 9.2.
[b] For Dominican Republic, Paraguay, and Venezuela the information available permits only the use of the age segments 0–11 (months) and 12–59 (months).

Table 9.5. Asymptotic t-values for the logit regression coefficients of variables measuring length of inter-birth intervals[a, b, c]

| | Age segments | | | | | | | | | | | | |
| | 0 | | 1-2 | | 3-5 | | | 6-11 | | | 12-59 | | |
Country	PI1	PI2	PI1	PI2	PI1	PI2	FC3	PI1	PI2	FC6	PI1	PI2	FC12
Colombia	3.29 (34)	3.46	0.82 (4)*	0.63	3.55 (23)	3.63	1.42	2.98 (27)	4.00	1.24	1.57 (21)	1.66	3.33
Costa Rica	5.26 (66)	3.52	3.29 (23)	3.84	2.04 (36)	2.67	5.32	1.51 (31)	2.33	4.79	2.28 (18)	2.13	2.85
Ecuador	6.60 (85)	6.90	4.80 (53)	4.56	5.08 (91)	4.62	7.64	1.62 (48)	4.00	5.37	1.65 (18)	3.01	2.77
Haiti	4.23 (79)	5.57	0.98 (23)	3.15	.33 (20)	3.42	0.30	2.17 (23)	2.94	0.94	0.33 (10)*	1.24	2.55
Jamaica	2.98 (17)	2.10	0.91 (5)*	1.00	1.23 (12)	1.32	2.96	2.29 (17)	2.53	1.87	0.48 (10)*	2.02	1.86
Mexico	6.16 (92)	4.72	0.30 (3)*	1.28	2.73 (32)	1.50	5.39	3.99 (43)	3.49	4.64	2.08 (19)	2.08	3.48
Panama	5.00 (56)	4.50	0.16 (1)*	0.73	1.44 (10)*	1.21	2.86	1.06 (3)*	0.85	1.35	1.14 (5)*	1.01	1.55
Peru	5.37 (77)	7.34	1.91 (20)	3.89	4.41 (44)	4.72	3.31	2.01 (68)	4.98	5.84	2.28 (55)	5.90	3.65
Trinidad	3.41 (52)	2.93	1.27 (10)*	0.85	1.33 (8)*	2.10	0.84	0.22 (6)*	2.00	0.34	0.97 (5)*	0.99	0.99
Dominican Republic[d]	5.21 (44)	5.15	—	—	—	—	—	—	—	—	0.83 (9)*	1.77	3.25
Paraguay[d]	8.26 (68)	5.32	—	—	—	—	—	—	—	—	0.42 (5)*	0.89	2.65
Venezuela[d]	4.95 (29)	3.85	—	—	—	—	—	—	—	—	1.09 (16)	1.37	1.16

[a] The definition of the variables is indicated in footnote (a) of Table 9.2.
[b] The numbers in parentheses represent the likelihood ratio value contrasting the model *including* the variables measuring birth interval dynamics with the baseline model. They are asymptotically distributed as X² . Starred entries indicate that corresponding value is insignificant at p <0.01 with 2 and 3 degrees of freedom for the first two and last three age segments respectively.
[c] Unless otherwise indicated all logit regression coefficients are properly signed.
[d] In these cases the first age segment corresponds to the interval 0–11 months. Lack of detailed age at death prevented a more refined treatment.

realization represented in Table 9.4 comes from a universe where a positive sign in the estimated coefficient is as likely as a negative one.

A second result emerges from an examination of Table 9.5: the asymptotic *t*-ratios reach significance in a substantial amount of cases. Among the variables representing the preceding interval the exceptions occur within the higher-order age segments (1–2, 3–5, 6–11, and 12–59). The insignificant coefficients for the variable FCX are equally distributed among all age segments. Of special importance are the high *t*-ratio values for PI1 and PI2, reached within the *first* age segments in all countries. Equally relevant are the high *t*-ratio values associated with PI2 and FCX across all age segments but exhibited only by some countries, namely Costa Rica, Ecuador, and Peru and, to a lesser extent, Haiti and Mexico. The metric of the coefficients displayed in Table 9.4 corresponds to the logit scale. However, since the average probabilities of surviving in each age segment are close to one, they can also be interpreted as approximated average percentage decrease in the probabilities of dying within each segment that will result from a small change of 1 per cent on and around the mean of the pertinent independent variables. With only a handful of exceptions the magnitudes involved are higher for PI2 and for PI1. Similarly, the effects are more powerful within the first age segment and weakest within the last one. The magnitude of the effects corresponding to the variable FCX indicates a clear progression from high to low values as the age segment increases.

A different and perhaps more useful way of gauging the actual importance of the estimated effects is through two alternative measures known as relative risks and population-attributable risks. The former represents the approximate ratios of the age-specific death rates in the most unfavourable categories to those in the most favourable one. The latter is the proportionate reduction in mortality expected to occur in one age segment if the most unfavourable category of individuals were eliminated. Tables 9.6, 9.7, and 9.8 display the corresponding results. In the first age segment the relative risks associated with a short preceding birth interval are at least 1.74 times as large as the ones associated with longer birth intervals. Relative risks close to or exceeding 2.0 occur in all countries with the exception of Colombia. The relative risks for higher age segments decrease both in magnitude and statistical importance. The relative risks associated with following conceptions are surprisingly high for the age segment 3–5—some values exceed 3.0—but decrease sharply in the higher age segments and are not always based on statistically significant coefficients.

From a population policy point of view, the relevant issue is the magnitude of mortality change that would follow if the pace of child-bearing were slowed down. The figures displayed in Tables 9.7 and 9.8 should give a rough idea about the direction and magnitudes of such changes. They indicate that elimination of short birth intervals would

Table 9.6. Relative risks of children with unfavourable inter-birth intervals[a,b]

| Country | Variable | | | | | | | |
| | PI Age segment | | | | | FCX Age segment | | |
	0	1-2	3-5	6-11	12-59	3-5	6-11	12-59
Colombia	1.74	1.23*	2.86	2.77	1.30*	1.55*	1.28*	1.48
Costa Rica	2.12	4.05	1.98	1.69*	1.81	3.51	2.46	1.73
Ecuador	2.44	3.11	2.42	1.65*	1.57*	2.92	2.08	1.45
Haiti	2.40	2.15*	2.25*	2.07	1.18*	1.18*	1.33*	1.41
Jamaica	1.80	1.78*	1.85*	2.51	1.65*	3.83	1.78*	1.51*
Mexico	1.99	1.54*	1.75*	2.25	1.46	3.74	2.23	1.59
Panama	2.41	1.31*	1.77*	1.40*	1.34*	3.34	1.52*	1.35
Peru	2.55	2.53	3.36	2.18	1.94	2.28	2.48	1.48
Trinidad	1.91	1.94*	2.73*	1.74*	1.52*	2.12*	1.19*	1.35*
Dominican Republic	1.94	—	—	—	1.29*	—	—	1.50
Paraguay	2.54	—	—	—	1.19*	—	—	1.60
Venezuela	2.03	—	—	—	1.48*	—	—	1.29

[a] An asterisk indicates that the relative risk has been calculated with at least one statistically insignificant coefficient.
[b] For ease of representation the effects of PI1 and PI2 were combined in a weighted average: the coefficients utilized to calculate the relative risks due to PI equals $\beta_1 W_1 + \beta_2(1 - W_1)$ where β_1 and β_2 are (minus) the logit regression coefficients of PI1 and PI2, and W_1 is the proportion among all index children in a favourable position (previous birth interval is longer than 18 months) whose previous sibling was born less than 36 months before.

Source: Tables 9.2 and 9.3.

Table 9.7. Population Attributable Risks (PAR) corresponding to the effects of preceding inter-birth intervals and observed probabilities of dying ($_nq_x$)[a,b]

Country	Age segments									
	0 q_0	PAR	1-2 $_1q_1$	PAR	3-5 $_3q_3$	PAR	6-11 $_6q_6$	PAR	12-59 $_{48}q_{12}$	PAR
Colombia	.0352	.16	.0098	.05	.0115	.32	.0164	.31	.0464	.07
Costa Rica	.0328	.23	.0093	.44	.0136	.37	.0168	.20	.0201	.17
Ecuador	.0413	.22	.0128	.30	.0336	.22	.0280	.12	.0310	.06
Haiti	.0648	.14	.0205	.12	.0216	.13	.0273	.11	.0906	.02
Jamaica	.0248	.13	.0039	.13	.0052	.14	.0101	.22	.0195	.11
Mexico	.0526	.17	.0046	.10	.0119	.14	.0194	.21	.0433	.09
Panama	.0290	.23	.0034	.06	.0046	.14	.0078	.08	.0198	.07
Peru	.0534	.25	.0210	.24	.0166	.33	.0278	.20	.0797	.16
Trinidad	.0297	.17	.0036	.18	.0050	.28	.0035	.15	.0087	.11
Dominican Republic[b]	.0904	.20	—	—	—	—	—	—	.0490	.07
Paraguay[b]	.0558	.21	—	—	—	—	—	—	.0225	.03
Venezuela[b]	.0457	.21	—	—	—	—	—	—	.0177	.11

[a] PAR is calculated as $\dfrac{Pe(R-1)}{1+Pe(R-1)}$ where Pe is the proportion of all births which occur less than 18 months after the previous birth and R is the relative risk calculated in Table 9.6.

$_nq_x$ is the probability of dying between ages x and x+n (in months).

[b] The value of q_0 corresponds to the age segment 0-11 months.

Table 9.8. Population Attributable Risks (PAR) corresponding to the effects of a following conception*

Country	Age segments		
	3–5	6–11	12–59
Colombia	.04	.05	.15
Costa Rica	.20	.20	.20
Ecuador	.10	.12	.12
Haiti	.01	.02	.07
Jamaica	.12	.09	.14
Mexico	.14	.15	.16
Panama	.12	.07	.10
Peru	.08	.17	.12
Trinidad	.07	.16	.10
Dominican Republic	—	—	.17
Paraguay	—	—	.14
Venezuela	—	—	.09

* PAR is calculated as in Table 9.7. Pe is now the proportion of all children whose mother experiences a conception (eventually leading to a live birth) before they reach age 3, 6, or 12 months.

produce changes within the range of 13 to 25 per cent in the first age segment, 5 to 44 per cent in the second, 13 to 37 per cent in the third, 8 to 31 per cent in the fourth, and 2 to 17 per cent in the last. The above changes would occur on account of a shorter preceding interval. Comparable gains are to be expected as a result of the elimination of rapid following conceptions (see Table 9.8): the gains are between 4 and 20 per cent in the age segment 3–5, 2 to 20 per cent in the age segment 6–11, and 7 to 20 per cent in the last segment. It should be emphasized that the estimated gains in Tables 9.7 and 9.8 are *not* additive and, hence, cannot be used to estimate total gains due to overall changes in the pace of child-bearing. They are useful, however, as bench-marks for estimating the lower and upper bounds of potential changes. Using as weights the distribution of ages at death within the interval 0–59 and applying them to the quantities appearing in Table 9.7 leads to a lower boundary in the changes of child mortality (0–59 months) of about 13 per cent in Jamaica and a maximum of 22 per cent in Peru. A similar calculation applied to the values presented in Table 9.8 shows that the changes in the probability of dying between 0 and 59 months resulting from the disappearance of rapid following conceptions can reach a minimum of 10 per cent for Haiti and a maximum of 20 per cent for Costa Rica. Thus, the elimination of conceptions occurring within *nine months* of the previous births should reduce cumulated mortality within the first five years of life by at least 10 per cent and at most 22 per cent. Naturally, the validity of these figures is strictly dependent on the validity of the estimated model.

The Effects of Cultural and Social Contingencies

Further insights into the nature of the relationships may be obtained by examining cross-country variations of effects. Tables 9.4 and 9.5 show no evident clustering of countries along geographical location, levels of mortality, levels of fertility, or other important characteristics such as breast-feeding patterns and contraceptive prevalence. Thus, for example, the magnitude of the effects of preceding interval in the first age segment are on average *higher* for high-mortality countries such as Ecuador, Haiti, and Peru than for low-mortality countries such as Costa Rica, Jamaica, and Trinidad. However, there are conspicuous exceptions in both groups: Panama, a low-mortality country, behaves like a high-mortality one, whereas two high-mortality countries, Mexico and Dominican Republic, behave like low-mortality ones. A lack of systematic variations is also evident in other age segments, particularly the last one, where the effects are *low* and *insignificant* for high-mortality countries such as Haiti and Dominican Republic.

The effects of FCX show little more country-based regularities. The only discernible pattern pertains, in fact, to exceptions: low and insignificant values are characteristic of Colombia, Haiti, and Trinidad within at least the first two age segments. Yet these three countries cannot differ more with respect to important variables such as contraception and breast-feeding on the one hand, and levels of infant mortality on the other. Examination of Table 9.2 shows that, at least in the case of Haiti, the rarity of the event may obscure important effects. In fact, proportions of index children in the least favourable conditions (FCX = 1) are the lowest observed among all countries. Long postpartum amenorrhoea periods induced by long periods of lactation are the most likely explanation of the rarity of the event.

A different search for patterns leads to the study of selected interaction effects. In accordance with the hypotheses suggested earlier, I studied two sets of interaction effects: those between mother's education and birth intervals on the one hand, and those between preceding and following birth intervals on the other. The most important results appear in Table 9.9. The table displays the interaction terms that were statistically significant. The estimates that are now shown were statistically insignificant, although they may have had the correct sign. It is encouraging to see that those which were statistically significant effects were also properly signed. However, they are somewhat exceptional and show no evident clustering. Note, for example, that if one considers only the first and last two age segments, that is, those containing a number of events sufficiently high to detect interactions, one would find that only 4 out of 48 possible interaction effects involving preceding and following interval were significant, 8 out of 144 involving preceding birth interval and education, and 1 out of 48 involving following interval and education. Quite clearly, these data and analyses provide little

Table 9.9. Summary of the magnitude and statistical significance of selected interactions between inter-birth intervals and mothers' education[a,b]

Country	Age segment (in completed months)	Pairwise interactions							
		Edu(2)* PI1	Edu(3) PI1	Edu(2)* PI2	Edu(3)* PI2	Edu(2)* FC	Edu(3)* FC	PI1* FC	PI2* FC
Colombia	12–59	—	—	—	—	—	—	−.5589 (.2794)	−.7806 (.3199)
Costa Rica	6–11	—	—	—	—	—	—	−1.087 (.4203)	—
Ecuador	6–11	.8019 (.3147)	—	—	—	—	—	—	—
Haiti	0	—	.9089 (.4137)	—	—	—	—	—	—
	12–59	—	—	—	—	−.7367 (.3588)	—	—	—
Jamaica	6–11	—	—	—	—	—	—	—	−.7186 (.3378)
	12–59	—	—	—	—	—	—	—	−.8383 (.3788)
Panama	6–11	2.286 (.9445)	1.943 (4.989)	4.783 (1.865)	4.552 (1.877)	—	—	—	—
Dominican Republic	12–59	—	—	—	—	—	—	—	−.6462 (.3286)
Venezuela	0–11	—	1.086 (.4121)	.9501 (.4532)	—	—	—	—	—

[a] The variables PI1, PI2, and FCX are defined as in Table 9.2. Edu(2) corresponds to primary education and Edu(3) corresponds to education levels at or beyond secondary.

[b] In parentheses appear the asymptotic standard errors of the estimated effects.

basis for arguing the existence of contingencies which weaken or reinforce the effects of pace of child-bearing on infant mortality. These results are not unlike those obtained in other investigations (Hobcraft *et al.*, 1983; Palloni and Tienda, 1986).

A More Complete Model: Measuring the Effects of Breast-feeding

The tenor of the propositions discussed earlier suggests that the models estimated before could be better specified. In so far as breast-feeding is an *intervening variable*, its absence from the model would not cause biases in the estimates but would leave in obscurity the mechanisms through which inter-birth interval affects mortality. One would expect that the magnitude of the estimates obtained above would be substantially reduced once the effects of breast-feeding are accounted for. Measuring the effects of breast-feeding is quite complex, and the appropriate procedures have been thoroughly examined elsewhere (Palloni and Millman, 1983 and 1985). However, three of the most relevant issues will be briefly mentioned here.

(*a*) In order to avoid truncation and simultaneity biases, the mortality risks in an age segment $x, x + n$, are examined as a function of a dichotomic variable representing breast-feeding. This variable takes on a value of 1 if the child was breast-fed for at least x months and a value of zero otherwise. This strategy conduces to loss of information but makes it possible to avoid exaggeration of effects.

(*b*) To control for the effects of pre-existing health conditions, two proxies of health status at birth are used: the proportions of total pregnancies that ended in wastage and of multiple births. These are far from perfect measures but do remove a fraction of confounding effects.

(*c*) A shift in the sample base is required. In fact, WFS collected information on breast-feeding only for the last and next-to-last births. This is a very selected sample and creates problems which have been described elsewhere (Palloni and Millman, 1983). It suffices to say here that selectivity biases created by the peculiar nature of the sample are not important for the estimation of effects of breast-feeding and birth intervals on infant mortality (Palloni and Tienda, 1986).

The baseline model estimated before was re-estimated on a restricted sample of last and next-to-last births. I will discuss the results obtained in two countries (Peru and Costa Rica), which contrast sharply in terms of levels of mortality, fertility, breast-feeding practices, and contraceptive prevalence.

The first panel of Table 9.10 displays the estimated effects from a model exactly analogous to (1). By and large the magnitudes of the coefficents are somewhat lower than those appearing in Table 9.4. However, they remain properly signed and statistically significant whenever they had been so

Table 9.10. Logit regression coefficients of alternative model specifications for the relations between breast-feeding, pace of child-bearing, and infant early and childhood mortality, Peru 1977 and Costa Rica 1976

Model 1[a, c]

	Peru					Costa Rica				
	Age segments					Age segments				
Variable	0	1-2	3-5	6-11	12-59	0	1-2	3-5	6-11	12-59
PI1	-.7001	-.4679	-.3102	.2691	-.1990	-.6551	-.5627	-.4877	.5653	-.8852
	(.1430)	(.2690)	(.2712)	(.2218)	(.1566)	(.2340)	(.3914)	(.4345)	(.3347)	(.3831)
PI2	-.9248	-.6226	-.7716	-1.195	-.5920	-.6833	-2.073	-.2616	-.6940	-.8658
	(.1694)	(.3156)	(.3381)	(.3116)	(.1879)	(.2732)	(.7420)	(.4743)	(.4075)	(.4461)
FCX	—	—	1.227	.8931	.5298	—	—	.8734	1.173	-.3396
			(.4507)	(.2789)	(.1535)			(.6324)	(.3498)	(.4731)

Model 2[b, c]

	Peru					Costa Rica				
	Age segments					Age segments				
Variable	0	1-2	3-5	6-11	12-59	0	1-2	3-5	6-11	12-59
PI1	-.4533	-.4367	.2867	-.2429	-.2023	-.3741	-.3093	-.3010	.4954	-.8674
	(.1534)	(.2691)	(.2713)	(.2224)	(.1569)	(.2453)	(.3960)	(.4372)	(.3376)	(.3860)
PI2	-.7836	-.5475	-.7398	-1.156	-.5969	-.5148	-1.882	-.1422	-.6767	-.8540
	(.1787)	(.3163)	(.3387)	(.3124)	(.1882)	(.2830)	(.7358)	(.4782)	(.4078)	(.4473)
FCX	—	—	1.128	.7937	.5413	—	—	.4356	1.055	-.3602
			(.4537)	(.2830)	(.1561)			(.6359)	(.3569)	(.4764)
BFX	-2.903	-.9486	-.5398	-.4194	.0544	-2.930	-2.093	-1.465	-.4596	-.1385
	(.1357)	(.2127)	(.2284)	(.1932)	(.1354)	(.2447)	(.3914)	(.3989)	(.3130)	(.3948)

[a] Model 1 includes the background and control variables already defined in the text but *excludes* the indicator of breast-feeding.
[b] Model 2 is as model 1 but *includes* an indicator of breast-feeding.
[c] Numbers in parentheses are standard errors.

before. Thus, the restricted sample of last and next-to-last births leads to conclusions that are in accord with those drawn from previous estimates. The second panel shows the coefficients in a model which *includes* the indicator of breast-feeding (BFX). First, note that the estimated effects of breast-feeding are strong, properly signed, and statistically significant everywhere except in the last age segment in Peru and the last two age segments in Costa Rica. These estimates, particularly those corresponding to the first age segment, should be taken with some caution, for they may be somewhat inflated as a consequence of having included only poor measures of health status. What is noteworthy, however, is a second feature of the figures presented in the second panel: with the exception of those corresponding to the first age segments, the estimated effects of PI1, PI2, and FCX remain almost unaltered if compared with those in the first panel. Taken at face value, the result should be interpreted as indicating that breast-feeding is *not* an important mediating mechanism between pace of child-bearing and survival status. This is a rather surprising and unexpected conclusion. Its complete verification, however, requires (*a*) an explanation of why attenuation effects *do* occur in the first age segment, (*b*) the accounting for alternative mediating mechanisms, and (*c*) discarding the possibility that systematic measurement errors are *not* affecting the indicator of breast-feeding. I will deal with each of these issues in turn.

The effects of PI1 and PI2 in the first age segment may be greatly attenuated when BFX is included in the model, precisely because there is no efficient control for pre-existing health conditions. Children who were born after very short intervals (less than 18 months) may have very low weight at birth, and as a consequence their general health status may be significantly impaired. Poor health status may simultaneously prevent breast-feeding and lead to death shortly after birth. Thus, breast-feeding and survival are associated through an artefactual relation. The first consequence of this is that the effects of BFX should be strongly attenuated when a proxy for pre-existing health status, such as length of preceding interval, is controlled for. This is, in fact, the case (figures are not shown). The second consequence is the converse of the first: the effects of length of preceding birth interval in the first age segment should be significantly reduced once the variable BFX is controlled. This is what happens in Table 9.10 (compare the first columns in the upper and lower panels).

Alternative mediating mechanisms have been reviewed elsewhere (Palloni and Millman, 1985). Among them, the most crucial appear to be competition for material resources and maternal care. Needless to say, their measurement and the assessment of their effects remain elusive. The only available methods of evaluating their importance appear to be of a residual nature.

Errors in reporting of breast-feeding durations which are systematically associated with survival status of the child could produce serious downward biases in the estimates of the effects of breast-feeding. Simultaneously, they may lead to playing down the attenuating effects of breast-feeding on pace of child-bearing. Elsewhere, it has been shown that there are compelling reasons and quite strong evidence to support this conjecture (Palloni and Millman, 1985). The use of a somewhat crude procedure to eliminate the distorting effects of errors in the reports of duration has been shown to produce two results: first, the absolute magnitude of the direct effects of breast-feeding increase without exceptions, and second, the attentuation of the estimated effects of pace of child-bearing becomes demonstrably strong.

Other measurement errors, however, may still be operating. First, the variable FCX (particularly FC12) is too crudely defined. It clearly does not permit an appropriate discrimination between index children whose health can be endangered by following conceptions occurring after their twelfth month and those whose mothers do not become pregnant again. As a consequence, introducing a control for breast-feeding—even if breast-feeding is accurately measured—can hardly tap the general mechanism leading from rapid conception to health deterioration. Second, even if no errors affected the *reports* on breast-feeding duration, there is still one major obstacle related to our inability to distinguish between the *existence* and the *intensity* of lactation. It is hardly believable that all children who were breast-fed for a certain length of time received the same amount of milk or were similarly engaged in supplementation. Variability in the intensity of breast-feeding is probably related to survival status. It may thus contaminate the estimates of the direct effects of breast-feeding as well as distort (downwardly bias) the magnitude of attenuation of the effects associated with pace of child-bearing.

In summary, the negative evidence regarding the role of breast-feeding as a mediating mechanism between pace of child-bearing and survival status of children is somewhat inconclusive. On the one hand it is very likely that other mediating mechanisms do operate. On the other hand, different types of measurement error may be responsible for the apparent failure of the models to show systematic attenuation effects.

Conclusions

The evidence presented in support of the hypotheses linking pace of child-bearing and early child mortality seems very strong. Without exceptions, the impact is large and statistically significant in the first month of life, less so during the periods 1–2 and 3–5 months, and again strong over the interval 6–11 months. An attenuation is evident during the age interval 1–4 years. The effects of preceding and following interval translate into more or less comparable average proportionate changes in mortality. By and large, however, those attributable to the latter are strongest over the age segments 3–5 and 6–11 months.

Relative risks and population-attributable risks highlight the enormous diadvantages associated with short preceding interval and rapid following conceptions. Relative death risks of those in the most disadvantages categories reaching values of 2.0 or 3.0 are common. In only one exceptional case do these relative risks turn out to be close to unity. On average, the hypothetical reduction in child mortality (below five years of age) that would result from a slowing down in the pattern of reproduction that eliminated disadvantaged categories, can reach values as high as 20 per cent and be no less than 12 per cent.

The evidence marshalled for the understanding of contingencies and mechanisms of operations is not as strong, however. In the first place, although there is substantial diversity in the magnitude and age patterns of the effects, it defies any systematic organization. Contextual or institutional properties such as countries' mortality levels, breast-feeding patterns, and contraceptive prevalence are of only limited utility as explanatory factors. Similarly, individual variables that serve as proxies for access to, and capability to use, information, and socio-economic standing do not depress the negative effects of shortly spaced births. Nor do the joint occurrence of short preceding birth interval and rapid following conception lead to any more deleterious consequences than those that each of them would generate separately. Secondly, little support was found for the hypothesis that breast-feeding is the main mechanism through which the negative effects of birth interval operate. Perhaps better measures of breast-feeding would bring its role into sharper focus or the utilization of structural equation models would tease out its real impact. For the time being, however, we should assign to other mechanisms as much priority as originally was assigned to breast-feeding.

References

Baldion, E. (1981), *Colombia: Aspectos socio-demograficos relevantes en el estudio de la mortalidad infantil y su asociacion con la fecundidad*, CELADE Publicaciones, ser. D, no. 102, UN Centro Latinoamericano de Demografia, Santiago, Chile.

Cantrelle, P., and H. Leridon (1971), 'Breastfeeding, Mortality in Childhood and Fertility in a Rural Zone of Senegal', *Population Studies* 25(3), 505–33.

Cleland, J. G., and Z. Sathar (1984), 'The Effect of Birth Spacing on Childhood Mortality in Pakistan', *Population Studies* 38, 401–18.

DeSweemer, C. (1984), 'The Influence of Child Spacing on Child Survival', *Population Studies* 38, 47–72.

Eastman, N. J. (1944), 'The Effect of the Interval Between Births on Maternal and Fetal Outlook', *American Journal of Obstetrics and Gynaecology*, 47, 445–6.

Federeci, N., and L. Terrenato (1980), 'Biological Determinants of Early Life Mortality', paper presented at the Seminar on Biological Aspects of Mortality and Length of Life, Italy, International Union for the Scientific Study of Population.

Federick, J., and P. Adelstein (1973), 'Influence of Pregnancy Spacing on the Outcome of Pregnancy', *British Medical Journal* 4, 753–6.

Gray, R. H. (1981), 'Birth Intervals, Postpartum Sexual Abstinence and Child Health in H. Page and R. Lesthaeghe (eds.), *Child-spacing in Tropical Africa: Traditions and Change*, Academic Press, New York.

Harfouche, J. K. (1970), 'The Importance of Breastfeeding', *Journal of Tropical Pediatrics* 16, 135–75.

Hobcraft, J. N., J. W. McDonald, and S. O. Rutstein (1983), 'Socio-economic Factors in Infant and Child Mortality: A Cross-national Comparison', paper presented at the annual meetings of the Population Association of America, San Diego.

Jain, A. K. (1969), 'Pregnancy Outcome and Time Required for Next Conception', *Population Studies* 23, 421–33.

Jelliffe, D. B. (1966), *The Assessment of Nutritional Status of the Community*, WHO Monograph Series no. 53, World Health Organization, Geneva.

Knodel, J. (1968), 'Infant Mortality in Three Bavarian Villages: An Analysis of Family Histories from the 19th Century', *Population Studies* 23, 297–318.

—— and A. Hermalin (1984), 'Effects of Birth Rank, Maternal Age, Birth Interval and Sibship Size on Infant and Child Mortality: Evidence from 18th and 19th Century Reproductive Histories', *American Journal of Public Health* 74, 1098–106.

Martin, L., T. J. Trussell, F. Reyes-Salvail, and N. Shah (1983), 'Covariates of Child Mortality in the Philippines, Indonesia and Pakistan: An Analysis Based on Hazards Models', *Population Studies* 37(3), 417–32.

Palloni, A. (1985), 'Health Conditions in Latin America and Policies for Mortality Change' in J. Vallin and A. Lopez (eds.), *Health Policy, Social Policy and Mortality Prospects*, INED/IVSSP, Ordina Editions, Liège, 465–92.

—— and S. Millman (1983), 'Effects of Breastfeeding on Infant Mortality', proposal submitted to the National Institute of Health.

—— —— (1985), 'Effects of Interbirth Intervals and Breastfeeding on Infant and Early Childhood Mortality', paper presented at the Population Association of America Meetings, Boston.

—— and M. Tienda (1986), 'The Effects of Breastfeeding and Pace of Childbearing on Mortality at Early Ages, *Demography* 23(1), 31–52.

Preston, S. H. (ed.) (1978), *The Effect of Infant and Child Mortality on Fertility*, Academic Press, New York.

Puffer, R. R., and C. V. Serrano (1973), *Patterns of Mortality in Childhood*, Harvard University Press, Cambridge, Mass.

Rutstein, S. O. (1983), *Infant and Child Mortality: Levels, Trends and Demographic Differentials*, WFS Comparative Studies: Cross-national Summary, no. 24 (September), International Statistical Institute, Voorburg, Netherlands.

Shapiro, S., E. Schlesinger, and R. E. L. Nesbitt (1968), *Infant, Perinatal, Maternal, and Childhood Mortality in the United States*, Harvard University Press, Cambridge, Mass.

Trussell, J., and C. Hammerslough (1983), 'A Hazards-model Analysis of the Covariates of Infant and Child Mortality in Sri Lanka', *Demography* 20(1), 1–26.

Winikoff, B. (1983), 'The Effects of Birth Spacing on Child and Maternal Health', *Studies in Family Planning* 14(10), 231–45.

Wolfers, D., and S. Scrimshaw (1975), 'Child Survival and Intervals Between Pregnancies in Guayaquil, Equador', *Population Studies* 29(3), 479–96.

Wray, J. D. (1971), 'Population Pressure on Families: Family Size and Child-spacing', *Reports on Population/Family Planning* 9, 403–58.

—— and A. L. Aguirre (1969), 'Protein Calorie Malnutrition in Candelaria, Colombia. 1. Prevalence: Social and Demographic Causal Factors', *Journal of Tropical Pediatrics* 15, 76–98.

Wyon, J. B., and J. E. Gordon (1962), 'A Long-term Prospective-type Field Study of Population Dynamics in the Punjab, India' in C. V. Kiser (ed.), *Research on Family Planning*, Princeton University Press, Princeton, NJ.

10 Mortality and Health Dynamics at Older Ages

GEORGE C. MYERS

Center for Demographic Studies, Duke University, Durham, North Carolina, United States

The continuing reductions in mortality rates and consequent increases in survival for inhabitants of many developed countries, even at advanced ages, have raised major issues of both theoretical and practical importance. How likely are future reductions in the face of seeming biological restraints on lifespan? Have the increases in survival been accompanied by increases in survival free of disease and disablement? What are the changing patterns of disease that have been responsible for these declines and which are apt to be involved in future trends? And of paramount importance, what are the implications of these developments on both individual and societal well-being in health in the face of modifications in the size and composition of populations?

Demographers have been generally remiss in failing to anticipate recent movements in mortality. Tied to fairly mechanistic conceptions of the process of mortality change, those engaged in preparing population projections and forecasting mortality failed to anticipate the reductions that have occurred in the past decade and a half in most developed countries following a period of relative stagnation. Mathematical and statistical approaches to forecasting mortality, for the most part, have not proved to be sufficiently flexible in handling fluctuating periods of levelling off and advance that have characterized experiences in this century. Whereas downward trends at earlier ages (such as in infant mortality) and for infectious diseases follow fairly well-defined patterns, trends at advanced ages, which mainly reflect the incidence and fatality from chronic diseases, have proved more difficult to handle.

Elsewhere I have suggested that population policy dealing with population ageing and mortality has been relatively neglected due to assumptions that (1) trends in these dimensions are fairly predictable, (2) the nature of the phenomenon is unmodifiable, and (3) mortality, in contrast to fertility, is not a major factor affecting population structure. There are solid grounds for questioning such assumptions for countries that have passed through the major stages of a demographic transition (Myers, 1982). Indeed, in spite of these past deficiencies there are a number of reasons why demographers should begin to address some of these important issues, especially as they relate to mortality trends at older ages.

First, in more developed countries a large majority of total deaths occurs at older ages. This trend has been continually upwards, as we will examine later in this chapter. Any study of mortality patterns and trends for these countries must necessarily emphasize the features at older ages, although this topic has received relatively little direct demographic attention in the past.

Second, mortality levels, although higher at older than at younger ages, have been declining sharply for many countries. This has led towards increasing survival levels both up to the older ages and throughout the later periods of life. Although earlier analyses generally showed that improved survival at younger ages played a predominant role in extending life expectancy at birth (United Nations, 1982), recent examinations demonstrate that mortality declines at later ages have contributed considerably to changes in life expectation at birth. Pollard (1982) found that in Australia during the period 1971–9 mortality changes at age 65 and above accounted for 35 per cent of the 2.89 year male improvement in life expectation at birth and half of the 3.16 year female gain. In Japan for the period 1975–80, 42 per cent of the 1.71 year improvement in male life expectation could be attributed to reductions at age 65 and above, as could 55 per cent of the 1.95 years gained by females. Furthermore, although numerical life expectation gains have been greater at birth than at exact age 65, the proportionate gains at both ages are very comparable.

Third, in spite of general declines in mortality at older ages, there is considerable variation in age-specific rates and levels of survival between countries at fairly similar levels of social and economic development. Moreover, important differentials exist within countries, as between urban and rural areas, by socio-economic levels, and by age, ethnicity, and sex. For example, Lopez (1983) points out that shifting sex–mortality differentials at older ages have accounted for over a half of the widening gap between life expectation at birth of males and females.

Fourth, in light of these developments, there are pragmatic reasons for furthering our understanding of mortality patterns. Dynamic changes in the size and structure of the aged population obviously require deeper knowledge of past mortality trends and greater attention to forecasting of mortality. To do so demands insight into the factors responsible for changes in mortality at adult and older ages, especially the disease process, modifications in individual health behaviour, and the role of the health services and interventions. Mortality changes simply do not occur in a mechanistic way, they are the product of complex interplay between biological factors and the environment, mediated by social forces. This is especially true of the broad shifts from communicable to non-communicable, chronic disease. This raises important issues about the scope for further mortality reductions, which may be constrained by any of the forces that are involved.

Demographers are able to elucidate the factual matters relating to mortality patterns, but they are also in a position to delve more deeply into the factors producing changes. In a sense this broadened commitment may be viewed as analogous to the consideration of the determinants influencing fertility. While the chapters in this book attest to the importance of biological and behavioural factors in determining mortality patterns at birth or childhood, it is no less the case that such concerns should be emphasized in studying mortality patterns and trends at later ages. Moreover, the methodological tools available to the demographer, in particular life-table and other survival method approaches, are eminently suitable for studying such a complex and dynamic process.

In this discussion we will examine developments in mortality patterns at older ages and consider ways in which morbidity and related disability are involved. Only evidence for more developed countries is drawn upon. The statistics reported are drawn from both published and unpublished data from the World Health Organization. It is assumed that the data are reasonably accurate for the 19 countries included in the major portion of the analysis. Horiuchi and Coale (1982) found that for such countries age exaggeration in both census enumeration and death registration is minimal and that in general model estimation of life expectation at age 65 would actually lead to higher estimates of expectation than those reported officially. None the less, recent analyses of data quality in the United States suggest that caution must be used in interpreting any data on the older population (US Bureau of the Census, 1984 appendix B).

Mortality Trends

Deaths at Older Ages

The importance of examining mortality at older ages is clearly pointed out by considering data on the proportions of all deaths that occur at ages 65 and above and 85 and above (Table 10.1). These figures express not only differences in composition of the population but also relative mortality conditions at various ages. The latter will be examined by considering rates later in the chapter.

For these 19 more developed countries, the unweighted average for deaths at age 65 and over indicates that over two-thirds of all male deaths (67.1 per cent) and nearly 80 per cent of female deaths (79.9 per cent) occur at older ages. In Sweden slightly over three-quarters of male deaths occur at later ages, and the other Scandinavian countries have similar proportions.

Table 10.1.   Proportion of all deaths at age 65 and over and age 85 and over, by sex, 1980 or 1981

Country	Male		Female	
	65 +	85 +	65 +	85 +
Australia	62.4	9.5	76.2	16.0
Austria	70.2	9.8	85.2	22.6
Bulgaria	64.7	8.0	77.2	14.5
Denmark	72.0	13.6	80.4	25.2
France*	67.4	11.5	84.3	31.6
Germany, Federal Republic	71.2	9.7	84.5	21.7
Hungary	62.1	6.6	77.4	15.4
Iceland	67.8	19.0	82.9	27.8
Japan	64.8	9.7	76.0	19.8
Netherlands	71.3	14.1	81.3	26.0
New Zealand	64.6	10.1	74.7	22.0
Norway	73.6	15.1	85.0	27.9
Poland*	56.2	5.6	72.8	17.1
Sweden	75.1	14.6	84.5	27.2
Switzerland	71.0	12.7	84.0	26.6
UK—England and Wales	71.8	9.8	83.1	25.6
UK—Scotland	68.3	8.3	81.1	22.1
United States	61.7	12.0	75.0	25.7
Yugoslavia*	58.8	6.6	72.0	13.5

* Data for 1980
Source: World Health Organisation, World Health Statistics Annual, 1983: US National Center for Health Statistics, Monthly Vital Statistics Report, vol. 33, no. 3 supplement, 1984; Australian Bureau of Statistics, Deaths Australia 1982, no. 3302, 1983.

In contrast, Poland and Yugoslavia report less than 60 per cent of male deaths at later ages. For females, 6 countries have more than 84 per cent of total deaths occurring at later ages.

At age 85 and over, the average for the 19 countries is nearly 11 per cent for males, with Iceland leading the way with 19 per cent and Norway, Sweden, and the Netherlands at over 14 per cent. The Eastern European countries have particularly low levels. Nearly 32 per cent of French females die after age 85, but noteworthy is the fact that over a quarter of all female deaths in eight other countries occur at these very advanced ages.

The relatively high proportion of deaths at older ages has obvious importance for the provision of medical services, in terms of facilities (hospitals), and such like the training of personnel, and the whole nature of treatment and care. It is also important in our understanding of mortality patterns and trends to recognize that deaths at older ages represent the great majority of total deaths in these countries and that relatively high proportions of these deaths are at extremely old ages. Yet most of the readily available mortality statistics (for example, published data from the

UN and WHO) are reported only for specified terminal ages of 80 or 85 years. With nearly a quarter of female deaths occurring at age 85 and over, more detailed age tabulation of data would seem to be recommended. Moreover, the proportions of deaths at older ages have been increasing rapidly in many countries. In the United States, for example, deaths at age 60 and over for both sexes increased from 70.2 per cent in 1967 to 75.0 per cent in 1979 (Myers and Manton, 1984).

Comparisons in Life Expectation

The data presented in Table 10.2 are drawn from the most current life-tables prepared by the World Health Organization using standardized methodo- logical procedures. Data for Australia and the United States are from recent national tables that were prepared using fairly comparable approaches.

Life expectation at birth for males exceeds 70 years for 12 of the 19 countries, with Japan leading the way with an expectation at birth of 74.1 years and Iceland only somewhat lower (73.4). The lowest levels among those countries are found for the Eastern European countries of Bulgaria, Hungary, Poland, and Yugoslavia. The same countries represent the extremes at age 65, but noteworthy is the high level of life expectation at this age for the United States and the low position of the Netherlands in comparison with other countries. At age 85, the US level is the highest. In contrast, levels of life expectation for males at age 85 in Iceland, Sweden, and Switzerland place these countries much lower in comparative terms. Comparative values for life expectation at later ages for some countries may differ sharply from similar comparisons of levels of life expectation at birth. This is indicated by a rank correlation coefficient of 0.67 between life expectation at birth and at age 85. In terms of survival, 80 per cent of Japanese males could expect to live to age 65 under the current mortality schedule, but only 61 per cent of males in Hungary. At age 85 the gap is even wider: 8.2 per cent of live births could expect to survive until then in Hungary, compared with 21.6 per cent in Japan.

To examine further variations at older ages, the percentages of life-table population surviving between ages 65 and 75 and ages 75 and 85 years are presented in the next two columns. Japanese survival, which was the highest up to age 65, also continues at the highest level after that point up to age 75. However, in the interval of 75 to 85 years, the survival levels for Iceland and the United States are much greater even than those for Japan.

Thus, we can see some quite divergent patterns of survival among countries from these aggregate life-table data for males. Some countries display low survival throughout the life course (such as Hungary and Poland), while high-survival countries reveal somewhat more diverse patterns. On the one hand, there is Japan with high survival levels up to an age 75; others such as Iceland, with moderate survival up to 65, but high

Table 10.2. Measures of life expectancy and survival by sex for selected countries, 1980 or 1981
(a) Males

Country	Expectation of life at age			Per cent surviving to		Per cent surviving between	
	0	65	85	65	85	65 and 75	75 and 85
Australia	71.4	13.9	4.7	74.6	17.4	65.2	35.8
Austria	69.3	13.0	4.4	70.6	12.6	62.3	28.6
Bulgaria	68.9	13.0	4.6	70.3	12.3	61.9	29.7
Denmark	71.4	13.7	4.7	73.9	16.2	64.6	33.9
France*	70.8	14.3	4.8	72.1	17.8	67.3	36.6
Germany, Federal Republic	70.2	13.1	4.4	72.8	13.5	62.3	29.7
Hungary	65.5	11.6	4.0	61.0	8.2	55.1	24.5
Iceland	73.4	15.2	4.6	76.9	24.0	69.2	45.1
Japan	74.1	15.1	4.9	80.2	21.6	71.7	37.6
Netherlands	72.8	14.1	5.0	77.7	18.2	65.6	35.7
New Zealand*	69.9	12.9	3.7	72.6	13.2	62.2	29.2
Norway	72.7	14.3	4.7	77.0	19.0	67.3	36.7
Poland*	66.1	12.2	4.3	63.3	9.5	57.6	26.0
Sweden*	72.8	14.4	4.5	77.4	18.9	68.3	35.8
Switzerland	72.5	14.4	4.6	77.0	19.2	68.1	36.5
UK—England and Wales	71.2	13.1	4.4	74.6	14.4	62.3	31.0
UK—Scotland	69.2	12.2	4.2	69.5	11.0	57.8	27.5
United States	70.4	14.4	5.2	71.2	18.5	66.0	40.0
Yugoslavia	67.8	13.0	4.2	68.5	12.4	61.8	29.4

(b) Females

Country	Expectation of life at age			Per cent surviving to		Per cent surviving between	
	0	65	85	65	85	65 and 75	75 and 85
Australia	78.4	18.1	5.7	86.4	37.7	81.1	53.8
Austria	76.4	16.4	4.8	85.2	28.2	77.8	42.6
Bulgaria	74.4	15.1	4.8	83.2	21.9	72.1	36.4
Denmark	77.6	17.9	5.9	83.9	34.5	79.9	51.5
France*	79.1	18.9	6.0	87.1	39.7	83.9	54.3
Germany, Federal Republic	76.9	16.9	5.1	85.5	30.3	78.9	45.0
Hungary	73.0	14.8	4.6	78.9	20.5	71.0	36.6
Iceland	79.9	18.4	6.8	89.3	37.0	81.1	51.1
Japan	79.6	18.4	5.8	89.0	38.2	83.2	51.6
Netherlands	79.6	18.8	6.3	88.0	39.6	82.8	54.3
New Zealand*	75.6	16.6	5.2	82.2	29.5	76.2	47.0
Norway	79.5	18.4	5.9	88.5	38.2	82.6	52.3
Poland*	74.6	15.7	5.0	82.0	23.9	74.8	39.0
Sweden*	79.1	18.2	5.7	87.6	36.9	82.2	51.2
Switzerland	79.4	18.5	5.8	88.2	38.4	83.6	52.0
UK—England and Wales	77.2	17.2	5.6	84.7	32.1	78.3	48.4
UK—Scotland	75.3	15.9	5.2	81.4	26.2	73.7	43.8
United States	77.9	18.6	6.5	83.7	38.6	80.6	57.2
Yugoslavia	73.3	15.2	4.5	81.3	22.2	73.0	37.4

* Data for 1980.

Sources: World Health Organization special tabulations, except for US National Center for Health Statistics, *Monthly Vital Statistics Report*, vol. 33, no. 3 supplement, 1984, and Australian Bureau of Statistics, *Deaths Australia 1982*, no. 3302, 1983.

levels thereafter; and the United States, with relatively low survival up to age 65, but relatively high survival thereafter.

The inter-country patterns of female life expectation and survival among countries are generally similar to males, but at much higher levels in all cases. Large sex differences in life expectation at birth are found for France (8.3 years) and Poland (8.5), although the relative levels differ greatly. There does not appear to be any pattern of male–female differences in life expectation with levels of life expectation. About 6–7 years difference in life expectation at birth seems average, with about 3–4 years at age 65 and no more than two years difference at age 85 (for extended discussion, see Lopez and Ruzicka, 1983).

The survival of females to later ages is considerably greater than for males, 87.1 per cent surviving to age 65 in France compared with 72.1 per cent of males, and in Poland 82.0 compared to 63.3 per cent. For France, 39.7 per cent of females survive to age 85 compared with 17.8 per cent of males. Comparable differences are found for the United States and the Netherlands. At the advanced ages, survival is particularly high for females in France between ages 65 and 85, Japan and Switzerland between 65 and 75, and in the United States between 75 and 85.

As is the case for males, some distinctive patterns of survival prevail over the life course in different countries. As countries move toward higher levels of life expectation, increasingly the improvements must necessarily occur at older ages. This is particularly true for females where life-table survival to older ages (that is, age 65) is in the 80–90 per cent range. Attention, therefore, must be directed at the mortality levels that prevail at specific older ages and how they have changed over time.

Comparison of Age-specific Death Rates

Two-year average death rates for males and females are presented in Table 10.3. Among the 19 countries considerable variation exists in age-specific rates, with the Eastern European countries having much higher rates than the others. For males, the rates are also very high for Scotland and New Zealand. In contrast, the levels for Iceland are uniformly low. What is particularly important is the lack of uniformity in relative levels over the older ages. The rates for Japan and Sweden are low up to age 75 (and Switzerland up to 80), but then deteriorate somewhat, while those for the United States are relatively low at ages above 75 and for the Netherlands above age 80.

These relative shifts also are found for females. US rates are among the lowest after age 75. Australia's rates also show relative improvement with age compared with other countries, and Iceland's rates became relatively low after age 80. French rates, which rank as lowest up to age 80, then become relatively higher, as do those of Switzerland. These shifts for both

Table 10.3. Average death rates at older ages, by sex and age, 1980–1 (in thousands)

	Male					Female				
	65–9	70–4	75–9	80–4	85+	65–9	70–4	75–9	80–4	85+
Australia	32.9	52.1	81.2	122.1	205.4	15.8	25.9	45.0	77.9	161.8
Austria	35.7	58.2	94.6	147.4	227.4	17.8	31.8	59.4	108.2	207.8
Bulgaria	36.9	60.0	95.3	148.7	229.1	22.7	43.1	73.9	130.8	215.9
Denmark	33.5	53.6	84.1	123.9	214.9	17.1	27.5	46.8	83.1	170.7
France	30.4	47.8	75.4	119.9	207.3	12.4	22.2	41.2	77.7	167.2
Germany, Federal Republic	35.6	58.5	93.0	141.8	225.0	16.9	30.3	56.2	99.9	192.8
Hungary	46.1	70.9	112.0	153.6	261.8	25.2	42.6	74.3	124.3	220.5
Iceland	25.3	42.8	62.0	134.2	192.5	15.3	23.9	44.0	73.3	144.0
Japan	24.8	42.8	74.1	120.7	206.6	13.2	24.3	46.8	85.4	174.1
Netherlands	32.0	52.0	79.7	119.3	198.4	13.7	23.8	43.4	77.2	157.8
New Zealand*	36.8	57.0	93.3	145.9	269.1	21.8	32.0	55.7	91.2	191.5
Norway	30.4	47.4	75.7	118.8	206.3	13.8	24.5	45.0	82.6	169.0
Poland*	42.7	66.2	103.2	158.4	230.4	20.9	36.4	65.1	118.2	200.8
Sweden*	28.4	47.0	75.9	123.7	222.1	14.0	24.7	46.0	84.2	174.0
Switzerland	29.2	47.3	73.9	121.7	215.8	13.1	23.4	44.8	81.6	175.0
UK–England and Wales	36.4	58.7	92.3	139.3	228.8	18.6	30.6	52.4	90.0	184.0
UK–Scotland	42.6	66.8	102.1	155.2	246.6	23.7	37.2	59.9	99.4	190.8
United States	33.4	50.1	73.5	130.6	184.7	17.1	26.3	41.5	71.2	144.8
Yugoslavia*	36.4	58.8	88.6	149.1	236.1	22.1	40.1	66.3	125.2	222.4

* Figures for 1980 only.

Source: World Health Organization, World Health Statistics Annual, 1983; US National Center for Health Statistics, Monthly Vital Statistics Report, vol. 33, no. 3 supplement, 1984; Australian Bureau of Statistics, Deaths Australia 1982, no. 3302, 1983.

males and females in relative levels by age do not permit any ready explanations, but do suggest the complexity of modelling age patterns of mortality at these advanced ages.

Sex–Mortality Ratios

The variations in age-specific death rates between countries and at different older ages produce some interesting differences in sex–mortality ratios. Table 10.4 illustrates that the differentials decline by age for all countries except Iceland, where they fluctuate (perhaps owing to the small numbers of deaths), and New Zealand. The highest ratios of excess male mortality are found for France up to age 80, which reflects the relatively low female death rates at these ages. The Eastern European countries, which have the highest relative death rates at older ages, actually have the lowest sex–mortality ratios. Higher ratios can, of course, result from various combinations of above- or below-average death rates for either males and females. Even disregarding the terminal age interval 85 and over, in which rates can be distorted by compositional factors, it seems clear that higher relative death rates for both males and females, especially the latter, produce lower sex ratios. High sex ratios most often appear to result from strikingly lower female death rates compared to males.

Table 10.4. Sex–mortality ratios at older ages, by age 1980–1

Country	Age 65–9	70–4	75–9	80–4	85 +
Australia	208	201	180	157	127
Austria	201	183	159	136	109
Bulgaria	163	139	129	114	106
Denmark	196	195	180	149	126
France	245	215	183	154	124
Germany, Federal Republic	211	193	166	142	117
Hungary	183	166	151	132	119
Iceland	165	179	141	142	134
Japan	188	176	158	141	119
Netherlands	234	218	184	154	126
New Zealand	169	178	168	160	140
Norway	220	194	168	144	122
Poland	204	182	158	134	115
Sweden	203	190	165	147	128
Switzerland	223	202	165	149	123
UK—England and Wales	196	192	176	155	124
UK—Scotland	180	180	170	156	129
United States	195	190	177	155	128
Yugoslavia	165	147	134	119	106

Source: Based on data from Table 10.3.

Changes in Death Rates at Older Ages

Temporal patterns in death rates at older ages between average rates for 1950–4 and 1965–9, and 1950–4 and 1980–1, are examined with the earlier period as a base of 100 (Table 10.5). It has been widely noted that there was a stagnation or even increase of death rates from the middle of the 1950s until the later years of the 1960s for many developed countries (United Nations, 1982). In the 1970s rates began declining again for many countries.

Table 10.5. Percentage changes in death rates at older ages by sex and age, 1965–9 and 1980–1 compared with 1950–4 (death rate 1950–4 = 100)

Country and year	Age 65–9	70–4	75–9	80–4	85 +
Australia					
1965–9					
Male	103.5	103.0	100.5	99.5	96.4
Female	88.3	88.5	86.5	89.0	90.1
1980–1					
Male	77.4	80.3	81.1	83.1	83.3
Female	63.5	61.2	61.6	65.4	74.3
Austria					
1965–9					
Male	107.4	105.3	100.4	96.7	96.2
Female	83.3	84.9	85.4	88.5	92.8
1980–1					
Male	84.0	89.4	92.2	90.4	86.2
Female	64.6	65.6	70.6	77.0	86.0
Bulgaria					
1965–9					
Male	75.6	101.4	122.7	96.5	97.7
Female	73.2	103.5	119.4	113.2	107.9
1980–1					
Male	81.4	111.0	115.6	106.0	107.0
Female	68.6	102.5	119.2	118.8	121.6
Denmark					
1965–9					
Male	117.5	107.4	99.6	97.1	94.1
Female	80.6	79.3	77.6	83.9	85.4
1980–1					
Male	113.4	106.9	102.2	91.3	87.5
Female	68.4	61.4	59.2	64.3	71.7
France					
1965–9					
Male	99.8	93.4	88.2	84.6	84.9
Female	74.7	76.2	76.7	78.5	84.9
1980–1					
Male	76.0	75.2	73.8	70.2	68.2
Female	52.83	53.2	56.6	60.8	69.2

Table 10.5.   cont.

Country and year	Age 65–9	70–4	75–9	80–4	85 +
Germany, Federal Republic					
1965–9					
Male	118.9	111.9	101.7	97.2	97.6
Female	81.9	81.0	82.2	86.1	91.7
1980–1					
Male	96.4	98.2	94.8	89.4	85.6
Female	60.6	60.5	64.2	69.0	79.4
Hungary					
1965–9					
Male	95.9	97.4	92.6	91.2	85.1
Female	78.7	81.9	84.2	85.8	89.6
1980–1					
Male	111.0	108.0	103.6	93.8	86.4
Female	79.8	78.7	79.7	79.8	85.4
Iceland					
1965–9					
Male	105.0	99.2	98.1	94.1	102.4
Female	97.3	87.3	92.9	110.0	106.8
1980–1					
Male	92.9	104.9	88.6	82.6	91.7
Female	78.2	69.4	81.8	81.4	78.6
Japan					
1965–9					
Male	78.3	82.3	90.9	98.9	91.0
Female	66.3	72.4	83.1	94.2	87.7
1980–1					
Male	51.4	57.0	66.8	74.4	77.4
Female	39.8	45.1	55.6	65.6	74.3
Netherlands					
1965–9					
Male	118.8	110.5	99.6	93.5	94.0
Female	76.1	77.5	79.4	83.2	91.3
1980–1					
Male	113.8	111.8	101.1	90.6	85.4
Female	58.0	57.2	58.6	62.5	72.8
New Zealand					
1965–9					
Male	106.0	108.1	108.1	103.4	106.0
Female	90.7	86.6	87.5	92.3	95.3
1980–1					
Male	97.0	99.0	104.0	104.1	112.3
Female	89.4	77.8	80.1	79.9	86.4
Norway					
1965–9					
Male	121.5	117.3	108.7	104.2	95.4
Female	89.5	90.6	92.0	93.3	89.7

Table 10.5. cont.

Country and year	Age 65–9	70–4	75–9	80–4	85+
1980–1					
Male	115.6	111.9	107.0	100.7	91.8
Female	71.0	69.4	71.6	75.6	77.4
Poland					
1965–9					
Male	83.0	84.3	82.9	83.2	108.2
Female	70.5	73.8	76.9	78.7	104.2
1980–1					
Male	88.9	89.3	91.7	95.6	114.7
Female	64.8	66.1	72.6	85.2	114.3
Sweden					
1965–9					
Male	99.5	100.5	98.0	93.3	89.6
Female	72.6	75.9	81.0	81.0	84.9
1980–1					
Male	94.0	95.2	91.9	89.5	87.2
Female	57.9	57.0	61.2	64.7	73.5
Switzerland					
1965–9					
Male	95.6	93.9	93.4	91.4	92.7
Female	75.1	76.5	81.3	85.5	93.1
1980–1					
Male	76.5	78.0	77.2	79.0	83.6
Female	50.3	51.9	57.5	62.2	77.0
United Kingdom—England and Wales					
1965–9					
Male	99.4	100.1	95.0	92.3	95.1
Female	84.4	83.6	81.7	83.0	91.4
1980–1					
Male	82.0	86.7	86.2	84.3	86.4
Female	73.2	70.2	68.8	70.8	83.4
United Kingdom—Scotland					
1965–9					
Male	104.7	103.2	95.4	87.6	93.9
Female	81.7	83.7	81.7	78.0	89.3
1980–1					
Male	91.1	94.4	90.1	86.6	87.1
Female	77.0	72.1	69.2	68.6	79.7
United States					
1965–9					
Male	101.7	101.3	99.7	96.2	107.2
Female	84.8	80.8	83.4	86.9	98.6
1980–1					
Male	81.8	85.3	84.2	83.8	91.6
Female	68.2	64.2	62.1	66.8	77.7

Source: Same as Table 10.3.

In the period centred between 1952 and 1967, a considerable number of countries experienced increases in male death rates at older ages. Three overall patterns emerge. In New Zealand, Norway, and the United States, male rates at each age tended to rise or stay the same over this period. A second pattern is found in which death rates increased up to age 75 or 80, but declined at the oldest ages, as in Austria, Bulgaria, Denmark, Germany, the Netherlands, and Scotland. A third group of countries, including France, Hungary, Japan, Sweden, Switzerland, and England and Wales, had declines at all the older ages.

It has been suggested that the increased death rates may reflect cohort differences arising from those groups that experienced deleterious conditions during World War II, for example those who were aged 65–74 in 1965–9 and 35–50 in 1940. However, the mixed categories of countries found in each group confound such a simplistic explanation.

In contrast to males, death rates declined for females at nearly all older ages during the earlier period. In general, death rates were 10 to 20 per cent

Table 10.6.   Chances per 1,000 live born of eventually dying from specified causes, by sex, *circa* 1980 (1970 values in parentheses)
(*a*) Males

Country	Causes of death			
	Cancer	Stroke	Heart disease	Respiratory
Australia	215 (163)	108 (115)	414 (438)	92 (102)
Austria	218 (198)	132 (126)	360 (309)	59 (91)
Bulgaria	140 (148)	206 (192)	349 (293)	93 (142)
Denmark	236 (206)	81 (102)	408 (426)	81 (70)
France	253 (208)	107 (128)	242 (229)	68 (72)
Germany, Federal Republic	225 (190)	119 (127)	366 (299)	72 (95)
Hungary	201 (183)	144 (133)	350 (385)	69 (56)
Japan	221 (163)	223 (278)	215 (169)	102 (90)
Netherlands	287 (235)	90 (103)	362 (364)	77 (85)
New Zealand	204	100	403	132
Norway	210 (178)	110 (143)	385 (375)	92 (91)
Poland	175	56	423	68
Sweden	209 (189)	85 (95)	466 (450)	60 (65)
Switzerland	261	96	372	68
UK—England and Wales	231 (208)	96 (111)	394 (381)	155 (170)
UK—Scotland	226 (206)	108 (123)	392 (392)	125 (134)
United States	209	78	437	72
Yugoslavia	154 (117)	98 (86)	398 (251)	66 (68)

Note: 1980 figures based on ICD-9   1970 figures based on ICD-8
   Cancer 08–14   Cancer A45–60
   Stroke 29   Stroke A85
   Heart Disease 25–8, 30   Heart Disease A80–4, A80–8
   Respiratory 31–2   Respiratory A89–96
Source: World Health Organization, *World Health Statistics Annual*, 1974 and 1983.

lower in 1965–9 than in 1950–4, declines particularly noteworthy in France. Death rate reductions tended to be greater at the earlier ages (65–74) than at the oldest ages.

The two-year average death rates for males in 1980–1 are lower than in the base period for a number of countries. In the case of Japan, rates are a half to three-quarters of the comparable rates in 1950–4. The exceptions are Bulgaria, Hungary, and Poland, in which increases are found. In some countries, such as Denmark, the Netherlands, and Norway, rates at earlier ages remain higher in 1980–1 than in the base period 1950–4, while in New Zealand they are higher at ages over 75.

Declines in female death rates continued in the later period at every age for nearly all countries, with the exception of Bulgaria, where they still remain above 1950–4 levels, and Poland, where rates at ages 80 and over increased. The most significant declines are found in Japan, where the female rates in 1980–1 were 40 per cent of 1950–4 figures at ages 65–9 and 45 per cent of those comparable figures at ages 70–4.

As in the previous discussion on death rate levels, it can be noted that certain countries, such as Japan, with high initial levels show remarkable

(*b*) Females

Country	Causes of death			
	Cancer	Stroke	Heart disease	Respiratory
Australia	176 (148)	188 (199)	419 (427)	55 (58)
Austria	190 (183)	189 (178)	390 (344)	51 (76)
Bulgaria	108 (108)	254 (258)	384 (340)	74 (116)
Denmark	232 (210)	113 (140)	393 (403)	72 (54)
France	178 (165)	154 (165)	279 (249)	58 (67)
Germany, Federal Republic	199 (180)	176 (179)	380 (309)	45 (66)
Hungary	174 (165)	196 (174)	398 (437)	46 (41)
Japan	155 (129)	255 (282)	254 (194)	82 (80)
Netherlands	223 (198)	139 (154)	356 (351)	58 (66)
New Zealand	184	165	366	111
Norway	191 (167)	173 (200)	344 (330)	105 (114)
Poland	146	82	477	43
Sweden	204 (185)	124 (132)	478 (441)	57 (66)
Switzerland	204	149	406	49
UK—England and Wales	198 (175)	152 (178)	357 (369)	153 (138)
UK—Scotland	199 (177)	172 (205)	357 (377)	114 (95)
United States	182	129	466	51
Yugoslavia	114 (92)	128 (109)	482 (294)	52 (61)

declines in both female and, to a lesser extent, male rates. The Eastern European countries show gains only for females. Countries with lower-level rates in 1950–4 for the most part show considerably more reduction of female rates throughout the period and mixed patterns of reductions for males.

The net impact of these trends has been to attenuate the inter-country variations in death rates among countries with low levels of mortality and to increase further the variations between the Eastern European countries and the other countries. This is particularly true with respect to male death rates at older ages. The sharp reductions in male rates made in the 1970s in such countries as the United States, Japan, and, to a lesser extent, France have produced a new set of countries setting the pace towards reduced mortality and greater survival levels. Interestingly, it is reductions at the ages 65–74 in Japan that have bought Japan to the forefront, while low levels at the very old ages have characterized the US mortality patterns. For France the changes are rather similar over all later ages.

Mortality by Cause

Comparison of Causes of Death

Inter-country studies of cause-specific mortality patterns at older ages have recently been reported by Lopez and Hanada (1982) and Manton (1983). They afford a general picture of the major patterns with respect to underlying causes of death. We will refer to findings from these studies in conjunction with data reported in Table 10.6, which indicate life-table proportions of the initial radix who would eventually die of these major diseases, given the schedule of existing rates. The four selected causes reported on represent about 70 to 80 per cent of the death probabilities for all causes. It should be noted that the relative levels over time are affected by reductions in other causes of death, such as infectious and parasitic diseases and other unspecified diseases. While there are known inter-country differences in diagnostic practices, the reporting of certain causes of death and, of course, changes in the classification system itself over time, recent analyses (Lopez, 1983; Manton, 1983) indicate that the reporting of ill-defined causes of death has declined over time for most developed countries.

Probabilities of dying from cancer and respiratory diseases are generally higher for males than females, but the probability is lower for strokes. The inter-country comparisons show quite similar patterns for males and females. Figures for cancer show that France, the Netherlands, and Switzerland have high levels for males, and Denmark and the Netherlands for females. For both males and females, the probabilities for cancer are low in the Eastern European countries.

For the combined cardiovascular diseases (stroke and heart disease), Bulgaria and Sweden have the highest levels. However, it is strokes in Bulgaria that are of greater importance, while for Sweden the stroke level is low, but the heart disease probability is extremely high. This is true for both males and females. Japan's stroke levels are extremely high for both sexes, but the proportion of deaths from heart disease are extremely low. The French levels for the two categories combined (and especially heart disease) are much lower than in other countries for both males and females, an anomaly that has sometimes been attributed to diagnostic practices.

The highest probabilities of dying from respiratory disease are found, not surprisingly, in the UK countries and New Zealand. Low levels for males are found for Austria and Sweden, and for females in Poland.

Trends in Causes of Death

For a number of these countries data are available to examine broad trends between 1970 and 1980. Figures in parentheses in Table 10.6 are 1970 probabilities. The chances of dying from cancer increased in every case (except Bulgaria for males) in the ten-year period, with increases generally greater for males than for females. This greater proportionate effect on males of cancer mortality is undoubtedly attributable to rapid increases in lung cancer mortality, as Lopez and Hanada (1982) point out. Increases were particularly noteworthy for both sexes in Japan, the Netherlands, and Australia. Manton (1983), in examining trends from 1950 to 1978 for a smaller number of countries, finds that the longer-term trend in probabilities of dying from cancer has been towards a steadily higher level for both males and females. However, it is also the case that the mean age at death from cancer increased steadily for both sexes, with the sole exception of Hungary in the 1970–8 period.

The changes in the proportion dying from strokes and heart disease present a more complex picture, which probably involves changes in diagnostic practice as well as true differences. Noted earlier were the high proportions of males dying from cardiovascular diseases in Bulgaria and Sweden, especially strokes in the former and heart disease in the latter. In the period 1970–80, Bulgarian levels increased for strokes, as did heart disease proportions for Sweden. The high male stroke proportion in Japan actually showed the largest decline, but there was correspondingly a very large increase for heart disease. For heart disease, the largest increase was in Germany and Yugoslavia, although the size of the latter change can probably be explained by reporting practices. Manton (1983) reports that increasing levels for heart disease can be attributed mainly to *declining* mean ages of death. In contrast, lowered levels for heart disease in the

United States have been accompanied by a higher mean age of death for males.

The findings for females are generally comparable to those for males, with some countries showing increasing levels and others a decline, and in certain cases a trade-off between strokes and heart disease. None the less, there has been a steady progression toward *older* mean ages at death for these major causes of death for females in most developed countries, quite in contrast to males (Manton, 1983). It may be noted that the greater rise in life expectancy at later ages for females than for males during the recent past is due in part to increased female mean age at death from heart disease in particular, and probably strokes as well.

Finally, with respect to the relative contribution of respiratory diseases the trend is mainly downward, with large declines for both males and females in Austria, Bulgaria, and Germany. England and Wales and Scotland, with the highest levels in 1980, had even higher levels in 1970 for males. Levels for females have risen for both countries.

The difficulties of modelling changes in mortality at older ages (ages 65–74) were borne out in the curve-fitting exercise that Lopez and Hanada (1982) conducted for the period 1955–78 for several main causes of death. This was particularly true for male death rates, which tended to rise then fall over the period for a number of countries. In some countries an increasing trend was noted, thus giving cubic and quadratic fits. For females the trends were more regular, with downward trends that could be fitted most commonly by cubic curves. While such exercises are useful in gaining further understanding of temporal trends, they do not yield any simple explanation of the overall transition in death rates from major causes of death.

While analysis of the timing of changes in death rates and life expectation reveals considerable variation, male levels (mainly for cardiovascular diseases) for certain countries seem to have declined in the 1970s. Undoubtedly, changes upward in the mean age of death are responsible for overall variations. The fact that countries with already low levels of mortality at the older ages continue to show large improvements suggests that any maximum levels of death rates and life expectation are not currently being reached. Similar conclusions have also been reached in examining the relative absence of age compression of deaths at the older ages (Myers and Manton, 1984). Horiuchi and Coale (1983) lend support to this view by examining the relative rate of decline in the proportional increment of death rates at very old ages. Finally, the existing differences in patterns of mortality and trends among countries suggest that intra-country factors are operating that to date have not been easily measured and assessed in international comparisons. Country studies, therefore, may yield important insights into the dynamic determinants of mortality and morbidity trends.

Mortality and Health Components

Health Expectation

An increasing number of studies are being conducted that use life-table functions to reveal various aspects of survival with or without certain health conditions (Colvez and Blanchet, 1983; Robine an Colvez, 1984; Manton and Soldo, 1984; Katz *et al.*, 1983; Dillard, 1983; Desjardins and Legare, 1984; Wilkins and Adams, 1982). A main aim of these studies is to capture the dynamics of mortality and related health states over the life course in a relatively standardized and easily conceptualized manner. There have been numerous efforts in the past to produce aggregate indices of the health status of the population. One use of indices is to examine how these measures are influenced and, in turn, influence mortality (Sullivan, 1971). The life-table and its various functions have long been regarded as suitable tools for examining both morbidity and mortality (see review by J.H. Pollard, 1982). But only recently have demographers become interested in applying these procedures for developing composite life-tables that capture a more complex pattern of interrelationships with health. Such procedures are particularly suitable for examining country patterns over time, although to date most efforts have been for single points in time.

To illustrate, Figure 10.1 gives a hypothetical picture of how survival curves for morbidity, disability, and mortality might operate. Survival curves enable us to assess the average period free of disease (or any specified disease), the mean period between the disease onset and disability, and finally the length of disability. Implicit in this model is the notion that the

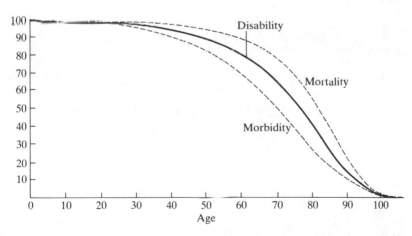

Figure 10.1. The mortality (observed), morbidity (hypothetical), and disability (hypothetical) survival curves for US females in 1980.

process follows a natural progression from disease to disability to death, which is consistent with the World Health Organization (1980) framework for the process, but not necessarily congruent with reality. With such a model, however, it is theoretically possible to assess a series of perspectives on mortality changes and measure improved survival at various ages and whether or not the increased expectation of life has been matched by increased health expectation or life years free of disability. Although most existing studies do not provide the type of evidence that is suitable for such assessments, some cross-sectional results can be examined that point the way toward further applications of these approaches.

The manner in which results form these studies are presented takes on two forms: (1) a graphical depiction of survival curves, shown in Figure 10.1, and (2) tabular data on life expectations in different states at specific ages (birth, age 65, and so forth).

The life-table health expectations have been widely used by French and Canadian health statisticians, building on earlier work by Sullivan (1971), to examine the heatlh conditions in the country as a whole and in certain provinces (for example Robine and Colvez, 1984; Dillard, 1983). For the Haute-Normandie area of France in 1978–9, Robine and Colvez found an expectation of life at age 65 of 13.3 for men and 18.0 for women. In contrast, the expectation of healthy life (measured by physical independence, mobility, and no major limitation of activity) was 8.7 years for men and 6.1 years for women. Data for comparable studies are presented in Table 10.7. Interestingly, these results show a strong gender difference in mortality and disability expectations, which is undoubtedly due to age patterns of survival and social supports available. Again these measures are for single points in time.

Table 10.7.   Results from four studies indicating years of life expectancy and years of life expectancy with incapacity at age 65, 1978–80

	Wilkins	Dillard	Colvez–Robine	Wilkins–Adams
Expectation of life	Quebec 1978	Quebec 1980	Haute Normandie 1979	Canada 1978
Male	13.7	13.9	13.3	14.4
Female	18.1	18.5	18.0	18.7
Expectation of life with incapacity				
Male	4.9	6.0	4.6	6.2
Female	8.0	10.0	11.9	9.6

Source: Robine and Colvez 1984.

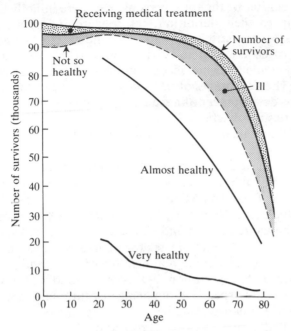

Figure 10.2. Survival curve and gradients of health loss for the female population of Japan by age and health status
Source. Koizumi, 1982.

Figure 10.2 shows survival curves for Japanese females in 1979, derived by Koizumi (1982) from both vital statistics and survey sources. This figure depicts not only the mortality and morbidity survival curve but also other functions such as medical treatment and perceived health status. Thus, using available data, one is able to characterize visually the current health status of a population in terms of a gradient of health loss and in terms of the age dynamics of the gradient. Koizumi derived curves for survivors and number living with no disease for four periods between 1940 and 1954. They appear to show steady improvement in life expectation but somewhat overlapping trends for health expectation over time.

Another study that has employed life-table procedures is the Massachusetts Health Care Panel Study, which involves an investigation of older persons begun in 1974 and repeated in 1976 and 1980 (Branch *et al.*, 1983). The first report from this study on active life expectation was recently published (Katz *et al.*, 1983). It reveals that at age 65 men have an expectation of living without major limitations of activity of 9.3 years, and women 10.6 years. After age 80, however, the amount of average remaining active years is greater for males. The non-poor also had higher active life expectation than poor persons at each age after 65. Notable in this study is the fact that a quarter of the total persons who were initially dependent in 1974, according to their definition, returned to independence after 15 months, and 18 per cent after six years. This indicates a far more dynamic process than is often assumed and gives support therefore to an integrated perspective that would take into account multi-state transitions (Keyfitz and Rogers, 1982). The advantages of this study are the use of longitudinal data and the rigorous development of a scale for measuring independence that is based on activities involved in daily life.

Of perhaps greater interest are several analyses that report changes over time in these measures of relative mortality and health. A report issued by the Quebec Council of Social and Family Affairs (Dillard, 1983) presents some data from Wilkins and Adams (1982) for Canada and work conducted on US data by the Canadian Ministry of Social Affairs, extending earlier efforts of Colvez and Blanchet (1983). Table 10.8 summarizes these findings. For the United States and Canada, the gains in life expectation over the different periods were greater for females than for males. In both countries, the years of expected good health were substantially fewer than were years of added life expectation. In this case, 'good health' was the total sum of years one could expect without being institutionalized and being free of temporary and permanent inactivity. Actually, the level of this measure fell in the United States between 1969 and 1976, which may reflect measurement changes in the survey data. The years of life with restriction of activities increased in both countries, and for both men and women. Particularly noteworthy was the sharp increase in such limitations among Canadian women between 1951 and 1978.

Evaluation

The studies to date that derive measures of health expectation have demonstrated that the general approach is sound and can contribute as a first step in conceptualizing and assessing the complex health and mortality process. However, even the cursory review made here illustrates a lack of co-ordinated efforts in addressing some central issues. The following points require consideration.

Firstly, there are *conceptual* issues in terms of what measures of health or ill health should be emphasized. Aside from problems encountered in determining the onset of morbid conditions of a chronic nature (disease incidence), a vast array of related health states have been suggested under the rubric of what we have referred to as disability. They include (1) restrictions of activity, which may encompass permanent or transitory interruptions in activities of daily living, (2) physical dependence, lack of mobility, physical infirmities—such as loss of sight, hearing, or body parts, (3) utilization of health services, ranging from doctor visits or hospitali-

Table 10.8. Expectation of life at birth and mean health expectancy in various states, by sex, United States 1962–76 and Canada 1951–78

	Males				Females			
	1962	1969	1976	Change 1962–76	1962	1969	1976	Change 1962–76
United States								
Life expectation at birth	66.8	66.6	68.7	+1.9	72.5	74.2	75.8	+3.3
In good health	56.8	57.0	57.1	+0.3	60.8	63.6	62.7	+1.9
With restriction of activity	10.0	9.7	11.5	+1.5	11.6	10.6	13.1	+1.5
Severe	2.8	3.7	—	—	1.5	1.6	—	+0.2

	Males			Females		
	1951	1978	Change 1951–78	1951	1978	Change 1951–78
Canada						
Life expectation at birth	66.3	70.8	+4.5	70.8	78.3	+7.5
In good health	59.8	61.1	+1.3	64.7	66.1	+1.4
With restriction of activity	6.6	9.7	+3.1	6.1	12.2	+6.1

Source: Council of social and family affairs, government of Quebec, *Durée ou qualité de la vie?*, tables 10 and 11.

zation to institutionalization in a nursing home, and (4) a range of subjective perceptions regarding one's health or life satisfaction. Another set of survival roles, such as social integration and economic sufficiency, suggested by the World Health Organization (1980), would further expand the list of other relevant health dimensions. In short, factors have often been selected on the basis of importance for health service assessment and planning rather than the interplay that such factors have on the health and mortality process. Moreover, there has been a lack of attention to reversibility in the survival process. Changes are not all unidimensional—diseases do remit and inactive persons are restored to activity, as noted earlier.

Secondly, most of the studies that have been conducted have relied on secondary data which have been obtained for other purposes (such as National Health Surveys). This may be advantageous from the standpoint of increased data use, but disadvantageous in terms of suitability. Some have been based on rather small samples and therefore lack national coverage. In all but one case—the Massachusetts Health Care Panel Study—the data are cross-sectional and transitional probabilities therefore synthetic. This has meant a reliance on period instead of cohort life-tables. Retrospective survey information could be obtained to overcome these limitations, but it raises questions of reliability. The result has been an over-reliance on point prevalence rather than incidence data, which has been shown to have major implications in determining individual rates of life-time institutionalization (see, for example, McConnel, 1984). Because most data sources have not been directed specifically towards collecting data on older persons, it has meant that information at extreme later ages may be lacking, which is a serious matter in life-table applications for the kinds of dimensions that are being examined.

Thirdly, in addition to conceptual and data problems there are some technical issues that have detracted from many of these studies. They include sampling and censoring issues, rather severe case losses in longitudinal studies, crude estimation procedures for terminal age intervals (which relate in part to lack of detailed information at older ages), and the general assumption of independence of causal rates in the actuarial procedures. In almost all cases, improper computational techniques are used, such as the conversion of $M(x)$ rate to $Q(x)$ probabilities in the Katz *et al.* (1983) study, where in fact it was not needed. The inadequacies in the data presented in most study reports make it impossible to recalculate the tables so that valid comparisons can be made.

In summary, it seems certain that the growing availability of survey and record information on various aspects of health status and related death information will engender a growing use of actuarial procedures for assessing the interrelationships between various dimensions of health and mortality. In time, this accumulating body of research should make it possible to examine the temporal process of change in these parameters and help us to assess the degree to which life prolongation has been accompanied by changes in related health dimensions. The knowledge to be gained is critical for dealing with the ageing process. This has implications not only for planning of health and social services; it should also contribute to an improved understanding of past mortality trends and enable improved forecasting of changes in the future. However, there remain a number of conceptual, data, and technical problems to be addressed. It is here that the demographer can make a strong contribution to these efforts, in collaboration with actuaries, epidemiologists, health statisticians, and health planners.

References

Branch, L. G., S. Katz, K. Kniepmann, and J. A. Papsidero (1983), 'A Prospective Study of Functional Status Among Community Elders', *American Journal of Public Health* 74(3), 266-8.

Colvez, A., and M. Blanchet (1983), 'Potential Gains in Life Expectancy Free of Disability: A Tool for Health Planning', *International Journal of Epidemiology* 12 (2), 224-9.

Desjardins, B., and J. Legare (1984), 'Le Seuil de la vieillesse', *Document de travail no. 14*, Demography Department, University of Montreal.

Dillard, S. (1983), *Duree ou qualite de la vie?*, Council of Social and Family Affairs, Government of Quebec.

Horiuchi, S., and A. J. Coale (1982), 'A Simple Equation for Estimating the Expectation of Life at Old Age', *Population Studies* 36(2), 317-26.

—— —— (1983), 'Age Patterns of Mortality for Older Women: An Analysis Using the Age-specific Rate of Mortality Change with Age', paper presented at the 1983 annual meetings of the Population Association of America, Pittsburgh.

Katz, S., L. G. Branch, M. H. Branson, J. A. Papsidero, J. C. Beck, and D. S. Greer (1983), 'Active Life Expectancy', *The New England Journal of Medicine* 17, 1218-23.

Keyfitz, N., and A. Rogers (1982), 'Simplified Multiple Contingency Calculations', *The Journal of Risk and Insurance* 49, 59-72.

Koizumi, A. (1982), 'Toward a Healthy Life in the 21st Century' in *Population Aging in Japan: Problems and Policy Issues in the 21st Century*, International Symposium on an Aging Society: Strategies for 21st Century Japan, Nihon University.

Lopez, A. D. (1983), 'The Sex Mortality Differential in Developed Countries' in A. D. Lopez and L. T. Ruzicka (eds.), *Sex Differentials in Mortality: Trends, Determinance and Consequences*, Department of Demography, Australian National University, Canberra.

—— and K. Hanada (1982), 'Mortality Patterns and Trends Among the Elderly in Developed Countries', *World Health Statistics Quarterly* 35, 203-24.

—— and L. T. Ruzicka (eds.) (1983), *Sex Differentials in Mortality: Trends, Determinants and Consequences*, Department of Demography, Australian National University, Canberra.

Manton, K. G. (1983), 'Mortality Patterns in Developed Countries, paper presented at the 1983 annual meetings of the Population Association of America, Pittsburgh.

—— and B. J. Soldo (1984), 'A Dynamic Model of Population Aging and Health Status Change: Implications for the Development and Implementation of National Health Policy', revised paper presented at the National Health Policy Forum, Washington, D C.

McConnel, C. E. (1984), 'A Note on the Lifetime Risk of Nursing Home Residency', *The Gerontologist* 24(2), 193–8.

Myers, G. C. (1978), 'Cross-national Trends in Mortality Rates Among the Elderly', *The Gerontologist* 18, 441–8.

—— (1979), 'Recent Trends in Mortality Among the Aged and their Implications' in J. M. Donald, A. V. Everitt, and P. J. Wheeler (eds.), *Ageing in Australia*, Australian Association of Gerontology, Sydney.

—— (1982), 'The Ageing of Population' in R. H. Binstock, W. S. Chow, and J. H. Schulz (eds.), *International Perspectives on Ageing: Population and Policy Challenges*, United Nations Fund for Population Activities, New York, 1–36.

—— and K. G. Manton (1984), Compression of Mortality: Myth or Reality?', *The Gerontologist*, 24(4), 346–53.

Pollard, A. H. (1981), 'The Interaction Between Morbidity and Mortality', *Journal of the Institute of Actuaries* (Australia) 107, 233–302.

Pollard, J. H. (1982), 'The Expectation of Life and its Relationship to Mortality', *The Journal of the Institute of Actuaries* 109(2), 225–40.

Robine, J. M., and A. Colvez (1984), 'Esperance de vie sans incapacite et ses composantes: De nouveaux indicateurs pour mesurer la sante et les besoins de la population', *Population* 39, 27–45.

Sullivan, D. F. (1971), 'Disabling Component for an Index of Health', US National Center for Health Statistics, ser. 2, no. 42.

United Nations (1982), *Levels and Trends in Mortality Since 1950*, UN New York.

US Bureau of the Census (1984), Demographic and Socioeconomic Aspects of Aging in the United States, Current Population Report, ser P–23, no. 138, US Government Printing Office, Washington, D C.

Wilkin, J. C. (1981), 'Recent Trends in the Mortality of the Aged', *Transitions of the Society of Actuaries* 33, 11–44.

Wilkins, R., and O. B. Adams (1982), *Healthfulness of Life; A Unified View of Mortality, Institutionalization, and Noninstitutionalization Disability in Canada, 1978*, Institute for Research on Public Policy, Montreal.

World Health Organization (1980), 'International Classification of Impairments, Disabilities and Handicaps: A Manual of Classifications Relating to the Classification of Disease', W H O, Geneva.

Part IV

Crisis Mortality

11 Crisis Mortality: Extinction and Near-extinction of Human Populations

ANDRE BOUCKAERT

Faculty of Medicine, Catholic University of Louvain, Belgium

Mortality Crises

Mortality crises deserve special attention in the study of mortality. They can be defined as unusually high mortalities arising from a common, unusual, causal factor operating for a limited amount of time across a given geographical area. The actual number of deaths should in no way be used as evidence of the severity of mortality crises. Obviously, the worst episodes of plague in small islands do not result in numbers of deaths that would match even mild infections in China or the United States. This statement of fact only supports the need for more extensive research on mild infections. However, plagues in small islands should not be forgotten: their study can perhaps enable us to reach interesting conclusions about plagues in large countries, where their deadly impact would soon exceed all consequences of mild infections, prevalent as those can be.

Severe critical mortality can sometimes end in the total annihilation of the victimized population, particularly when the latter is small: as in the case of food poisoning or thirst on a small ship, which may lead to its ultimate transformation into a powerless derelict. Such a fate is not restricted to small ships, however, as is shown by the Viking settlements in Greenland (Utterstrom, 1955). These devastations are much more likely to occur in sparse and isolated populations; they will be called *extinctions*. Extinction requires a very high mortality reaching its peak in a very short time, giving no opportunity for escape and no chance for reproduction. Extinction seems to have occurred at some stages in prehistoric societies but is distinctly uncommon in literate societies. A bias is obvious here: total disappearance is likely to be associated with lack of adequate reporting except in mythological tales, and such tales are not poor in accounts of disastrous extinctions (such as Atlantis). However, because of the infrequency of their occurrence or the lack of documentation, our interest will be drawn mainly to disasters slightly less total in their scale, which we will call *quasi-extinctions*. We will make use of this denomination to refer to a significant reduction of the population size, sometimes associated with a recognizable cultural or genetic discontinuity. We will try to collect information about the social behaviour of communities at the edge of destruction, with the avowed aim of being able, at some stage, to systematize such findings as parts of a quasi-extinction syndrome.

Whatever the causes and circumstances of critical mortality, it seems obvious that it will reduce the population to some extent. But this is not a rule; the two World Wars did not significantly depress the European or Asian populations. Conversely, mortality is probably very seldom the sole explanation of episodes of population shrinkage. The study of catastrophes of the past will often leave no choice other than the use of population data to estimate the magnitude of critical mortalities, but this is misleading, and birth rate evolution is usually crucial in shaping the evolution of populations struck by critical mortalities.

After the shock of disaster, the birth rate may remain unaltered, or it may decrease or increase. Given M, the critical mortality rate, and m and n, respectively the common death and birth rates, it can be shown that:

$$T = Log(1 - M)/(m - n)$$

where T is the time required for return to the previous population size. If, for example, M = 0.20 (a high but still not uncommon figure for famines), for a moderate population increase ($n = 0.016$ and $m = 0.0086$, United States 1981), T = 30 years.

Depressed birth rates are a common finding during wars and famines and in succession to cultural breakdowns. The finding of a low birth rate associated with a high death rate is even considered as diagnostic of famines. Psychological and purely physiological processes are involved, but a certain degree of birth rate depression may also result from an unequal sensitivity of the age groups to disaster conditions, since any increased sensitivity of the young age class will decrease the number of potential progenitors.

Increased birth rates are observed in the aftermath of some disasters, and seem to be common in refugee settlements. From the point of view of survival, increased birth rates are certainly an adaptive strategy for societies as soon as their basic needs are satisfied. In a context of shortage, survival of the individual is certainly better served by a pause in births: it should be no surprise therefore to witness sudden behavioural changes in this respect during the study of critical mortality.

Emigration is not unusual after disasters. Emigration is sometimes the only way out during epidemics and famine: one needs only to remember the story of Hebrews migrating to Egypt during a drought; in addition, the prophylactic value of pilgrimages during plagues was well known during the Middle Ages, as there was no other method of avoiding infectious contacts. Emigration is also a consequence of material destruction brought by earthquakes and hurricanes, since such losses may hamper work and employment opportunities. Emigration is a selective subtraction of young skilled manpower from the victimized population. It brings about a further collapse in the social structure of the non-migrants but it also creates difficult problems of integration for migrants and for their hosts. Slavery was one of the possible adaptive mechanisms, again quoted in the Biblical story of the Hebrews in Egypt. Another possibility, not so different as may be perceived, is the confinement of migrants in refugee communities without any prospect for the future. Yet another possibility is a violent clash between migrants and hosts: it should not be forgotten in the picture of emigration that Germanic and other people who settled in the Roman Empire and brought its final collapse were initially refugees from over-population in Central Asia; the whole story of barbarian invasions is perhaps to be understood in this perspective.

The present problems of Lebanon, Assam, Sudan, and Thailand—to quote just a few cases—give ample ground for fearing further violence stirred up by unaccepted refugees in crowded countries. This does not mean that peaceful or even mutually profitable relations between refugees and hosts are impossible. Looking to the past for examples, we find that the Jewish refugees from Portugal were quite successful and quite useful to their Dutch hosts. Palestinian refugees have recently given a decisive economic impetus to the neighbouring Arab countries, where they were able to offer much-needed skilled assistance. North America as we know it would not have achieved its fast development without the continuous influx of refugees from all the European countries. However, it means that we must scrutinize very carefully the slightest opportunities for integration, by looking specifically at the social gaps that could best be filled by migrants, instead of allowing the refugee communities to grow in a mood of fear and distrust. The problem is nowhere more pressing than in Africa; in that part of the world there are at least five million acknowledged refugees, and the real picture is certainly worse. By their size alone, such communities would qualify as a kingdom or republic of their own. The preferential treatment of some refugees by international institutions, acting out of good will but without any real knowledge of African life and conditions, has already been observed to stir xenophobic feelings (for example, Cabinda refugees in Zaire, Nomads in Sahel, Falashas in Sudan). Taking into account the continental nature of the problems of Africa, there is no real ground for believing that displacement across borders can solve them, and resettlement in the mother country is perhaps a better alternative. But such a resettlement cannot be successful without international assistance, as was shown by the difficulties involved in the reinsertion of Ghanaian migrants expelled from Nigeria when the latter country experienced its first disillusionments after the oil boom.

Disasters

Any aetiological classification of disasters will attempt to distinguish between those of natural and man-made origins. The former will include earthquakes, volcanic eruptions, violent winds, flood, drought, and fast climatic modifications. The latter classification will essentially be concerned with war and with industrial pollution. Famines and epidemics will require special consideration, since they very often result from natural weather conditions but may also do so from wars or from pathological social structures. Moreover, natural causes show a variable amount of impact that depends on the social response they elicit.

Hence, we suggest that it is desirable to distinguish first between primary and secondary disasters. Most life losses, it will be demonstrated, do not occur as a result of the action of those physical forces liberated during the early stage of disasters. Social and other human reactions can either alleviate or amplify the magnitude of the first impact. In fact, even before any disaster strikes, the social structures can be analysed in order to forecast whether they would be able to mitigate or be likely to intensify the initial disturbances. Social structures always show some potential for reducing the disturbances brought about by disasters, and such a potential can be seen as a kind of social immunity. However, social immunity—like any other—is not effective across the full range of disturbances. It may be overwhelmed; it may also be counter-productive and achieve much more destruction than the disaster itself. This social ambivalence is nowhere clearer than in the famines of Africa today.

Drought is part of cyclical rainfall evolution in many parts of Africa. Predictions on a year-to-year basis are still out of reach because of large random or poorly understood fluctuations. However, the probability of drought on a broad time-scale can be known quite accurately, and there is no excuse for surprise at the news from Eastern—and, probably very soon—Western Africa. The following questions should be made a mandatory part of routine monitoring. What is the relationship between rainfall and harvests, giving proper probabilistic weight to all figures—unpleasant as they might seem—for rainfall? Is it possible to substitute less sensitive crops for those used (as was the case for potatoes in Northern Europe)? Is it possible to dispatch extra local surpluses to areas of shortage in a limited time? And with the available manpower and logistics? What about land allocation? Is it possible to shift from export cultures to nutritionally valuable crops? Is it possible to import acceptable food using export benefits? What is the capacity of the transportation network? The answers to such and other questions can be used as a basis for *pre-disaster diagnosis*. Obviously, according to the answers, a given shortage of rain can lead to completely different situations. The socio-economic nature of the extreme vulnerability of Africa to drought is best understood by comparison with the spectacular harmlessness of the West European drought of 1976 (Morren, 1980). To take the contrast a step further, the severe Australian drought of 1983 shows how much a prepared society can survive without experiencing real famine.

The Ethiopian drought of 1973 (Rivers *et al.*, 1976) was no more severe and no more unpredictable than drought in Europe or Australia. The following factors were crucial in precipitating famine. Isolated hilltop villages with virtually no contact with the outside world were conveniently allowed to starve to death without anybody knowing or caring. Although redistribution of local surpluses could have brought relief, no such redistribution was ever attempted. Had attempts been made, they would have failed, since no practical transportation system was available. There was no planning of agricultural production in the context of dietary requirements. A general distrust of traditional rulers and a too well-founded suspicion that they were unable to manage the crisis paved the way for civil war, attempted secession, international conflict, and finally a tragic exodus of refugees. The war operations made famine worse. Since the starting-point was the same in Ethiopia and Western Europe three years later, the importance of socio-economic factors in disaster immunity is clear. The Ethiopian case also illustrates the fact that most losses of life are a consequence of social inadequacies (the secondary disaster) rather than of natural forces themselves.

Famines

According to Cepede and Lengelle (1953), China experienced an average of one famine every thirteen months between 108 BC and AD 1929. While this could be perceived as an unusually high frequency by comparison with the recent history of developed countries, it should not be forgotten that Northern Europe was used to famine every two years up to the eighteenth century (Imhof, 1979). The irregular pattern of weather and the effect of population size on the number of births are good explanations of the recurrent famines in history. More basically, the lack of an effective fertility response to nutrition in our species, a consequence of the unusual length of pregnancy, offers a sufficient explanation of the permanent threat of famine. Another explanatory factor is the sedentary life-style of most human groups, and their extreme reluctance to adapt to environmental changes. Since the sedentary life itself can be seen as the logical consequence of a long pregnancy and lactational investment, proneness to famine seems to be a typical, rather than an exceptional, aspect of human evolution. Some societies developed into nomads and were able to exploit wide strips of unfavourable environment, but such an economic organization is clearly not compatible with large population sizes. Hence, human societies have no choice but to develop a certain amount of famine immunity by mastering environmental challenges.

Causes of famine include:

(*a*) Drought, as in the Sahel and Eastern Africa;
(*b*) Flood: Bangladesh, Indonesia;
(*c*) Frost: Northern Europe before the nineteenth century;
(*d*) Plant or animal pests (epiphytics): the cause of the Irish famine.

Poor potato harvests throughout Europe in 1846 resulted from: (1) the narrow genetic polymorphism of potatoes; (2) the increasingly large areas of contiguous planting, offering exceedingly favourable conditions of propagation for pests. Both mechanisms are reasons to fear famines in modern times. Since the use of large areas for the culture of genetically homogeneous strains is likely to increase to meet increased food requirements, special attention should be given to the potentially disastrous effects of parasites on plant populations (Barrett, 1981).

(*e*) War: combinations of war and famine are common. War can obviously result from famine, as shortage heightens competition. But war also precipitates famines for one or several of the following causes:

(1) Deliberate interference with the satisfaction of needs in order to obtain surrender or to crush resistance (Mayer, 1971). This can be accomplished through blockade (as during the two World Wars) or through intentional harvest destructions (American Civil War, Vietnam). Although this is not popularly recognized, such interference was also carried out by pro-Allied groups operating in continental Europe during World War II.

(2) Various forms of looting and confiscation by occupation armies.

(3) Decreased agricultural manpower caused by mandatory conscription, forced labour, and so on.

(4) Destruction of the transportation network.

(5) Interference of battlefields with transportation: this happened in the Netherlands in 1945, when the characteristic geography of this country, with its huge urban population separated from its agricultural hinterland, proved to be exceedingly dangerous, since the country was virtually separated into conflicting halves during the last stage of the war.

(6) Local overpopulation resulting from uncontrolled population displacements: this was typified in the case of the Biafran conflict. Even without any military confrontation, famines are much more likely during cold-war-like strained international relations than during more peaceful periods. Relief, if offered, is likely to be inadequate because it will be limited by public opinion or other political constraints. Moreover, wherever whole countries are perceived as hostile, it cannot be seriously expected that major efforts will be attempted to bring them relief.

(*f*) Pollution: this unusual cause has been observed only once up to now. In Iceland in 1773, a volcanic eruption in the uninhabited central part of the island was followed by sulphur fallout to such an extent that crops and livestock were poisoned. People could only escape starvation by emigration. The population reduction averaged 20 per cent (Whittow, 1980). Sulphur pollution by natural disaster is an unusual occurrence. But industrial sulphur pollution is a growing problem and acid rains are now a real threat to lakes, rivers, and forests.

(*g*) Epidemics: mass mortality among peasants interferes with agriculture and precipitates famine among city-dwellers and dependents. This was observed during the European plague of the fourteenth century, better known as the Black Death (Hecker, 1859; Nicol, 1971; Bowsky, 1971). As a generalization, any kind of mass mortality is likely to be followed by famine for the survivors.

(*h*) Locust migrations: responsible for the Rajputana famine of 1868–9 (Passmore, 1951).

(*i*) Systematic allocation of agricultural tasks to unskilled persons, exemplified by the Khmer Rouge rule of Cambodia from 1975 to 1979. That the aim of such a policy was to lower the population size to a level compatible with primitive agricultural practice cannot be ruled out; such was certainly the result (Ponchaud, 1978). Incidentally, the Morgenthau proposal for the future of Germany after World War II would have had, if followed, similar consequences.

(*j*) Systematic allocation of unsuitable and infertile lands to some populations: exemplified by the policy of the Indian reservations in the United States during the nineteenth century.

(*k*) Monoculture: in addition to the risk of epiphytics, monoculture leads to desertification by erosion, as was found in the Caribbean. The dust bowl of Oklahoma during the thirties is more recent evidence of the same process.

(*l*) Overgrazing: also leading to desertification (Northern Africa).

(*m*) Destruction of the irrigation network: by neglect (Spain during the *Reconquista*) (Hollingsworth, 1969) or with the aim of turning the country into a desert (the Mongols in Mesopotamia).

(*n*) Sudden climatic fluctuations: the general cooling of the Northern Hemisphere during modern times culminated during the Little Ice Age of the seventeenth century. The agricultural production of Western Europe was depressed. Agricultural societies of the North were wiped out. The extinction of Viking settlements in Greenland is certainly the most impressive testimony of the vulnerability of human societies to minor temperature changes (Le Roy-Ladurie, 1967).

High-order Disasters

A natural way to investigate the sequence of events leading to high mortality is to dissociate the initial physical events from their social and economic consequences. As already quoted, the primary impact of natural disasters is usually quite limited. The concept of secondary disaster will be used here to outline the impact of disturbed social and economic forces on mortality. The unsatisfied need for decent living conditions intensifies competition among disaster survivors. Since the normal course of events has been altered, totally new strategies of behaviour are likely to be contemplated. Different and conflicting solutions will attract different segments of the social body, and, without recognized rules that would lead to the pursuit of one way rather than another, violent clashes may result. These are unlikely to occur unless violence is seen as the only way out for a desperate population. However, whenever a disaster leaves plenty of people in unbearable misery, with a feeling that they are neglected, abused, or betrayed by their political rulers, the struggle for survival assumes the shape of a violent rejection of the rulers. This was observed, for instance, after the Ethiopian famine of 1973, the Bengal cyclone of 1970, and the earthquake in Nicaragua of 1972. Civil war achieves a degree of redistribution of the available resources, but only at the cost of additional mortality; in fact, the victims of civil war soon outnumber the casualties of the primary natural disaster.

Civil war may also initiate famine where there is none, and it may increase any already present food shortage. Since no other option is left in these circumstances, whole populations leave their traditional territory in a desperate attempt to find asylum abroad. Population displacement can be considered as the *tertiary disaster*.

Competition between native and migrant settlers is likely to develop very quickly, generating a new civil war. This can be considered as the *quaternary disaster*: Lebanon is a good example of the propagation of disasters by unsettled refugee problems. The starting-point in this case was the genocide of European Jews by the Nazis. Survivors settled in Israel and problems with the native Arabs quickly led to civil war and dismembering of the country. The Arab refugees first attempted to settle in Jordan, where the competition with native inhabitants was soon to develop to a point where a genocide of the refugees could be feared (Carre, 1970). Consequently, the Palestinian refugees moved to Lebanon, where their coming shifted the delicate balance of power between the heterogeneous populations of this tiny country. This time, a genocide of Christians could not, at first, be ruled out. Any final solution, after the involvement of Israel and Syria and the further displacement of the valid refugees—now scattered among several other Arab countries—seems remote, to say the least. Hence, it seems obvious that refugee problems are not easily or satisfactorily solved by time alone: unless an active policy of peaceful resettlement is followed, further clashes are almost certain on an overcrowded planet.

Evaluation

A quantitative evaluation of mortality is needed for all kinds of disasters. First, comparative studies of major disasters are required for an understanding of the importance of prognostic factors. For example, how should we forecast the effects of drought under the worst hypotheses? Such estimates are necessary as soon as we want to select relief policies on a rational basis. Since available resources are not sufficient for all kinds of policies, a cost–benefit computation is mandatory, using the maximum and average of the number of deaths averted by each action. Second, we need objective criteria to enable us to delineate disaster mortality from its background of non-disaster, random, fluctuations of the death rate.

In all cases, it is imperative to take the population size into account. Should we forget it, any cause of death in any large country would be considered as disaster. It can be very difficult to estimate the size of the population at risk, since catastrophes can occur in regions located at the intersection of many national borders. In such circumstances, the death count will sort casualties by national groups, thereby obscuring the magnitude of the event. The same phenomenon is likely when the disaster area overlaps many administrative circumscriptions in one country.

Hollingsworth's index (1979) takes into account the death rate and the time-scale of the disaster, and is used for historical research. Using the index, mass mortalities of the past are not attributed to disasters unless restricted to a short time-period. The effect is that short-lived disasters will easily be recognized while long disastrous episodes will not.

For example, the Lisbon earthquake of 1755 gives an index value of 95. This should be compared with the value of 249 for the Mexican crisis of 1519/1608 (Ashburn, 1947; Chaunu, 1981; Cook, 1973; Borah, 1960; Cook and Borah, 1960). In the war of Paraguay against the Triple Alliance, the index reaches 700 (Richardson, 1960; Coser, 1971; Sanchez-Albornoz, 1974).

Whenever mortality is estimated by the reduction of population size, allowance should be made for the decreased birth rate. This is the more important because reduced natality is the key factor in population size shrinkage (Chaunu, 1981). Moreover, emigration will specifically result in population depletion, and allowance should be made for this.

Catastrophic mortalities do not usually show strong age biases, but decreased natality undermines the pyramid of ages. The mean age of the population increases, and the birth rate is lowered. Emigration has a similar effect: migrants are usually younger than non-migrants. Hence, any post-disaster demographic monitoring should pay special attention to the birth rate and age structure.

Genetic Consequences

The complete extinction of a human population is associated with the disappearance of the genes carried by its members. This explains the importance of catastrophes for evolution: any large-scale mortality is associated with changes of the genetic structure of mankind. In quasi-extinctions, according to the magnitude of mortality and to the genetic specificities of the victims, survivors can be considered as a comprehensive or partial sample of their parent population. Gene disappearance is likely to occur wherever there is a genetic bias in mortality, but may also take place because some genes are specific enough to be absent from the survivor population through the effect of selection or gene drift.

Epidemics offer a good example of the evolutionary consequences of large mortalities. For example, the Mexican crisis of the sixteenth century and the rapid reduction of the Maori population of Hawaii and New Zealand during the nineteenth century were both related to the introduction of new viral diseases like measles, smallpox, and influenza, in populations where no genetic resistance had developed because of a lack of previous exposure (Beaglehole, 1940; Cumberland, 1949). In such cases, a fast reduction of the population size is associated with a shift in gene frequencies. Blood groups have been thoroughly studied in this perspective: their frequencies reflect the paths followed by lethal epidemics of the past because the genes linked with resistance genes are strongly selected at the expense of the others.

Another interesting feature of the aftermath of large epidemics is the growth of mixed-blood populations. In mixed-blood groups, the native genes find protection against the new infective agents; such groups can be considered as the only effective survival opportunity for the native gene population after the introduction of foreign pathogens. Cultural biases in historical reporting often fail to acknowledge the simultaneous occurrence of the native population decrease and of the growth of the mixed group. In fact, the so-called native population probably diverges from its unselected ancestors as much as the mixed-blood population, since it will finally include only the genetically resistant strain while the new mestizo group carries a recombination of native and foreign genes.

Interestingly, genetic discontinuities are easily overlooked when no obvious cultural changes are associated with them. The war of the Triple Alliance (Brazil, Uruguay, Argentine) against Paraguay is a well-known example of an extreme man-made disaster. During the final stage of the conflict, the Paraguayan male population was virtually exterminated. The next generation was obviously of mixed ancestry, since Brazilian soldiers assumed the biological fatherhood. But the Paraguayan mothers raised their children in their unique Paraguayan spirit, teaching them the Guarani language and so on. A strong commitment to the country of their (maternal) grandfathers was soon to develop in the post-war generation. National pride showed its strength during the Chaco War thirty years later.

Cultural Consequences

The scars left by catastrophes in the cultural superstructure are often very deep. In a country where volcanic activity is felt everywhere, such as Iceland, awareness of danger and a basic knowledge of survival tactics permeate all the facets of daily life. After a catastrophe, the political structure shows usually a shift towards an authoritarian style and a militaristic organization. This course of events is well documented: for example, for China after the Taiping rebellion (Kuhn, 1970). The systematic use of female workers in Europe during the two World Wars resulted in a permanent pattern of women's involvement in the industrial activities of these countries. The population reduction caused by the Black Death in Europe in 1348 was associated with a change in social structures and the development of a class of free peasants in place of the previous serfs.

World War I exerted a lasting influence on the attitudes and tastes of Europeans. The reduced natality combined with the disappearance of many key characters and with the ageing of the population produced a strange feeling of doom (the lost generation). To a certain extent, even the possibility of catastrophe, such as the nuclear threat, could achieve a similar result today. Ancient memories of catastrophes could also explain why many popular cosmologies include the notion that the human species will be wiped out by a general cataclysmic event. However, the most radical cultural consequence of disasters is the destruction of beliefs and values of the past and their replacement by a cultural system that, at first, seems to be a copy of a foreign model. For example, the native Meso-American culture vanished completely during the sixteenth century. The mixed blood group that was to develop as the future Mexican society seemed to have rejected all links with the pre-Columbian culture. However, its cultural evolution was completely divergent from that of its Spanish models. Later, it became obvious that a synthesis had been born the native cultural elements giving a distinct and original touch to the Mexican way of life.

The mechanism of post-disaster cultural breakdown is poorly understood. Since important cultural changes followed both World War I and the 1962–73 prosperity wave in Europe, without any critical reduction of the population by mortality, and since no such changes were reported after such mass mortalities as the Black Death or the war of the Triple Alliance, it is not unreasonable to associate such changes with a decreased birth rate rather than with population reduction. In cases of depressed natality, cultural parent-to-child transmission is no longer homogeneous but restricted to a small group of large families. The cultural background of those families is likely to be very different from that of society as a whole. Moreover, such a family culture is probably too narrow to be used as a template for the culture of a complete society, and an imaginative new synthesis is needed. Cultural and genetic changes could then be ascribed to the same basic causes.

Strategies for Survival

It is now commonplace to speak of strategies even for behaviour with no conscious background, provided it can be shown that they are associated with a successful evolution aimed at a stated objective. In disasters some consistent strategies seem to be discernibly associated with the search for survival. Such strategies are observable either during the emergency or as a part of the disaster immunity syndrome.

(*a*) Emigration

Emigration can result from economic destruction during natural disasters; it can also be the only escape left from famine, war, or epidemics. The adaptive value of emigration follows from the relief it brings to demographic pressure in an impoverished environment (for the non-migrants) and from the discovery of new and possibly better environments (for the migrants).

(*b*) Depressed Birth Rate

A consequence of physiological disturbances in famine, psychological disturbances by war, and economic depression, a depressed birth rate enhances the potential for survival of the adult population by cancelling the burden of rearing infants and by lowering the demographic pressure.

(*c*) Unequal Share of Natural Resources

Already present in most pre-disaster situations, it usually increases during and after emergencies. While the uneven distribution of available food is the actual cause of starvation after poor harvests, it also has an adaptive value, since a completely homogeneous distribution would probably leave everybody below the level of vital needs.

(*d*) Cultural Collapse

Since advanced stages of disaster disorganization can be considered as the evidence of failure of the previous culture, the use of the mental concepts of a successful group is an obvious case of learning by trial and error.

(*e*) Miscegenation

The recombination of local with foreign genes can allow the former to survive in the presence of adverse conditions, as has been already remarked.

Conclusions

Our knowledge of past historical catastrophes is still in its infancy. It is very important to understand why some societies manage to escape, sometimes narrowly, impending destruction. In order to be able to reach such an understanding, more attention should be given to behavioural strategies and to their relative efficiencies in a variety of circumstances. More attention should also be given to some demographic traits of societies during disasters. The careful observation of birth and death rates should allow the—at least partial—prediction of the evolution of societies after disasters, and their ultimate fate. The adaptive value of some reactions, which might at first appear as totally negative, should also be scrutinized. Finally, a better knowledge of the cause of death and age-specific mortalities during disasters would be profitable for early disaster diagnosis and for adequate recognition of the stages of the quasi-extinction process.

References

Ashburn, P. M. (1947), *The Ranks of Death: A Medical History of the Conquest of America*, New York.
Barrett, J. A. (1981), 'The evolutionary Consequences of Monoculture' in J. A. Bishop and L. M. Cook (eds.), in *Genetic Consequences of Man Made Changes*, Academic Press, London.
Beaglehole, E. (1940), 'The Polynesian Maori' in L. G. Sutherland (ed.), *The Maori People Today*, Wellington.
Borah, W. (1960), 'Population Decline and the Social and Institutional Changes in New Spain in the Middle Decades of the Sixteenth Century', *Akten des 34 Internationalen Amerikanistenkongresses* Vienna, 172–8.
Bowsky, W. M. (1971), *The Black Death: A Turning Point in History?*, New York.
Carre, O. (1970), *Septembre noir*, Juillard, Paris.
Cepede, M. and M. Lengelle (1953), *Economie alimentaire du globe*, M. Th. Genin, Paris.
Chaunu, P. (1981), *Histoire et decadence*, Librairie Académique Perrin, Paris.
Cook, S. F. (1973), 'The Significance of Disease in the Extinction of the New England Indians', *Human Biology* 45, 485–508.
—— and W. Borah (1960), *The Indian Population of Central Mexico 1531–1610*, University of California Press, Berkeley, Calif.
Coser, L. A. (1971), 'The Termination of Conflict' in C. G. Smith (ed.), *Conflict Resolution: Contribution of the Behavioral Sciences*, University of Notre Dame Press, Notre Dame, Ind., 486–91.
Cumberland, K. B. (1949), 'Aotearoa Maori: New Zealand about 1780', *Geographical Review* 39, 401–24.
Hecker, J. F. C. (1859), *The Epidemics of the Middle Ages*, transl. by Babington, Trubaer, London.
Hollingsworth, T. H. (1969), *Historical Demography*, The Sources of History, London.

—— (1979), 'A Preliminary Suggestion for the Measurement of Mortality Crises' in H. Charbonneau and A. Larose (eds.), *The Great Mortalities: Methodological Studies of Demographic Crises in the Past*, Ordina, Liège, 21–8.

Imhof, A. E. (1979), 'Recherches macrorégionales sur la mortalité en Europe septentrionale sous l'ancien régime' in H. Charbonneau and A. Larose (eds.), *The Great Mortalities: Methodological Studies of Demographic Crises in the Past*, Ordina, Liège, 139–52.

Kuhn, P. A. (1970), *Rebellion and its Enemies in Late Imperial China: Militarization and Social Structure (1796–1864)*, Harvard University Press, Cambridge, MA.

Le Roy-Ladurie, E. (1967), *Histoire du climat depuis l'an mil*, Flammarion, Paris.

Mayer, J. (1971), 'What Kind of Organization and what Type of Trained Personnel are Needed in the Field? in *Famine: Symposium of the Swedish Nutrition Foundation*, Stockholm, 178–84.

Morren, G. E. B. (1980), 'The Rural Ecology of the British Drought', *Human Ecology* 8, 33–64.

Nicol, B. (1971), 'Causes of Famine in the Past and in the Future' in *Famine Symposium of the Swedish Nutrition Foundation*, Stockholm, 10–14.

Passmore, R. (1951), 'Famine in India: A Historical Survey', *Lancet* 2, 303–7.

Ponchaud, F. (1978), *Cambodia: Year Zero*, Holt, Rinehart, Winston, New York.

Richardson, L. F. (1960), *Statistics of Deadly Quarrels*, Boxwood and Quadrangle, Pittsburgh.

Rivers, J. P. W., J. F, J. Holt, J. A. Seaman, and M. R. Bowden (1976), 'Lessons for Epidemiology from the Ethiopian Famine', International Colloquium on Disaster Epidemiology, Antwerp.

Sanchez-Albornoz, N. (1974), *The Population of Latin America: A History*, University of California Press, Berkeley, Calif.

Utterstrom, G. (1955), 'Climatic Fluctuations and Population Problems in Early Modern History', *Scandinavian Economic History Review* 3.

Whittow, J. (1980), *Disasters: The Anatomy of Environmental Hazards*, University of Georgia Press, London.

12 Famine in China 1959-61: Demographic and Social Implications

PENNY KANE

Cardiff University Population Centre, University College, Cardiff, Wales

Famine has been endemic in China's history, with recurrent drought in the northern and central provinces as well as floods, both along the meandering rivers which frequently burst their banks or changed their course, or resulting from typhoons hitting the coastal provinces. But famine is, as Tawney long ago pointed out, a matter of degree: There are districts in which the position of the rural population is that of a man standing permanently up to the neck in water, so that even a ripple is sufficient to drown him (Tawney, 1932). The number of those standing up to the neck in water increased immeasurably during the 1940s, as a consequence of war. Few tasks were more urgent, for the new Chinese government after 1949, than to ensure some minimal food security.

Structures and Stresses in the 1950s

An improved agricultural base was needed, not only to feed the people but also to provide a surplus for the development of China as an industrial nation. Following the Soviet model of an essentially extractive policy towards agriculture, the First Five Year Plan (1953-8) gave overwhelming budgetary priority to industry, with agriculture, forestry, and water between them being allocated only 7.6 per cent of the funds. It was assumed that economies of scale, increased irrigation, and the intensification of traditional agriculture would lead to the necessary increases in productivity.

Economies of scale were to be achieved in the long run by collectivization. Land reform—of which the Communists had already considerable experience in the Liberated Areas—was extended to the whole of China by 1952. It involved redistribution, largely to the poor and middle peasants, with every family member receiving a share. Cultivated land, always in short supply in China, had dwindled from 120 million hectares in 1936 to 98 million in 1949, when it had to support some 550 million people. Improving productivity and extending the area under cultivation required access to

Table 12.1.   China's grain output 1952–7

Year	Total grain (million tons)	Grain per head (kg)	Rice	Wheat	Corn	Other
				(million tons)		
1952	163.9	278	68.4	18.1	16.9	25.8
1953	166.8	283	71.3	18.3	16.7	26.6
1954	169.5	281	70.9	23.3	17.1	26.1
1955	183.9	299	78.0	23.0	20.3	28.0
1956	192.7	300	82.5	24.8	23.1	32.1
1957	195.1	301	86.8	23.6	21.4	32.0

Source: State Statistical Bureau, 1983.

tools, agricultural equipment, and fertilizer, which the peasant family simply did not possess. Land reform was thus followed first by mutual aid teams sharing equipment and labour, and then by co-operatives which, by the end of 1957, included the collective ownership of land.

Efforts to increase irrigation and water conservancy culminated in massive projects undertaken during 1957 and 1958, with an original target for the area to be irrigated within a year being increased twice, and still over-fulfilled within the first four months. Unfortunately, not all the projects were well chosen, and some resulted in increases in salinity, and serious losses to agriculture, particularly in Hebei, Henan, and Shandong.

Nevertheless, grain output during the 1950s increased steadily until 1957. Much of the extra grain produced was kept by the peasants for their own use. From 1953 onwards, the state assumed a monopoly of the purchase of grain and offered regularly increased prices. Agricultural taxes also continued to be called for in grain and during the First Five Year Plan period were set at an overall level of some 16.5 per cent of an assumed normal yield. Neither measure was adequate to assure a sufficient supply of grain for the cities, the army, the feeding of grain-deficit areas, and the provision of national reserves. In 1955 each unit was given a fixed quota to produce, and quotas for compulsory purchase by the state were introduced, together with quotas to be sold to grain-deficit areas. The first result of this policy was a fall of 4–5 per cent in the quantity of grain procured by the state, despite a favourable harvest, and in the following two years the compulsory sales percentage had to be raised. Between 1953 and 1956 the grain taken by the state in tax and compulsory purchase has been estimated as amounting to between a fifth and a third of total output (Donnithorne, 1970).

However, as there was a critical shortage of storage capacity at the state level, much of the grain produced had to be left in village granaries, hampering the prospect of its effective use elsewhere. Poor transport systems also limited the possibility of quick and effective grain transfers. Between 1953 and 1957, less than 10 million tons of grain, or only 4.8 per cent of the total procured, went to the state reserves.

These were concerns of the State, rather than individual families. For them, the return of normalcy and a share in the land meant that good times were not merely just around the corner, but coming within reach. Fei Xiaotong captured the mood when he returned in 1957 to Kaixian'gong village, first studied in his classic *Peasant Life in China* (1936).

The land was divided, the irrigation channels were repaired, and crops were better and better each year. Such things had never happened before . . . this was the first year that one could replace the old cotton-padded jackets with new, better-made ones. In summer, people made western-style cotton shirts. If going barefoot was uncomfortable, they bought a pair of rubber boots. The young people were even more proud in their uniform jackets. At New Years [*sic*] the pigs had already been raised and, since it was meant that one did not have to put out cash to buy, they butchered the fat ones to have feasts, invite guests, have a little extra food, and so regain a little self respect. . . . One cannot say that the villagers actually wore too much clothing or ate too much . . .

but, he was afraid, they were consuming more than was safe (Fei Xiaotong, 1983).

The Great Leap Forward

The Great Leap Forward has been the focus of considerable attention, in particular from MacFarquhar (1983). Here it is sufficient to note that the Chinese leadership, and Mao Zedong especially, content neither with the success of their policies (industrial production increasing at an annual rate of 18 per cent) nor with their limitations (annual increases in agriculture of below 4 per cent) turned to ideology and the massive available labour power to lift China into a modern, industrial nation. If, as has been argued, the Chinese revolution from 1927 onwards had achieved victory less by objective causes than by a supreme exertion of human will and intelligence, the growth among its leaders of a hubristic self-confidence and a belief in the almost infinite possibilities of manipulating the Chinese people appears intelligible, though disastrous (Rodzinski, 1984).

One facet of the Leap was the mobilization of millions of people to produce steel through decentralized small-scale smelting, expected to result in a fourfold increase in production. By September 1958, 20 million people were involved, and at the height of the campaign the number rose to 90 million. It was estimated that during the last four months of the year the work involved would have amounted to 90 million workdays in a normal year. Much of the iron and steel which was made was useless.

More importantly, however, the campaign siphoned off peasant labour in a year when everything pointed to a bumper harvest. Much of the crop had to be abandoned and rotted for want of harvesters. Such labour as there was came predominantly from women, whose agricultural participation rates peaked at around 80 per cent at this time (Thorburg, 1978). Many—perhaps even the majority—were totally inexperienced in farm work.

Peasant enthusiasm for the Leap was blunted by the introduction of communes in place of the still-new co-operatives. Between August and November 1958, 98 per cent of the farm population was said to have been organized into communes, each containing, on average, some 30 co-operatives or around 25,000 people. Communes took over all agricultural and industrial resources, collected taxes, absorbed the old administrative functions of a town or district, ran banks, cemeteries, schools, and so on. The administrative problems consequent upon such a huge shift in responsibilities are easily envisaged.

In addition, there was no indication of how the peasants were to be compensated for their possessions. Many tried to sell them, rather than hand them over to the commune—but the market was saturated. In the case of food and draught animals there were obvious solutions: families ate their private stores, and the brigades (the old co-operatives) hid what they could. A further reason for hiding or consuming food was the introduction with the communes of community mess-halls, which it was feared would encourage extravagance and subsidize the poorer or less hard-working families at the expense of the rest. Often badly managed and providing an inadequate diet, the mess-halls proved rapidly unpopular (Croll, 1983).

Probably the final discouragement for many peasants were efforts in some communes to remove the private plots on which they grew vegetables to supplement their diet and for sale. Such plots as were left became, under regulations of 1958, taxable.

The prospect of a bumper harvest, and the euphoria of the early period of the Leap, led to absurd targets for agriculture. These, in turn, led to falsified reports and those, in their turn, to new and more impossible targets and equally impossible claims of units surpassing them. Alleged over-fulfilment of quotas also led to increased compulsory sales demands, which provinces could not meet. After 1958, some provinces manipulated statistics the other way—under-reporting production to get their quotas reduced, if they were grain exporters, or raised if they were gain-deficit regions.

Grain procurement at the central level became, in any case, more difficult with Great Leap policies of decentralization. Provinces were authorized to adjust targets for procurement and sales within their borders, with central government retaining control only over interprovincial transfers. Government power to extract grain from the richer provinces diminished. Sichuan, for instance, believed that it had been over-milched in the mid-1950s; during the famine, demands for additional transfers met with passive resistance (Donnithorne, 1970). Local self-sufficiency for products like grain which took up much space in transport was even encouraged, partly because transport was dislocated by the needs of the iron and steel campaign, and also by the military movements associated with the bombing of Quemoy and the revolt in Tibet, and later, the war with India. The quantity of grain crossing provincial boundaries, around 10 per cent of procurement between 1954 and 1957, was reduced to some 7.5 per cent in 1958.

The Extent of the Famine

The publication of time-series of statistics from China has at last made possible an attempt to examine the famine of 1959-61 (State Statistical Bureau, 1983). While there has been no year since 1949 in which less than 8 million hectares of land suffered from natural disasters, and most years have seen some 20 to 30 million hectares affected, the period 1959-61 shows disaster on a much larger scale.

Table 12.2.   China: Areas of natural disaster (million hectares)

Year	Total area covered by natural disaster	Disaster-affected area*	Flood-covered area	Flood-affected area*	Drought-covered area	Drought-affected area*
1957	29.2	15.0	8.0	6.0	17.2	7.4
1958	31.0	7.8	4.2	1.4	22.4	5.0
1959	44.6	13.7	4.8	1.8	33.8	11.2
1960	65.5	25.0	10.2	5.0	38.1	16.1
1961	61.8	28.8	8.9	5.4	37.9	18.7
1962	37.2	16.7	9.8	6.3	20.8	8.7
1963	32.2	20.0	14.1	10.5	16.9	9.0
1964	21.6	12.6	14.9	10.0	4.2	1.4

Note: The areas covered or affected by drought and flood do not necessarily equal the totals, which also include frost, typhoons, and hailstorms.
* Disaster-affected areas are those where crop production was reduced by 30% compared with normal years.
Source: State Statistical Bureau, 1983.

The harvest of 1959 was poor but not fatally so. In 1960 drought attacked every province except for Xinjiang and Tibet, while the coastal provinces were also hit by typhoons and flood. In 1961 the situation was almost as bad. Compared with the normal year of 1957 when total grain output was 193 million tons, output in 1960 and 1961 was reduced by a third. Over the whole period between 1959 and 1963, grain output was significantly below that of 1957. Other crops were also badly affected, largely from 1961 as, presumably, more resources were turned over to the vital grain.

Other indicators of the impact of famine on the economy are provided by what the Chinese call the total output of society—the sum of the gross output value of industry, agriculture, construction, transport, post and tele-communications, and commerce (Li Chengrui, 1984). The total output fell

Table 12.3.   China's grain output 1958–64

Year	Total grain (million tons)	Output per head (kg)
1958	200.0	303
1959	170.0	253
1960	143.5	217
1961	147.5	223
1962	160.0	238
1963	170.0	246
1964	187.5	266

Source: State Statistical Bureau, 1983.

by a fifth between 1960 and 1961 and did not recover its previous levels until 1964. Declines were contributed first by agriculture, and then from the other sectors from 1961 as reserves dwindled and funds had to be allocated to grain imports. Transport increased its share of total output by a quarter in 1959 and still more in 1960, in part reflecting efforts to redistribute supplies. (There was a 16 per cent increase in the daily average number of grain wagons, for instance, between 1959 and 1961, as compared with 1955–7.)

Mortality Impact of the Famine

The effect of the famine on the population can be seen from the population totals and vital rates (State Statistical Bureau, 1982). Death rates, which had been steadily declining during the 1950s, more than doubled between 1958

Table 12.4.   China's population and vital rates 1953–64

Year	Population (thousands)	Birth rate per 1,000	Death rate per 1,000	Growth rate per 1,000
1953	587,960	37.0	14.0	23.0
1954	602,660	38.0	13.2	24.8
1955	614,650	32.6	12.3	20.3
1956	628,280	31.9	11.4	20.5
1957	646,530	34.3	10.8	23.2
1958	659,940	29.2	12.0	17.2
1959	672,070	24.8	14.5	10.1
1960	662,070	20.9	25.4	−4.6
1961	658,590	18.1	14.4	3.8
1962	672,950	37.2	10.1	27.1
1963	691,720	43.6	10.1	33.5
1964	704,990	39.3	11.6	27.8

Source: State Statistical Bureau, 1982.

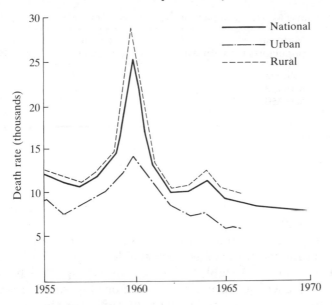

Figure 12.1. National, urban, and rural death rates, China 1955-65
Source: Wang Waizhe, 1984.

and 1960. In this latter year the population growth rate became negative. Although the mortality increase was greater in the rural areas, reflecting both the low margin of peasant life and the greater ease of distribution of food reserves in the cities, urban death rates appear to have doubled as well.

From the population totals and vital rates, it is possible to estimate the excess deaths during the famine period, taking the average of the death rates for the years 1956-8 and 1962-4 as an indication of the expected number of deaths which, under normal circumstances, would have occurred between 1959 and 1961. Because, during a famine, death is more likely to occur to those who are already elderly or otherwise weak, the death rates immediately following famine years tend to be lower than usual. An average which includes those years will thus somewhat increase the contrast between expected and actual deaths. On the other hand, it is likely that in the administrative confusion of the Great Leap and afterwards, registration of births and deaths was very defective, especially as in 1958 the fledgling Household Registration System established in 1955 was transferred from the Ministry of the Interior to the Ministry of Public Security. As a result, the averages for the pre-famine years and the famine years may also be on the low side. All in all, the estimate of 14 million excess deaths—2 per cent of the population—shown in Table 12.5 would seem to be a minimum one. The magnitude of the additional losses is not unique: 2 per cent of the

Table 12.5.   China: Mortality impact of the 1959–61 Famine

Year	Mid-year population (thousands)	Deaths Actual	Expected*
1959	666,005	9,657,072	7,326,055
1960	666,070	16,943,578	7,337,770
1961	660,350	9,508,752	7,263,630
		36,109,402	21,927,455

Difference: 14, 181, 947

* Based on the average death rates 1956–8 and 1962–4.

Bengal population is estimated to have perished during the famine in 1943 (Greenough, 1982).

The old, and the very young, are known to be at particular risk during famine. Such rudimentary data as are available for China indicate a similar pattern of mortality. A table presented by Wang Waizhe gives the percentage differences between age-specific mortality rates in selected years from 1957 to 1978, and mortality rates in 1981, for the populations of various ages between 45 and 85 (Wang Waizhe, 1984).

Table 12.6.   Percentage changes in the age-specific death rates of people of specified ages, from the years given to 1981.

Individual age	Changes from 1957	1963	1975	1978
45	− 46.85	− 26.23	− 5.81	− 12.90
55	− 23.21	− 1.81	− 18.33	− 11.52
65	− 11.46	+ 59.45	− 18.23	− 15.14
75	+ 10.51	+ 137.52	− 14.89	+ 2.00
85	+ 18.38	+ 213.87	− 16.85	+ 5.19

Source: Wang Waizhe, 1984.

The existence of the 1981 abridged life-tables (Jiang Zhenghua *et al.*, 1984) makes it possible to estimate age-specific mortality rates for the ages and years shown in Wang's table. Despite the impressive declines in the crude death rates since the 1960s, the age-specific death rate in 1981 of the population aged 55 was less than 2 per cent below the rate in 1963, while it was nearly 60, 140, and more than 200 per cent above the corresponding rates in 1963 for those aged 65, 75, and 85 respectively.

Wang suggested as a possible explanation of the extremely low death rates of the oldest age groups the survival of the fittest theory: the situation in 1963 may be regarded as a special case. During the three-year period of calamity, a great number of feeble old persons died, resulting in the death

Table 12.7.   Estimated age-specific mortality rates 1957-78

Age	1957	1963	1975	1978	1981
45	7	6	5	5	4.8
55	15	13	15	14	12.4
65	36	13	39	38	32.8
75	73	31	94	80	82.0
85	152	87	218	177	186.3

Source: Based on 1981 abridged life-tables (Jiang Zhenghua *et al.*, 1984) and Table 12.6 above. I am grateful to Dr Lado T. Ruzicka for the calculation of these estimates.

rate to be on the low side after the period of calamity. However, the depressed rates of 1963 appear to be so low as to suggest that some under-registration of deaths of the very old may also have occurred—a not unlikely happening if, in the post-famine period, the administrative apparatus was only slowly recovering.

The effect on the very young may be assessed by an examination of the 1964 census. The cohort aged 3-5 years in 1964 represents the survivors of all those born during the famine, between 1959 and 1961. The 6-8-year-olds are the survivors of all those born before the famine, between 1956 and 1958; because children tend to suffer disproportionate mortality in a famine, that cohort may also have been depleted rather more than would be expected under normal conditions. The cohort aged 0-2 in 1964, representing the survivors of those born between 1962 and 1964, includes the products of the post-famine baby boom, and thus may be larger than would normally be expected. However, by taking the average of the 1964 census population aged 0-2 and that aged 6-8, it is possible to get a rough indication of the expected size of the surviving population born between 1959 and 1961.

Table 12.8.   China: Cohorts aged 0-2, 3-5, and 6-8 in 1964

Age in 1964	Population (thousands)		Ratio	
	Actual	Expected	Actual	Expected
0-2	74,301.2	74,301.2		
3-5	40,724.2	66,545.9	0.548	0.896
6-8	58,790.7	58,790.7	1.444	0.883

Source: Population Census Office under the State Council, 1982.

The difference between actual and expected numbers in the famine-affected cohorts reflects the decline in births during that period, as well as excess deaths, and it is not possible to separate the relative contributions of each. All that can be said is that neither the very high mortality rates for China during 1959 to 1961 nor the much reduced birth rates are as visible in this calculation for all China as they might be for badly affected provinces.

Three provinces—Hebei, Henan, and Zhejiang—have so far had single-year age and sex compositions reported for the 1982 census, and I have the single-year breakdown for Anhui—which is known to have suffered badly in the famine—from the 1964 census.

Each of the four provinces was traditionally subject to drought or floods. A classification of provinces according to grain output per head in 1955–7 put Hebei, with 197 kilograms per head, almost at the bottom of the list of provinces for which data were available; Zhejiang at the top of the adequate range, with 307 kilograms; and Anhui just into the grain-rich provinces with 341 kilograms: there were no data available for Henan (Walker, 1981, 233). By comparison, each of the provinces except Hunan was classified as grain-rich in 1978–80.

Among the four provinces, there are differences in the overall level of mortality. A national retrospective sample survey of mortality, carried out between 1973 and 1975 in 24 provinces of China, gave life expectancy at birth for males as 67.1 years in Hebei, 66.4 years in Zhejiang, 65.1 years in Henan, and 64.5 years in Anhui. Each province had, at that time, life expectancy for males of above the national average of 63.6 years (Rong Shoude *et al.*, 1981).

Hence, if a similar procedure to that used above is adopted to estimate the impact of famine on mortality, the deficit in the number of survivors from the famine-affected cohorts may reflect not only differential exposure to the severity of the famine in each province, but also differences in mortality levels among the provinces.

By contrast with the figures for all China, the difference between actual and expected numbers in the famine-affected cohorts in Anhui is considerable. The actual surviving population, in 1964, of those born between 1959 and 1961 is a little less than a third of the expected size.

Table 12.9.   Anhui province: Cohorts age 0–2, 3–5, and 6–8 in 1964

| Age in 1964 | Population (thousands) | | Ratio | |
	Actual	Expected	Actual	Expected
0–2	3,756.9	3,756.9		
3–5	943.8	3,039.4	0.251	0.809
6–8	2,321.9	3,321.9	2.460	0.764

Source: 1964 Population census.

Following the same method, the 1982 census data can be used for Hebei, Henan, and Zhejiang. The two cohorts which were born before and after the famine were 18–20 and 24–6 years old in 1982. The famine-affected cohort was 21–3 years old. There is no reason to assume that within each of these three provinces the normal mortality experience of those born immediately before, during, or after the famine will have been particularly different (except, of course, for the impact of the famine itself). Thus, although the cohorts are smaller in 1982, an average of those surviving from the births of 1956–8 and from births of 1962–4 should indicate the expected number of survivors from the birth cohorts of the famine years.

The number of persons enumerated in 1982 in each of the birth cohorts followed here is not only made up of survivors, of course, it has also been affected by migration to and from the province during the intervening years. Unfortunately, there are no data available for estimating this component of change, and so the results given below should be interpreted with caution. A further reason for caution is that the army is enumerated separately in the census results and does not appear to be included in age and sex breakdowns (Caldwell *et al.*, 1984), so that young men in their twenties are under-represented in the cohorts with which we are concerned.

Comparing the affected cohorts in each of the three provinces with the national pattern, it can be seen that Hebei and Zhejiang approximate fairly

Table 12.10. Cohorts aged 18–20, 21–3, and 24–6 in 1982: China 10 per cent sample

| Age in 1984 | Population (thousands) | | Ratio | |
	Actual	Expected	Actual	Expected
18–20	6,808	6,808		
21–3*	3,927	6,217	0.577	0.913
24–6	5,626	5,626	1.433	0.904

* Survivors of the cohorts born 1959–61
Source: Population Census Office under the State Council, 1983.

Table 12.11. Cohorts aged 18–20, 21–3, and 24–6 in 1982: Selected provinces of China

| Age in 1982 | | Population (thousands) | | Ratio | |
		Actual	Expected	Actual	Expected
	Hebei				
18–20		3,420.5	3,420.5		
21–23*		2,356.5	3,349.1	0.689	0.979
24–26		3,277.7	3,277.7	1.391	0.979
	Henan				
18–20		5,166.5	5,166.5		
21–23*		2,272.7	4,514.6	0.444	0.882
24–26		3,912.7	3,912.7	1.721	0.867
	Zhejiang				
18–20		2,796.6	2,796.6		
21–23*		1,792.1	2,607.5	0.641	0.932
24–26		2,418.5	2,418.5	1.370	0.928

* Survivors from the cohorts born 1959–61.
Source: Population Census Office under the State Council, 1982.

closely to the national experience of the famine years. Both have a closer correspondence between the actual and expected ratios of those aged 21–3 and those aged 18–20 than the country did as a whole. This is because the number of 20-year-olds in each province is noticeably smaller than the number aged 18 and 19 in 1982; it may be inferred that both provinces took longer to recover from the famine than did the country as a whole. Henan, in contrast, has a low rate of survivors aged 21–3: that cohort was much more severely reduced.

Demographic Mechanisms for Survival

The demographic mechanisms through which the hungry population attempted to limit the impact of the famine were probably the same as had prevailed in previous disasters, and they are similar to those found, for instance, in the Bengal famine of 1943 (Greenough, 1982) or the Bangladesh famine of 1974–5 (Alamgir, 1980).

In the early part of the famine, marriages appear to have been postponed. The number of women aged 15–49 who married for the first time, as a proportion of all women of those ages, fell between 1957 and 1960 (Zhao Xuan, 1983). In 1961 it recovered to the level which prevailed in the 1950s, and in 1962 it increased considerably. During 1957–8 marriages may have been postponed because of the increasing involvement of women in the work-force and the emphasis on production during the Great Leap: in the subsequent two years it seems reasonable to attribute the situation at least in part to the famine. Postponing marriage during a period of scarcity was often the result of an inability to provide the bride-price and money for the marriage, as well as due to the reluctance on the part of the man's family to take in another mouth to feed.

Table 12.12. Number of women aged 15–49 marrying for the first time, per 1,000 women aged 15–49

Year	Women marrying	Year	Women marrying
1956	35.2	1961	35.1
1957	33.6	1962	40.2
1958	32.6	1963	36.1
1959	26.7	1964	28.7
1960	31.9	1965	26.3

Source: Zhao Xuan, 1983.

Single or married, the effect of famine on a woman, whose priority in food distribution was always low, could be devastating. In the village of Kaixian'gong, of the 35 divorced men studied in 1981, 23 had lost their wives who went away to beg during the famine years (Fei Xiaotong, 1983).

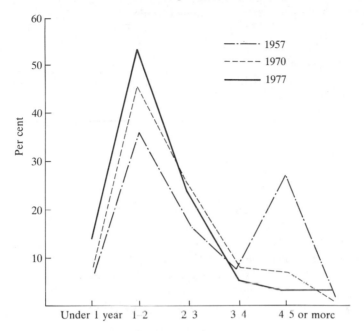

Figure 12.2. China, percentage distribution of intervals between marriage and first births, for marriages taking place in 1957, 1970, 1977
Source: State Family Planning Commission, 1983.

Even when the marriage was not postponed, the first birth often was. The only years for which figures are available on the intervals between marriage and first birth are 1957, 1970, and 1977 (Ran Yuguang and Xie Quibin, 1983). It is possible that the changes shown in Figure 12.2 reflect, to some extent, rises in the average age of marriage leading to a departure from a more traditional pattern of very early marriage which did not involve immediate consummation. Nevertheless, the very high percentage of women marrying in 1957 who waited for four or more years to have a first birth suggests that the famine may have at least increased the likelihood of a postponed birth.

This view is confirmed by the birth rates during the period 1959–61. The birth rate may have been at an unusually high level in the early 1950s, as a result of recovery from the war period. It showed a dramatic deceleration from 1959, and reached a mere half of its 1954 level by 1961. Taking an average of the birth rates for the years 1956–8 as an indication of the expected number of births under normal circumstances, the expected number of births between 1959 and 1961 can be calculated. (Birth rates after 1961 can be expected to be inflated by the inclusion of deferred births from the famine period and are thus not included in the calculation of the average.)

Table 12.13.   Fertility impact of the 1959–61 famine

Year	Mid-year population (thousands)	Births Registered	Expected*	Deficit (thousands)
1959	666,005	16,516,924	21,178,959	4,662
1960	667,070	13,941,763	21,212,826	7,271
1961	660,350	11,951,973	20,998,494	9,047
		36,109,402	63,390,279	20,980

* Based on the average birth rates 1956–8.

The estimate of 21 million missing births is probably too high. In the administrative confusion of the period, birth registration, like death registration, was probably inadequate. It is possible that in some instances registration occured much later than the actual birth. In addition, it is known that even today some births followed shortly by the infant's death are not registered in China (Gu Xingyuan and Chen Mailing, 1982). During the famine it can be assumed that a considerably increased proportion of infants died within a short time of birth, and thus a larger proportion remained unregistered.

Another reaction to the famine may be surmised from an examination of the sex ratios of the cohorts born between 1959 and 1961 (Johansson, 1984). In the 1964 census, the sex ratio for those under one year of age was 103.8, and it rose with each cohort back to those who had been born in 1959–60. Under normal circumstances a slight decrease in the sex ratio might be expected, as more boys than girls die in the first year of life. On their own, therefore, the sex ratios from the 1964 census suggest that girl babies suffered disproportionate mortality during the famine. However, if those same cohorts are followed through to the 1982 census, two of the cohorts of girls appear to be larger than they were in 1964. The overall female losses during the period 1964–82 appear to be only a little less than half (4.8 per cent against 9.3 per cent) those of the males. This provides some support for the assumption that a number of births were not registered, but also that some children were not reported in the 1964 census, and it was females who

Table 12.14.   Sex ratios of cohorts born 1959–64, China

Cohorts	1964 Census
1963–4	103.8
1962–3	105.3
1961–2	106.4
1960–1	107.0
1959–60	108.7

Source: Johansson, 1984.

were likely to be excluded. (In considering the sex ratios of these cohorts as they appear in the 1982 census, the missing male group of young men in the army also has to be taken into account.)

Table 12.15 also suggests some misreporting of age, which makes it difficult to analyse each cohort separately. It seems reasonable to assume, though, that there was excess female mortality among young children, though the 1964 census may overstate it. Excess mortality is also found among older female children in the 1964 census. Those girls born between 1948 and 1953 had declined by 10.8 per cent by the time of the 1964 census, while boys born in the same years had only declined by 8.7 per cent. There is, unfortunately, no way of establishing what proportion of these excess female deaths took place during the famine, as compared to the other years of the period.

Table 12.15. Cohorts born 1959–64, as enumerated in the 1964 and 1982 censuses, China

Cohort	Males: Number 1964 (thousands)	Remain 1982 (per cent)	Females: Number 1964 (thousands)	Remain 1982 (per cent)
1963–4	14,510	87.6	13,974	88.7
1962–3	15,515	88.0	14,733	93.2
1961–2	8,025	95.8	7,544	104.8
1960–1	5,961	89.1	5,574	96.2
1959 60	7,450	98.3	6,855	101.8
1959–64	51,462	90.7	48,680	95.2

Source: Johansson, 1984.

Although there are data on the numbers by sex for single years reported for the three provinces in the 1982 census, the analysis of the sex ratios of those born around the period of the famine would describe, by 1982, what would be young adults. The number of survivors in 1982 reflects the impact of differential mortality between birth and the census, which may also have changed over time, and the ratios will also reflect past migration patterns which may be quite significant in these age-groups. As a result it is impossible to separate these factors from any impact of famine-related sex differentials in mortality.

However, sex ratios for single years are available from the 1964 census for Anhui province, and that census was sufficiently close to the famine years for some assessment of the differential mortality impact of the famine to be possible.

Anhui's population–sex ratio was always and continues to be deplorable, but girls born between 1955–6 and 1959–60 seem to be missing in particularly large numbers, despite national declines in mortality during the

Table 12.16.   Sex ratios: Anhui province 1964

Cohort	Sex ratio	Cohort	Sex ratio
1963–4	105.4	1957–8	120.8
1962–3	106.5	1956–7	118.8
1961–2	107.6	1955–6	116.4
1960–1	107.8	1954–5	113.5
1959–60	116.3	1953–4	111.5
1958–9	120.7	1952–3	110.7

Source: 1964 census.

1950s. Such females, under the age of five but past the age of weaning, would have been especially vulnerable to discriminatory feeding practices during a famine.

The demographic data thus suggest an attempt to mitigate the impact of famine by avoiding increasing the number of mouths to be fed, through postponing marriage and births, together with nutritional concentration on the strongest and most productive—or potentially productive—members of a family.

Given the Chinese system of controls on population movement in the 1950s, migration may have been less of an option for the famine victims than was traditionally the case. Migration figures for the period are lacking. However, the official communiqué listing the ten tasks for adjusting the economy in 1962 gave, in fourth place, the 'need to reduce the urban population and the number of workers and functionaries to an appropriate extent by persuading, first of all, those workers and functionaries who had come from rural areas to return to rural productive work and strengthen the agricultural front' (Robertson, 1962). The Great Leap and the introduction of the communes had themselves encouraged rural-to-urban migration: Mao quoted a commune whose work-force of 20–30,000 had been reduced by 10,000 who left after pigs and poultry had been taken over by the commune (MacFarquhar, 1983). The still somewhat mysterious episode of the border crisis in early 1962, when some 63,000 refugees who had apparently received encouragement to leave China were apprehended by the Hong Kong government, may have stemmed in part from Chinese official recognition that returning vast numbers of urban migrants to the countryside was fraught with difficulties (Walker, 1962, 51).

Anecdotal evidence suggests that many rural people, perhaps without relatives in towns or other hopes of sustenance there, nevertheless left their homes during the famine and drifted aimlessly in search of food; in some provinces, whole villages were deserted as the few survivors straggled off.

Societal Mechanisms for Survival

Virtually nothing is known about other societal mechanisms which may have mitigated the effects of the famine: such indications as are presented here come largely from the remembrances of survivors. As in the past, those villagers who had more (perhaps because of a greater number of productive members) helped their hungrier kin. Land reform and the redistribution of goods had put an end to the old lineage holdings, however, and the amount the wealthier kin members had to offer was limited. In place of the unreliable charity of lineage or landlords, destitute peasants turned to the team, which guaranteed a subsistence level of food to all its members. Teams and brigades had managed, in 1958, to keep back substantial stores of grain, and it seems that this local hoarding stemmed from a traditional mechanism for averting disaster. It has been argued (Thaxton, 1983) that a fundamental tenet of peasant belief was that grain needed for survival should not be sent out of the county. This stored grain provided the rations for the poorer families, and the poorer work-teams within a brigade. It is possible, I think, to assume that at higher levels too—commune and provincial—there was an attempt to ensure that food stores were distributed as equitably as possible.

Those migrants who descended on friends or family members in areas less hard-hit than their own had no entitlement to subsistence. It was up to those who took them in to support them, and for the migrants—where possible—to contribute through sideline activities, or through helping on the private plot, for example.

It is unlikely that remittances from wealthier, or city-based, relatives played much of a part in relieving famine, for two reasons. The amount of food which could be bought—mainly from private plots or brigade and commune markets—was comparatively small and hardly included grain. Prices of what little was available became astronomical. In addition, the areas of natural disaster were so widespread that a surplus for sale was seldom accessible to a famine-hit family. It seems that it was only in the earlier stage of the famine, before successive bad harvests eradicated any surpluses, that peasants who were most desperate could barter such private possessions as they had for food, so that a man seeking food for a wife in childbirth gave a wristwatch for a chicken, for example.

When food became unobtainable, in some parts of the country, the peasants reverted to eating wild plants, of which there was a traditional knowledge. The intensive nature of Chinese agriculture and land use, though, meant that few had access to such plant foods on a significant scale: hence the frequent references (as in previous famines) to eating the bark from trees. As in previous famines, when the bones of the dead were burned and eaten by the living victims (Thaxton, 1983), the most desperate turned to the bodies of those who had already died.

The final group of societal mechanisms designed to limit the famine were governmental. These assumed a much greater importance than in past famines in China, or indeed elsewhere, because of the state monopoly of grain and the political philosophy of collectivization. Grain was not a marketable commodity: grain-surplus areas distributed what remained after state purchase and tax (and after allocating grain to local reserves and for the next year's seed) to rural individuals or families according to the work-points they had earned. Grain-deficit areas bought grain from the State from the proceeds of other farm output, or had grain rations allocated to them. Thus State intervention was of crucial importance.

By the end of 1958, opposition to the Great Leap and to the communes had become widespread, and the following year saw the beginning of the disaggregation of the communes in terms of size: by the early 1960s there were around 74,000 of them, or three times as many as in their original form. Some of their administrative functions were returned to the districts or townships; others, such as the allocation of work and the distribution of income, became the responsibility of more manageable units—the brigades or work teams. In the long run, such groupings functioned, but the short-term effect was to introduce further administrative chaos, with functions being transferred back and forth, units grouped and regrouped, and few clear channels of local direction (Eckstein, 1977). Between 1959 and 1961, however, the provinces began to exempt private plots from tax, and those communes which had absorbed them returned the plots to the peasants. Both moves encouraged increases in productivity and helped to create additional supplies of vegetables for the families.

Further attempts to ameliorate the food problem came from the use of reserves. If, as has been calculated (Donnithorne, 1970), total reserves held by the state at different administrative levels may be guessed (rather rashly) to have been somewhere around 20–5 million tons, it can be seen that even to bring the 1960 grain supply up to the level of the first famine year would have eliminated a large part of the central reserves. In fact, it is unlikely that all those reserves—some held at local level and some at provincial—could have been transferred to deficit provinces, given the difficulties of inter-provincial transfer which are apparent from the low level of such transfers in previous years.

To some extent it had been recognized throughout the 1950s that equitable distribution was impossible in a country so large and with a limited communications network. Provinces which could not meet their own grain needs (Hebei, Shanxi, and Jiangsu in 1956, and Hebei, Shanxi, Shandong, and Shaanxi in 1957) did not necessarily have them augmented to the desirable per capita level. Thus, in 1956 Hebei's per capita supply, even after state intervention, was only 56 per cent of that retained by Heilongjiang.

By 1961, stocks of grain had been depleted to the point where, for the first time since the revolution, the Chinese Government decided to import grain on a large scale. Shortages of currency meant that the decision also involved the reduction of imports of capital equipment, though such a reduction might have occurred in any case, because reductions of investment during the famine years led to an order, in 1961, that all capital projects should be stopped forthwith.

Following the famine, the policy of local self-reliance, already an integral part of Mao's doctrines, was extended. Store grain became one of Mao's most persistent themes, to the end of his life: campaign after campaign encouraged the peasants to put aside realistic quantities of grain for seed and as a reserve. Each local community was expected to cover itself for the bad harvests; each was largely expected to do the best it could in its own conditions. Investments in transport continued (between 1966 and 1976 four major rail networks were constructed), but on a scale which did not attempt to provide for the massive movement of grain around China. Wheat imports continued, too, to feed the cities and provide for central reserves, though increasingly they were balanced by rice exports.

The other major consequence of the famine was the policy, initially enunciated in 1961, of putting agriculture first. This meant a higher rate of investment in agriculture, compared with the emphasis during the 1950s on an industrial base. In fact, however, achieving a balance between investment in heavy industry, light industry, and agriculture was, and continues to be, extremely difficult. Nevertheless, there was an increased production of fertilizer and agricultural machinery. These agricultural investments, after 1963, tended to be concentrated in areas of high and stable yield which could be relied on to produce large surpluses. These areas received priority for investment grants, agricultural credit, and rural electrification as well as in the allocation of fertilizer and machinery. Another effort to maximize output was to encourage double and triple cropping. In many areas this was undoubtedly successful, but efforts to introduce it wholesale and regardless of local conditions meant that, in a less suitable climate, the total yield from two crops might be no more than the yield from one which was well watered and fertilized (Field and Kilpatrick, 1978 369–84).

Throughout the most critical period of the famine (1959–60) the country's leaders were preoccupied with other issues: first, the internal disputes resulting from the Great Leap itself, and then with the dispute with Russia, which led, in July 1960, to the abrupt withdrawal of all Russian experts and the blueprints from the projects on which they had worked. Mao later admitted that the Sino-Soviet quarrel had prevented the leaders paying adequate attention to internal affairs during 1960 (MacFarquhar, 1983). Early warning signs of the disaster, like the reduction of rations in the cities in the winter of 1958, were ignored because of the assumption that they all stemmed from local hoarding. Although the most impossible advance harvest estimates were revised downwards, the claims of what had

Table 12.17. China: Grain imports and exports by volume 1957–63

(Calendar years)	1957	1958	1959	1960	1961	1962	1963
Imports (thousands of tonnes)							
Wheat	—	127	—	—	2,622	4,419	4,394
Rice[a]	110	12	—	28	62	5	97
Barley	—	—	—	—	1,099	487	25
Maize	25	31	—	—	44	491	13
Rye	—	—	—	—	100	247	—
Oats	—	—	—	—	65	47	27
Other	4	—	—	—	—	24	—
Flour[b]	—	1	—	—	451	280	1
Total imports	139	160	—	29	4,445	5,999	4,557
Exports (thousands of tonnes)							
Wheat	2	1	158	112	121	89	110
Rice[a]	485	1,265	1,661	1,153	446	573	628
Maize	12	16	92	71	30	1	110
Total exports[c]	507	1,302	1,967	1,397	596	668	859
Net imports (+) exports (−)	−368	−1,142	−1,967	−1,368	+3,849	+5,332	+3,698

[a] Milled equivalents, [b] Wheat flour, grain equivalent, [c] Includes barley, rye, oats, and wheat flour.
Source: Donnithorne, 1970.

been gathered in were still well above reality. As late as 1965, Mao was accusing the peasants of minimizing output returns while exaggerating natural disasters (Snow, 1974).

The statistical system had been one of the first casualties of the Great Leap, and its collapse both helped to conceal the extent of the disaster and made planning to cope with it almost impossible. Governments have not infrequently attempted to disguise famines, especially during periods of international tension or internal unrest (Sen, 1981; Alamgir, 1980), and China was no exception. The struggles against Russia, India, and Taiwan, which had considerably increased international tension, made China reluctant to expose her vulnerability. As it was, from refugees and other sources, foreign commentators guessed enough to have serious doubts as to whether the regime could survive the remorselessly descending spiral which had descended on the country since the Great Leap. Only a good harvest in 1962, one of them suggested, could save it (Alsop, 1962 21-37).

Mao, and his followers, were equally reluctant to have the extent of the disaster documented in a way which would provide ammunition for opponents of this great experiment. Thus began the practice of concealing statistics—on population, on production, on a whole range of social and economic indicators—which lasted until the late 1970s and did much to undermine China's credibility with foreign observers.

Distrust of statistics, and lack of interest in rebuilding statistical systems, were also factors in another governmental reaction to the famine: a refusal to consider the implications of population growth. Discussion on the significance of a rapidly growing population for China's development plans was not a casualty of a clampdown on intellectuals following the Hundred Flowers movement: it continued into the famine years. It was the decline in the birth rate, the 14 million or more extra deaths, and the negative rate of growth, at a time when China was under a serious threat of war and was trying to mobilize all possible labour power to rehabilitate its farmland, which lost the issue such support as it had previously commanded. What might have been a temporary reaction, however, hardened into dogma in the absence of population studies and population projections. The result was a lost decade in population planning and control, through lack of a clear direction in population policy.

Finally, government response to the famine was—at least to some extent—to leave the peasants to their own devices. Although in subsequent years there were occasional efforts to do away with private plots, or to eliminate local markets and reduce incentives for private production, and there were of course continuing political education campaigns, these were, when compared to the successive convulsions of reform to which the peasants had been subjected in the 1950s, minor upheavals. The Cultural Revolution impinged on the peasants to a far lesser extent than on urban dwellers. It was not really until the early 1970s, when the campaign to learn from the model commune Dazhai switched its emphasis from increased production to extending political awareness, that a significant attempt was again made to heighten the collective organization of peasant farming. Even that campaign was leisurely in the time-scale it allowed for transition to brigade-level accounting and organization, in contrast with the almost overnight transitions of the 1950s. The fragile balance between China's food supplies and her population had been demonstrated yet again, and nothing was risked which might tilt that equilibrium.

References

Alamgir, M. (1980), *Famine in South Asia*, Oelgeschlager, Gunn, & Hain, Cambridge, Mass.

Alsop, J. (1962), 'On China's Descending Spiral', *China Quarterly* 11, 21–37.

Caldwell, J. C., M. Bracher, G. Santow, and P. Caldwell (1984), 'Population Trends in China: A Perspective Provided by the 1982 Census, paper presented to an international seminar on China's 1982 population census, Beijing, March 1984.

Croll, E. (1983), *The Family Rice Bowl: Food and the Domestic Economy in China*, UNRISD and Zed Press, London.

Donnithorne, A. (1970), *China's Grain: Output, Procurement, Transfers and Trade*, Chinese University of Hong Kong.

Eckstein, A. (1977), *China's Economic Revolution*, Cambridge University Press, Cambridge.

Field, R. M., and J. A. Kilpatrick (1978), 'Chinese Grain Production: An Interpretation of the Data', *China Quarterly*, 74, 369–84.

Fei Xiaotong (1983), *China Village Close-up*, New World Press, Beijing.

Greenough, P. R. (1982), *Prosperity and Misery in Modern Bangladesh: The Famine of 1943–44*, Oxford University Press, Oxford.

Gu Xingyuan and Chen Mailing (1982), 'Vital Statistics', *American Journal of Public Health* 72 (supplement).

Jiang Zhenghua, Zhang Weimin, and Zhu Liwei (1984), '*The Preliminary Study to the Life Expectancy at Birth for China's Population*', paper presented to an international seminar on China's 1982 population census, Beijing, March 1984.

Johansson, S. (1984), '*A Swedish Perspective on Sex Ratios and Other Intriguing Aspects of China's Demography*', paper presented at an international seminar on China's 1982 population census, Beijing, March 1984.

Li Chengrui (1984), '*An Analysis of China's Statistical Sources and Their Reliability during the Decade of Turmoil (1967–1976)*, paper presented to an international seminar on China's 1982 population census, Beijing, March 1984.

MacFarquhar, R. (1983), *The Origins of the Cultural Revolution Vol. 2: The Great Leap Forward 1958–60*, Oxford University Press, Oxford.

Population Census Office under the State Council, and Department of Population Statistics, State Statistical Bureau (1982), *The 1982 Population Census of China (Major Figures)*, Economic Information and Agency, Hong Kong.

—— (1983), *Major Figures By 10 percent Sampling Tabulation on the 1982 Population Census of the People's Republic of China*, Beijing.

Ran Yuguang and Xie Qibin (1983), 'Brief Analysis of Women in their First Marriage and the First Birth in Connection with Women', 'An Analysis of A National One-per-thousand-population Sample Survey in Birth Rate', *Population and Economics* (special issue), Beijing (in Chinese, contents in English).

Robertson, F. (1962), 'Comment on China's Descending Spiral', *China Quarterly* 12, 42–5.

Rodzinski, W. (1984), *The Walled Kingdom: A History of China from 2000 BC to the Present*, Fontana, London.

Rong Shoude, Li Junyao, Gao Runquan, Dai Xudong, Cao Dexian, Li Guangyi, and Zhou Youshang (1981), 'Statistical Analysis of the Life Expectancy in the Population of China in 1973–1975', *Symposium of Chinese Population Science*, ed. by the Institute of Population Economics, Beijing College of Economics, China Academic Publishers, Beijing (in Chinese, contents and summaries in English).

Sen, A. (1981), *Poverty and Famine: An Essay on Entitlement and Deprivation*, Oxford University Press, Oxford.

Snow, E. (1974), *China's Long Revolution*, Penguin, Harmondsworth.

State Statistical Bureau (1982), *China Official Annual Report 1982/3*, New China News Photos and Kingsway Publications, Beijing and Hong Kong.

—— (1983), *Statistical Yearbook of China 1983*, Economic Information and Agency, Hong Kong.

Tawney, R. H. (1932), *Land and Labour in China*, Allen & Unwin, London

Thaxton, R. (1983), *China Turned Right Side Up: Revolutionary Activity in the Peasant World*, Yale University Press, New Haven, Conn.

Thorburg, M. (1978), 'Chinese Employment Policy in 1949–78 with Special Emphasis on Women in Rural Production', *Chinese Economy Post-Mao Vol. 1*, paper submitted to the joint Economic Committee, Congress of the United States.

Walker, K. R. (1962), 'Comment on China's Descending Spiral', *China Quarterly* 12, 45–51.

—— (1981), 'China's Grain Production 1975–80 and 1952–57: Some Basic Statistics', *China Quarterly* 86, 215–47.

Wang Waizhc (1984), *Preliminary Analysis of Population Death Rate in China*, paper presented to an international seminar on China's 1982 population census, Beijing, March 1984.

Zhao Xuan (1983), 'State of Women's First Marriage in Forty-two Years from 1940 to 1981', 'An Analysis of a National One-per-thousand-population Sample Survey in Birth Rate', *Population and Economics*, (special issue), Beijing (in Chinese, contents in English).

Index